The Proven

7-Step Program

for

Saving Your Marriage

THE DIVORCE REMEDY

MICHELE WEINER DAVIS

SIMON & SCHUSTER

NEW YORK   LONDON   TORONTO   SYDNEY   SINGAPORE

SIMON & SCHUSTER
Rockefeller Center
1230 Avenue of the Americas
New York, NY 10020

This publication contains the opinions and ideas of its authors and is designed to provide useful advice in regard to the subject matter covered. It is sold with the understanding that the authors and publisher are not engaged in rendering legal, therapeutic, or other professional services in this publication. Laws vary from state to state, and if the reader requires expert assistance or legal advice, a competent professional should be consulted.

The author and publisher specifically disclaim any responsibility for any liability, loss, or risk, personal or otherwise, that is incurred as a consequence, directly or indirectly, of the use and application of any of the contents of this book.

Manufactured in the United States of America

1 3 5 7 9 10 8 6 4 2

Library of Congress Cataloging-in-Publication Data

Weiner Davis, Michele.
The divorce remedy : the proven 7-step program for saving your marriage /
Michele Weiner Davis.
p. cm.
Includes bibliographical references and index.
1. Marriage. 2. Interpersonal relations. 3. Communication in marriage. 4. Marital
psychotherapy. I. Title.
HQ734 .W4374 2001
306.81—dc21   2001042634

ISBN 0-684-87354-0

Acknowledgments

◡

This book is about partnership, without which this book would not have been possible.

My lifelong partner and husband, Jim, has been my biggest fan on this marriage-saving journey. Your creative ideas, never-ending support, encouragement, and incisive feedback are invaluable to me. You are the best. Our friendship nourishes me. I love you more than words can express.

Virginia Peeples, my assistant and incredibly dear friend, handles *all* the details in my life with such incredible expertise that all I ever have to do is "show up." You make me look good. Don't ever stop. I don't know what I'd do without you. I love you. Joe Peeples, Virginia's husband, deserves thanks for graciously putting up with his wife's long hours, out-of-town trips, and my many inopportune phone calls. Thanks for your patience.

My parents, Elizabeth and Harry Weiner, and parents-in-law, Leah and Byll Davis, are enormous emotional supports in my life. Mom, thank you for giving me the rare gift of unconditional love. Dad, thanks for teaching me the importance of achievement and success. Leah and Byll, thanks for being living proof that marriage and strong family bonds are the most important things in life.

Diane Sollee invited me to offer a keynote address at a professional conference in the late eighties called Divorce Busting. The rest, as they say, is history. I have never forgotten this catalyst to wonderful things happening in my career. Her continued support does not go unnoticed.

I want to thank Suzanne Gluck, my agent, for continuing to believe in me and my work after so many years.

I also want to thank Sydny Miner, my editor, for helping me realize that when it comes to words, "Less is more." I'm certain my husband will appreciate this discovery too.

I am appreciative of Betty Wilson's keen eye and help with the manuscript in its last editing round.

And last, but certainly not least, my clients and loyal Web site visitors are owed special gratitude. I feel enormously privileged that they have allowed me to become an intimate part of their lives and trusted me to help them restore their love and keep their families together. I have learned so much from you, the real experts. Thanks for your faith in me.

To Danielle and Zachary:
This book is dedicated to the two of you,
our wonderful children. Your dad and I believe in the sanctity of
marriage and in the importance of enduring family bonds. We hope
you both take these lessons to heart because they will greatly
enrich your lives; they are lessons to love by.
We love you very much.

To Jim:
Thank you from the bottom of my heart for your three most
precious gifts: your love, your commitment,
and our children.

Contents

Introduction

"I love you, but I'm not *in* love with you anymore." "We got married for all the wrong reasons." "I'm not attracted to you anymore." "Why can't you admit that we just made a mistake?" "My affair *isn't* the reason our marriage isn't working." "I never really loved you in the first place." "It's time to tell the kids it's over."

Does any of this sound familiar? If so, my heart goes out to you. There is little that is more painful than the feeling of love slipping through your fingers. It hurts to wake up in the morning. You feel disoriented and dizzy. Nothing else matters. Your life, your thoughts, your feelings, your entire being is about your spouse falling out of love with you. How could this happen? What went wrong? Didn't you both promise to love, honor, and cherish each other through good times and bad, through sickness and through health, for richer or poorer until death do you part? What happened to the dreams you had for the future?

If you have picked up this book, there is a reason, a good reason. You are someone who, though hurt and devastated by your spouse's proclamation that your marriage is over, refuses to accept it as a marital death sentence. I applaud you. You know that ending a marriage is no way to solve relationship problems. You feel surer than you've ever felt about anything in your life that, no matter how tough things are right now, they can get better. And most of all, you know that the fight for your marriage is well worth it. The trouble is, your spouse doesn't know this yet. And, chances are, what you've been doing to convince him or her hasn't been working too well. That's why you've picked up this book. You want to keep your marriage together but you aren't quite sure what to do next.

In hopes of finding answers to your marital problems, you've searched the Internet, read magazine articles and even taken up residence at your local bookstore. But unfortunately, your search for solutions has come up short. Although there is an inordinate amount of information for people whose relatively stable marriages can stand some tweaking, there is a dearth of practical, psychobabble-free tools for people teetering on the brink of divorce. You pray that there will come a day in the not-too-distant future when solving garden-variety marital problems will be your biggest concern. But for today, you have bigger obstacles to overcome. You need to save your marriage. And I will help you do just that. First, let me tell you a little bit about myself.

For the last two decades, I have been a marriage therapist, specializing in helping couples make their marriages work. But it wasn't always that way. Early in my career, like many therapists, I assumed that if people were unhappy in their marriages, they should just get out. After all, I told myself, life is short and we all have the right to be happy. But I soon learned the truth about divorce. It doesn't necessarily bring happiness. In fact, in most cases, divorce creates more problems than it solves.

Once I figured this out and truly took it to heart, I stopped being neutral about the benefits of working things out and the pitfalls of getting out. I became a zealot for marriage. I stopped pretending that the pain from divorce is only temporary. I grew determined to help people keep their families together. I focused all my energies on developing methods to help couples fall back in love again. And I succeeded. I created the Divorce Busting program; a method that has enabled me to help thousands of couples restore their love, even couples in what I would have once deemed "dead on arrival marriages."

Then I knew I had to spread the word and proceeded to write my bestselling book, *Divorce Busting*. And save marriages it did! What a wonderful blessing my work has been in my life! See for yourself:

Dear Michele,

My husband and I have been having a really rough past couple of years. We have two kids, ages four and six. Until recently, we were on the verge of separation and possible divorce. I found your book, and am now seeing real hope in my marriage. I am now finding that the things I saw as unsolvable problems are really communication issues between my husband and myself. I am using the techniques I found in *Divorce Busting* to really turn myself and my marriage around. I am amazed at how just changing some interactions with him has made such a HUGE difference in my marriage!

By showing my husband more patience with his moods, and giving him his time alone, I have found that he is less and less in his cave and more with the family. We have both shown each other more love and respect than we have in over two years. We have even been able to make love again. Thank you so much, Michele, for helping me not to give up! All my friends said leave him, but you gave me a great deal of hope and insight . . .

I thank God for helping me find the love and support I needed to save my marriage! God Bless You!

Letters like this make me feel passionate about my work. But that's not the only reason I'm passionate. There are personal reasons as well.

I grew up in a "Walton family." We had a wonderful home. I loved both my parents and my two brothers. My father was a successful businessman and my mother, a stay-at-home mom. We celebrated holidays with relatives and always had an overabundance of good food. I did well in school, had lots of friends, and went on memorable family vacations. My parents never fought.

Then one day in my senior year in high school, my mother called us in for a family discussion and announced her intent to divorce my father after twenty-three years of marriage. "I've been unhappy for a long time," she confessed, "and I'm ready to throw in the towel." With those words, my family life ended forever.

As an adult I asked my mother how she had decided to divorce my father. Because she felt unhappy in her marriage, she sought the help of a professional. After several years of weekly meetings, the therapist advised my mother to get a divorce because she believed the differences between my mother and my father were irreconcilable. She told my mother that leaving her marriage would help her find herself. That was all the encouragement my mother needed.

My parents' divorce was one of the most significant events in my life.

Although their divorce was amicable by most standards, it was devastating to me. I was leaving home to become a freshman at college, a difficult transition in the best of situations. I was launched from my nest just as the nest was crumbling. My parents were so immersed in their own pain and confusion that I had to rely on my own strength to get me through.

Today, despite an incredibly wonderful family, a fantastic career, and loving friends, I can easily understand why many people, regardless of their age when their parents divorced, see that event as having caused "a hole in their heart." The terrible thing about divorce is that it not only destroys relationships, it destroys families. I can still hear faint signs of pain when my brothers and I talk . . . and it's been almost thirty years!

From a personal standpoint, I have decided that, no matter what, I am going to make my own marriage work. My husband, Jim, and I have been together since 1973. We are best friends and lovers. I adore him and, on most days, I think he'd say the same about me. This is not to say that we don't have our ups and downs. Lord knows we do, but we are determined to work through them and come out the other side. And we do. We make up and laugh and love. Our marriage gets better with each passing year. I've learned a tremendous amount about making relationships work because of my determination to avoid divorce at all costs and give our kids the gift of growing up with both their parents.

As you can see, my parents' divorce made me a believer in the sanctity of marriage. I'm convinced that, unless you are in an extremely dysfunctional relationship—one in which there is physical abuse, chronic substance abuse, or chronic infidelity, for example—and your spouse isn't willing to change, you are better off solving your problems than getting out. Because of my conviction, I've devoted myself to helping people like you beat the divorce odds.

It is precisely for this reason that I have written this book. I want to take the guesswork out of marriage-saving. And, unlike *Divorce Busting*, where I inadvertently gave some readers the faulty impression that they had to find a therapist like me to help them save their marriages, I am going to show you how to become your own marriage expert . . . quickly! I have extracted the best and most effective ideas from my last book, and broken them down into specific steps you can take—by yourself—to make your marriage work again. Plus, I have had the benefit of hearing from thousands of readers who have asked fantastic questions about the application of my ideas to their own unique situations. It has forced me to become clearer and more specific about my Divorce Busting program. In fact, I have distilled it to seven steps. These steps will be the road map you need to save your marriage.

And if the road to marriage recovery has been a lonely one so far, that's all about to change. Even though we've never met, you'll be surprised by how well I know you and the issues with which you've been struggling. By the time you're done with this book, you will think I've been camping out in your living room for years! You'll read about communication breakdowns, emotional alienation, the Walkaway-Wife Syndrome, depression, infidelity, Internet obsession, midlife crises, sexual problems, and more. You'll eavesdrop on the trials and tribulations of others in your shoes. And best of all, you'll be able to savor, word for word, the incredible success stories of those who have risen above marital adversity and reclaimed their love.

So although you have probably been feeling pretty miserable, you have reason to come out of your funk right this very minute. I don't know everything, but I know a lot about saving marriages. People don't call me the Divorce Buster for nothing. I will give you the inside scoop about getting your marriage back on track. It will restore your faith in yourself, in your reluctant spouse, and in your marriage. So stop worrying. Start reading. Keep praying. And come learn everything you need to know to divorce-proof your marriage.

Part 1

The Divorce Trap

CHAPTER ONE

The Not-So-Great Escape

People who are unhappy in their marriages often speak of feeling trapped. They yearn to be free from the tension, loneliness, constant arguments, or deafening silence but worry that divorce may not be the right decision. After all, they took their marital vows seriously. They're not trying to hurt their spouses. They don't want to hurt their children. They panic at the thought of being alone. They worry about finances. They fear the unknown.

Yet the idea of living in a loveless marriage starts to feel like a death sentence. Over time, many of these people slowly convince themselves that the benefits of leaving their marriages vastly outweigh the benefits of staying. They tell themselves, "Kids are resilient, they'll bounce back," or "In the long run, this will be better for everyone." It's not until they embark on the path to divorce and begin to piece their lives back together that they discover the real price they paid for their so-called "freedom." Regretfully, this painful discovery comes too late. They have fallen into the divorce trap.

Dear Michele,

I was married for eighteen years and we have three terrific children. I instigated a divorce. It was final six months ago. Now, I am having second thoughts.

I never imagined that I would feel this way because, for years, I was so miserable in my marriage. I thought that once I got out, we all would be better off. At first, it *was* a relief to get away from all the arguing. However, I could not anticipate how quickly the feelings of relief would turn to pain. The look on my children's faces when they talk to their dad on the phone or when they come back from weekend visits has been more than I can bear.

What surprises me the most though is the fact that I find myself thinking about my ex all the time. He is far from perfect, but I now realize I could have made more of an effort to learn how to deal with the things that irritated or hurt me. Now I am haunted by the fact that my divorce destroyed not only a marriage but a family.

Joan

Dear Michele,

I feel like a fool writing to you, but I don't know where else to turn. After twenty-four years of marriage, I told my wife I wanted a divorce. I had been pretty unhappy in our marriage for a long time. Our sex drives were totally incompatible. Whenever I approached her, she never seemed to be in the mood. At first I thought I was doing something wrong, but after a while I got sick of all of her excuses.

Then I met a younger woman at work who respected me and seemed attracted to me. Although I never thought I would be the kind of guy who would have an affair, after spending hours together working on late night projects, the temptation just became too great. Although my wife suspected something, I kept my affair secret.

Eventually, I realized I couldn't live this lie any longer, so I filed for divorce. My wife was devastated. She begged me to stay. She tried to explain away my feelings—insisting that I was in the midst of a midlife crisis or that I was depressed. Still, I couldn't wait to get out on my own. I knew the kids would survive and I believed our marriage had died long ago.

The divorce became final a year ago during which time I have made some painful discoveries. It didn't take long before I lost my infatuation with the other woman. I started missing my wife. But she has made a whole new life for herself and I am not part of it.

If you have any suggestions, I will be forever grateful.

Mark

Mark and Joan are not alone. The divorce trap seduces over one million people each year. It promises peace and tranquility. It offers a fresh start, a second chance at romance, contentment, and self-discovery. It lures people into thinking that by walking out the door they can eliminate life's seemingly insurmountable problems. When you're desperately unhappy, these so-called guarantees are hard to resist. But there are good reasons for doing so. If you or someone you love is contemplating divorce, you will want to know what I have learned about the truth about divorce.

In my work, I've had a bird's eye view of what happens in people's lives after divorce. I have seen the intense pain and despair that linger for years. I have seen times when every birthday, holiday, or other causes for celebration have been nothing more but painful reminders of a divorce. I have seen the triggering of unpredictable, hurtful events such as the total rejection by the children of the parent seeking the divorce. I have known children who, even many years after the divorce and their parents' subsequent remarriages, still want to know if Mom and Dad will ever get back together.

Now, after three decades of our social experiment with rampant divorce and disposable marriages, I know it isn't a matter of people keeping their marriages together because they *can*, it's a matter of people making their marriages work because they *should*. Divorce stinks! Why? Recent findings about the long-term effects of divorce speak for themselves.

- Except in very extreme conflict-ridden families—and most families *do not* fit this criterion—children are better off when their parents stay married.
- Children are more likely to finish school and avoid problems such as teenage pregnancy, drug abuse, and delinquent behavior. Plus, they are more likely to have good marriages themselves.
- Even if a parent is happier as a result of divorce, there is no "trickle down effect." Children still struggle emotionally regardless of how the parent feels.
- Married men make better fathers. They are more likely to provide guidance, role modeling, and financial support.
- Marriage is good for most adults. As compared to single, widowed, or divorced people, married people are healthier, have

better sex lives, engage in fewer high-risk activities such as substance abuse, live longer, and are happier!

- Depression is almost three times as prevalent in women who divorce once, and four times as prevalent in women who divorce twice than in women who have never divorced.
- A random sample of over 8,600 adults revealed the percentages of those who felt lonely. The results are as follows. Marital status and percent reporting loneliness:

  Married—4.6

  Never Married—14.5

  Divorced—20.4

  Widowed—20.6

  Separated—29.6 (Page and Cole)

- Those in healthy marriages tend to be better, more productive employees. Married men miss work less often.
- Divorce increases the cost of many public health and social service programs. Single-parent households often mean children are raised in poverty or on public aid.
- A single mother's standard of living almost always decreases significantly after divorce.
- As compared to 50 percent of first marriages that end in divorce, 60 percent of second marriages end in divorce.

Many people considering divorce say they wish they could have a crystal ball that would allow them to see into the future. Actually, the crystal ball is here for the taking. Research has enabled us to be "clairvoyant." But many people choose to ignore or discount the facts because they've been hoodwinked into believing that divorce provides answers to an unhappy marriage. But how are myths about divorce being perpetuated?

The divorce trap is a powerful conspiracy that is invisible to the naked eye. Like carbon monoxide, the odorless killer, the divorce trap is an insidious influence, invading your thoughts without your knowing it. What are the forces behind the divorce trap?

WELL-MEANING FRIENDS AND FAMILY

Oddly enough, some of the people nearest and dearest to you are part of the problem. This is not to say that they don't have your best interests at heart. They do. They love you. They can't stand to see you in pain. More than anyone, they know you and know how much you deserve happiness in your life. Their caring is genuine. Why then do I say that your loved ones can be misdirecting you?

The Biased Shoulder

When you share your unhappiness with loved ones, what they hear is *your* side of the story, and your side only. Even though your feelings about your spouse and marriage are valid, they are, nonetheless, biased. Needless to say, if your spouse were in on the conversation, the story about your marriage would take a not-so-slight different turn. But the people who love you don't care about objectivity; they want you to feel better. Although this makes perfect sense, the end result is that the people in whom you are confiding offer potentially life-changing advice without a complete set of facts. If you follow that advice, you may create an even bigger rift in your marriage. Let me give you an example of how this works.

Sue was miserable in her marriage; she felt that she and her husband, Jeff, had completely grown apart. Sue decided to talk to her sister, Ann, about her predicament. Sue told Ann that she was really upset about how things had changed in her marriage. When she and Jeff got married, she explained, they were crazy about each other. They did everything together, spent hours talking, weekends doing fun things, and sex was great. They were best friends. As Sue recalled these memories, she cried. Seeing Sue in such pain, her sister's heart went out to her. Ann asked Sue to tell her more about what had been troubling her. Through her tears, Sue filled in the blanks.

She said that Jeff had turned into a completely different man from the one she married. He worked long hours and when he was home, he showed little interest in talking to her or in being with her. On weekends, he occupied himself with projects or watching sports on television. When Sue approached Jeff about her feelings, Jeff responded coldly, "Why are you always hassling me?" Sue tried to get through to Jeff and tell him how much his distance was hurting her, but Jeff seemed to withdraw even more.

Jeff's insensitivity to her feelings made Sue angry and hurt. She stopped doing thoughtful things for him, trying to engage him in conversation, and even refused his advances to be intimate. Now, instead of just being distant, Jeff had become critical and unpleasant, never passing up an opportunity to say or do something to hurt Sue's feelings. Sue couldn't understand why Jeff had become such a "jerk," especially since all she wanted was a closer relationship.

Upon hearing Sue's rendition of their marital interactions, Ann immediately came to her defense. "I can't believe he's acting this way! This isn't the same Jeff I used to know. What do you think is going on with him?" For the next half hour, they speculated about the possible causes of Jeff's ugly behavior—an affair, depression, a midlife crisis, or perhaps just bad genes from his father. Although they were uncertain as to the real reason Jeff had transformed into the unlikable man Sue had portrayed him to be, they agreed that Jeff was to blame for Sue's unhappiness. Ann consoled Sue. She hugged her and told her that she "would be there for her anytime she was needed." Ann also offered a few suggestions—counseling, giving Jeff an ultimatum, a trial separation—and Sue said she would consider her ideas. Sue thanked Ann for her support and understanding. She felt so much better.

Sue did follow through with Ann's suggestion to give Jeff an ultimatum. "Either you change, or I'm leaving," she warned him. But Jeff became even colder. In the weeks that followed, Sue regularly sought comfort in Ann's company. Sue complained, Ann commiserated. Although Sue felt validated by Ann's feedback, it did little in the way of helping her find solutions to her marital problems. As time passed and nothing improved, Sue's despair grew, as did Ann's determination to encourage her sister to leave her marriage. "You've tried everything," Ann told her. "It's time to throw in the towel."

It's easy to see how Ann arrived at this conclusion. Sue appears to be the spouse who is working on the marriage while Jeff is the inconsiderate, unloving one. But now let's eavesdrop on Jeff's conversations with his life-long buddy, John. Jeff is a very private person and, though he rarely opens up with friends and family, his unhappiness with Sue prompted him to discuss his marriage with John.

He told John that he was frustrated and angry at Sue. All she ever did was nag. Nothing he did ever seemed good enough. She asked for help in the kitchen and when he cleaned it, the only comment he heard was, "I can't believe the way you loaded the dishwasher, it's so sloppy," or "You forgot to wipe off the counters." All Jeff heard was criticism, never appreciation. So, after a while he just stopped trying.

A married man himself, John knew that relationship problems didn't happen overnight, so he asked about the circumstances leading up to their current situation. Jeff felt that Sue had bailed out on him as a partner long ago. "When we met, she was fun to be with. We went to sporting events, out to dinner, we socialized with friends, and had common interests. We golfed, played tennis, and biked all the time. We both loved the outdoors." But Sue stopped showing interest in their activities together. She seemed more interested in her job, church activities, friends, talking on the phone, and going shopping. Sometimes she would stay on the phone with her girlfriends or her mother the entire evening! "But the biggest change in Sue," Jeff said, "is that she never wants to have sex, and it's been that way for a very long time. That definitely bothers me the most."

Jeff went on to explain how hurt and angry he felt because of Sue's constant rejection. "I don't know what's with her. Sue used to love sex. I always prided myself about how connected we were physically. But now she's never in the mood. She's got a headache, she's mad at me, she's too busy, it's the wrong time of month . . . He told John that Sue's cold shoulder had taken its toll. He admitted to being irritable and snapping at Sue fairly often. He was hoping that at some point Sue, the woman who used to be his best friend and lover, would, just once, reach out to him and be affectionate. Instead, all he ever got was criticism.

After hearing Jeff's dilemma, John said, "Sounds really tough. I heard about some women with hormone imbalances losing interest in sex. You ought to check it out." Then he suggested that Jeff do something to spice his sex life up a bit. "Get a bottle of wine, buy a sexy nightgown, and make her a candlelight dinner. Stay at a nice hotel next weekend. Tell her you want to be closer physically."

A few days later, Jeff approached Sue with the idea of a little romantic weekend getaway. Sue didn't seem too interested. Jeff made a comment about not being intimate anymore and Sue snapped, "Of course we're not intimate! You don't expect me to want to have sex with you when our relationship stinks, do you?" Jeff replied, "Have you ever thought about the fact that our relationship stinks because you don't want to have sex anymore?" This chicken-or-egg argument played like a broken record for weeks before the couple decided to split.

Imagine how Ann or John might have reacted differently had they heard "the whole story." Ann might have realized that Jeff wasn't the villain Sue made him out to be; that he was feeling rejected and hurt. With this in mind, Ann might have suggested that Sue do things that would help Jeff feel more connected to her such as go biking or hiking together, or being more playful and affectionate. There's no question that Jeff wasn't handling his hurt feelings in the best way, but unfortunately, instead of sharing openly about their feelings of vulnerability, some people lash out. Since Ann was totally in the dark about Jeff's feelings about the marriage, her suggestion—give him an ultimatum—was bound to fail.

Had John heard Sue's side of things, he might have understood that for Sue the prerequisite for being close physically is emotional closeness and that Sue and Jeff had not been close for some time. He might have suggested that Jeff spend more time talking and paying attention to her, and being her friend. It's easy to see how John's well-meaning advice to spice up their sex life fell flat on its face.

Protectors and Rescuers

Another reason friends and family can increase the odds you will be divorce-bound is that, because they can't bear to see you in pain, they will steer you to what they think is the quickest escape from the emotional torture. They convince themselves and then you that since your spouse is the problem, you should get rid of him or her. "You don't deserve this. Just get out."

But you need to be aware of a couple of things when you listen to this advice. First of all, although your friends and family care about you, their advice is also self-serving. It will make *them* feel better if you aren't so sad. It will be a relief *for them* when you stop feeling so torn. *They* want an end to this unhappiness. The problem is, if you follow their advice and make *them* feel better, *you'll* be divorced and supporting yourself (and your kids), changing your lifestyle, and starting all over, *they* won't. Even if your loved ones are divorced themselves and believe that their divorce has improved their lives dramatically, it doesn't mean that you will feel this way too.

Second, although it might be tempting to believe that divorce will free you of your spouse, when children are involved, *there is no such thing as divorce.* Your spouse will be in your life forever. And I mean forever. You'll be in constant communication about visitation, decisions about your children's welfare, holidays, money, vacations, issues pertaining to the relationship between the children and new male or female friends/marital partners. The list is endless.

One woman wrote me,

I've been divorced for twenty-three years. I realized that my ex and I would be in touch weekly because of our kids, but I guess I thought that when the kids got older, he would just disappear from my life. My grown daughter is about to give birth next week and for the first time, I realized that my ex and I are going to be "the grandparents" together. What was I thinking? Spouses don't disappear.

Spouses don't disappear with a divorce, and neither do your problems. Although a person may be hard to get along with, the truth is, when you're experiencing marital problems, it's almost always the result of how *two* people interact. In other words, two people develop relationship habits, and if you leave, you take your habits with you when you go. Let me give you an example.

Deb and Ron had a great marriage in the early years. Deb admired and respected Ron's decisiveness and take-charge personality. But as years passed, Ron's tendency to tell Deb what to do and how to do it left her feeling less enamored of his so-called take-charge personality. Now, she thought he was overbearing and dominating.

At first, she tried to tell him to stop being so controlling, but he defended his actions and brushed her feelings aside. Deb kept her resentments and bitterness inside. She walked around most days being furious at him, without his even knowing it. Over time, she could no longer stand the bottled-up anger and filed for divorce. After all, she thought, if I get rid of this controlling man, I will be able to find myself again and make my own decisions. After a long, drawn-out battle, they finally divorced.

The problem is, by thinking that Ron was the sole cause of their marital breakdown, Deb was blind to the ways in which *her own* behavior contributed to their problems. Let's assume that Deb's perception of Ron is accurate and she tried to get Ron to back off. When her requests fell on deaf ears, however, instead of trying a new and more dynamic approach, Deb backed down and did nothing. The more Deb did nothing, the more Ron took over. In a sense, Deb created her monster.

And the sad part about all this is, when Deb divorces Ron, she will feel relieved momentarily to be free of his presence, but if and when she remarries, she will enter her new relationship unenlightened about how to deal with the differences that naturally occur between any two people. That's because she ran away from her relationship problems rather than solved or learned from them. And since she failed to see her role in the demise of their relationship, she is destined to make one of two common mistakes.

The first is to marry someone similar to Ron and re-create the exact same problems. The second is to fool herself into thinking marriage will be infinitely easier if she marries someone who is *totally* different from Ron. And that's what Deb did. She purposely sought out a man who was gentle and laid back. At first, it felt like her life's dream. She didn't have to walk on eggshells because no one was looking over her shoulder. She didn't have to be afraid to voice her feelings because her husband would listen rather than criticize. She felt she could be herself for the first time in years.

Time passed and now Deb felt that her laid-back, gentle man was wimpy and unmotivated. He made less money than her first husband. He wasn't overly ambitious. She disliked that she now had to help him support the children financially. When she asked him what he wanted to do on weekends, he always said, "I don't care, it's up to you." Although she used to appreciate his easy-going attitude, now she was frustrated by his indecisiveness. When she talked to him about her feelings, he got emotional and cried. Deb wanted to avoid feeling controlled in her life, but this was more than she bargained for. Rather than find productive ways to get through to her husband and get more of her needs met, Deb found herself thinking about divorce once again. And as before, she reassured herself that the problems in her marriage had nothing to do with her.

The obvious lesson here is that when a marriage fails, no matter how tempting it might be to put all the blame on one spouse's shoulders, both spouses have contributed to its downfall. I know that. But your friends and family don't know that. They just see your spouse's shortcomings.

Look, we all need people on our side, people who will stand by us, no matter what. But before you are too quick to heed the advice of your personal fans, you must remember this. Their opinions are biased. They can't always see the forest for the trees. If you leave conversations feeling supported but solutionless, be wary. You might be in the midst of being initiated into the divorce trap's steering committee.

WELL-MEANING THERAPISTS

Often people recognize that friends and family can be biased and, for that reason, decide to seek professional help for their marriage. Unfortunately, going to a therapist when you are having marital problems doesn't guarantee you will leave with your marriage intact. Some therapists see divorce as a challenging, yet viable solution to marriage's many problems. They appreciate the impact of divorce on children, but they prefer to focus on children's resiliency and their ability to adjust. Although they might initially try to help couples move beyond their differences, if the path to solution is rocky, they are quick to suggest calling it quits. They see divorce as a rite of passage. But why?

To begin with, you need to know that, first and foremost, therapists are people. No matter how well trained they may be, it's impossible for therapists to check their personal values, morals, and perspectives at the door at the start of a therapy session.

A therapist's views about marriage are influenced by many things, including the quality of his/her own parents' marriage. For example, if the therapist's parents had a highly combative marriage and made no attempt to improve things, making it miserable for the kids, the therapist might believe that people are better off divorcing when there is tension and steer the sessions in that direction. If a therapist's father had affairs and the therapist observed the hurt that it caused in the family, he might believe that marriages cannot heal after infidelity. If a therapist grew up with two parents who calmly talked things out when there was trouble, and if you and your mate have a more hotheaded problem-solving style, she might believe that you are incompatible and suggest you separate when research shows that many hotheaded couples manage to solve problems just as well as those who are more controlled. If, in growing up, a therapist had a really stormy relationship with her father, it's possible that she might have negative feelings about men and continually side with the woman in the couple. This sort of bias is likely to result in resistance on the part of the man (who feels outnumbered), or in his dropping out of therapy, neither of which bodes well for the marriage. In short, therapists can't separate who they are from what they do.

The same is true for me. Do you remember what I told you about the impact of my parents' divorce on my own marriage and in my work with couples? It made me a true believer in the sanctity of marriage. How does this pro-marriage bias affect what I do when I work with people?

For starters, each time I meet a person or couple and hear about their marriage problems, my default position is, "This marriage can be saved." Obviously, I am not always right and some marriages do end in divorce, but my positive attitude has served my clients well. Most couples stay together and find renewed happiness with each other.

I don't panic or become discouraged when I hear people's doubts about their marriages or when I'm told about complicated marital problems. I've worked with people who have had multiple affairs, a divorce in the works, months of separation, a loss of love and/or lust—and, in the eleventh hour—were able to fall back in love. I mean, *really* fall back in love. So, as I've said before, problems aren't roadblocks, just bumps in the road.

Contrast this "Never say die" philosophy with the approach many other therapists take with couples. Many therapists assess the viability of people's marriages based on the types of problems they are having, the severity of these problems, how long they have lasted, and how optimistic both partners are about the possibility for change. If the problems are long-standing or if one partner expresses intense doubt about the marriage, the therapist becomes pessimistic, starts to doubt that the marriage can be saved, and begins to work toward separation.

I, on the other hand, completely understand why people feel pessimistic. Anyone who has suffered in a marriage over a long period of time will, by definition, feel despondent. I see the hopelessness as a normal reaction to a painful situation rather than a sign about the marriage's future. I proceed with the knowledge that, once we find workable solutions, the hopelessness will vanish. Hopelessness doesn't derail me.

Too many therapists give people the message that divorce is a reasonable solution when hopelessness exists. How? For example, people often go to therapists for affirmation that getting out is the right thing to do. They feel really torn and they are looking for that "expert opinion." Some people even ask their therapist outright, "Don't you think I've tried everything?" "Do you think my marriage is over?" The truth is no matter how many degrees a therapist might have, or how smart s/he might be, there is *absolutely no way* for a therapist to know when a marriage has reached a dead end.

But this doesn't stop many therapists from acting as if they have a crystal ball. They say, "If your husband won't attend therapy, it means he's not committed to your marriage and nothing you do will make a difference," or "It seems as if your wife has lost feeling for you, why don't you just get on with your life?" or "As long as your husband is having an affair, you might as well assume your marriage isn't going to survive," or "Why are you hanging on to this marriage? Your wife has already filed for divorce?" Although these predicaments make marital repair more challenging, none of them is, by any means, a marital death sentence. Telling people that their marriage is doomed is, in my opinion, fortune-telling at best and unethical at worst.

Besides therapists' personal experiences, there are other reasons they might not be advocates for marriage. Their professional training may stand in the way. Although it may seem strange, the whole premise upon which traditional therapy is based may not be conducive to helping people work out problems when the going gets tough. For instance, therapists are trained to encourage people to pursue the parts of their lives that will bring *personal* happiness and satisfaction, even if these goals are at odds with what's best for the marriage, the children, or even the individual in question in the long run. The therapist wants you to feel good and do whatever it takes to make that happen.

I once saw a couple on the verge of divorce—thanks to a therapist the man had seen. The wife and child had moved back to their hometown, several thousand miles from their current home, in order to receive family support for their disabled child. Because they were having a hard time selling their home, the husband decided to remain with the home until it was sold. During the time they were separated, he had a great deal of freedom. He had no day-to-day responsibilities as a husband or father. He could work, go to his health club, and be with his friends as much as his little heart delighted. And he did. He was having a ball. That's when he started to question his marriage. He thought to himself, "I really enjoy my life as a single person. I wonder if there is something wrong with my marriage." So he sought the help of a professional.

The therapist helped him to uncover feelings of discontent with his marriage and his life as a family man. She suggested that perhaps he had always been a "pleaser," that is, he put effort into making everyone happy but himself. Her solution? "Get out of your marriage. Start anew. Be self-determining. Follow your heart." Psychobabble poison.

He eventually confessed his ambivalence to his wife, who was devastated. She had no idea he was unhappy in their marriage! They agreed to schedule an appointment with me. When I saw them, I understood the therapist's assessment: the husband *had* lost himself in the marriage, rarely openly expressed his desires, and often went along with the program, despite his own wishes. However, instead of thinking that his path to happiness was for him to abandon his marriage and family, I saw a better route; to help him become more forthcoming with his wife and find ways to meet his needs within the context of his marriage. Believe me, it was a no-brainer. After only three sessions they were happier than ever! He became more honest with his wife—only agreeing to do that which he really wanted to do and letting her know when he was disappointed about things—and she loved it. She no longer had to wonder whether he was doing things to placate her that only backfired later. Their marriage flourished. I placed a follow-up call to them a year later and they were pregnant with their second child. So much for a marriage doomed for divorce!

Another significant aspect of therapists' training that makes marriage preservation more challenging is the idea that in order to solve problems, people must first understand what caused the problems. What this means is that if a couple is having marital difficulties, instead of helping that couple identify things they can do *immediately* to feel closer and more connected, many therapists first gather lots of information about how each spouse was raised. This is unfortunate because research shows that the average time a couple experiences problems before initiating therapy is six years! Six years! So, that by the time most couples seek help, they are in desperate need of answers. They don't need to become experts on why they are stuck! If therapy fails to offer an immediate sense of relief or hope that solutions are possible, most couples become more despondent and more likely to throw in the towel.

Another belief inherent in most theories of therapy is the idea that people will get along better if they just express their feelings openly and honestly. In general, this is true. However, when a marriage is really in trouble, in most cases, the couple know precisely how their partner feels—they just don't have a clue as to what they can do to *resolve* the differences between them. Therapists are usually more skilled at helping people identify and express hurt and angry feelings than they are at helping people negotiate their differences, so therapy often ends up being more like a blame session than a problem-solving session. As a result, people end up feeling their marriages are really in bad shape and not worth preserving.

I don't mean to imply that all therapy is bad. It isn't! Therapy can be a lifesaver! There are lots of competent, caring therapists out there. But if you *do* decide to seek professional help, you need to make sure that you are seeking the help of an individual who believes that marriages are worth saving and who has been trained specifically to work with couples. Later in this book, I will offer some guidelines for choosing a good marital therapist.

THE MEDIA MYTH-MAKERS

I once worked with a man who told me that he needed to divorce his wife because he didn't think he loved her anymore. I asked him, "What makes you think so?" He replied, "It's just not the way I see it in the movies." I had been a therapist for approximately fifteen years at the time and I thought I had heard everything. I was wrong.

Hollywood cannot be faulted for offering unrealistic portrayals of what really goes on behind closed doors; after all, it's the silver screen's job to entertain, not to educate us. Yet in a media-saturated society, it's hard not to be influenced by the images with which we are bombarded; perfect hard bodies; impassioned, breathless sex, and heart-stopping romance. If our relationships don't quite measure up, we start to think we're being short-changed, and want to upgrade to a new and improved model.

But the truth is, good marriages can be incredibly boring. There's nothing sexy about making dinner, paying bills, caring for elderly parents, changing diapers, and chauffeuring kids to soccer games. The really good things about marriage—the comfort spouses feel in one another's presence, the unspoken glances that speak volumes, the little things people do for their spouses, the certainty that they will wake up next to each other in bed every morning—are about as compelling to watch as watching paint dry. That's why realism is in short supply on the movie screen. It wouldn't sell.

Nowadays, if Hollywood isn't busy glamorizing marriage, it's busy taking the sting out of divorce. Sitcoms, movies, and cartoons depicting nontraditional families are the norm, and everyone seems to be doing just fine. The message is clear—the nuclear family is a thing of the past and we're no worse for the wear. Viewers aren't exposed to the real trials and tribulations of blending families or of raising children as a single parent. We don't see the *War-of-the-Roses*-type arguments that often occur between spouses as they pit their biological children against their stepchildren. We're not told how these arguments often account for the fact that 60 percent of second marriages end in divorce. We don't hear about the poverty and other challenges that often accompany single parenthood, especially for women. Television makes life after divorce seem easy.

Beyond making marriage look more glamorous than life, and divorce less noxious than in reality, the media biases people's perspective about marriage by being obsessed with bad news. The National Marriage Project at Rutgers University released a report that received more than its fair share of attention. It said that the U.S. marriage rate has never been lower, births to unmarried women have skyrocketed, the divorce rate remains high, and Americans' marriages are less happy than in the past. Wire services, newspapers, and magazines had a field day. Radio talk shows were buzzing with guests hypothesizing why the institution of marriage is headed for disaster.

Although few could debate the data offered by this now famous report, it is equally undebatable this news reflects just one side of the coin. For instance, did you know that *The Wall Street Journal* reported that a long-term marriage is a new status symbol? Or, were you aware that surveys tell us that Americans continue to say that a happy marriage is their number-one goal and that approximately 85 to 90 percent of us are still getting married? Did you know that in a recent survey of America's wealthiest people—those in the ninety-ninth percentile of taxpayers—it was noted that 71 percent were married to their first spouse?* Do you know about the most popular and longest-running column in magazine history—"Can This Marriage Be Saved?"—in *Ladies' Home Journal?* It is an upbeat, positive column describing the steps different couples take to solve their marital problems. People can't get enough of it. Unless you have been living on another planet, you know that 50 percent of first marriages end in divorce, but have you ever wondered why 50 percent of marriages *last?* Have you ever considered what makes these long-term marriages different?

I strongly believe that the constant barrage of negative data about marriage takes its toll on society. We start to believe that divorce is one of life's normal rites of passage; we fall in love, we get married, we have children, and we divorce. This acceptance of divorce as the norm makes it more likely that, rather than do what it takes to make marriages work when the going gets rough, we just leave.

---

*"How to Get Rich: Work Hard, Stay Married, Save a Lot and Invest Wisely," *Barron's,* Sept. 20, 1999, p. 36.

Imagine for a moment, that instead of all the doom-and-gloom predictions about marriage, we were inundated with love's success stories. We'd read in-depth interviews about couples who have been married fifty years or more and case studies of those who had risen above difficult marital problems such as infidelity, and about the hundreds of thousands of couples whose lives have been changed by taking a simple marriage education course. We'd receive updated information about the ways in which long-term marriage benefits men, women, children, and society as a whole. Just think about how our collective unconsciousness might be altered if the media spent a fraction of the time investigating why marriage works instead of informing and warning us about the death of marriage!

THE LEGAL SYSTEM

"If there is one lawyer in town, he will starve to death. If there are two, both will make a good living."

Sometimes, when people are unhappy in their marriages and unsure about whether they should leave or not, they go to an attorney to check out their rights. This, in and of itself, is not a bad idea, but there are some things you should know before you pick up the phone.

When you go to a divorce attorney, what you get is someone who specializes in the divorce process, not reconciliation. People often seek legal advice, not because they are 100 percent sure they want to divorce, but because they want to get information and to feel that they are protecting themselves. Although many attorneys pick up on people's ambivalence and suggest counseling, this is not necessarily always the case. It's an attorney's job to facilitate a divorce, not to suggest reconciliation. Besides, the thinking goes that by the time you schedule an appointment with an attorney, you have already considered all the alternatives and you are ready to terminate your marriage.

Once you start the legal ball rolling, it becomes your lawyer's primary responsibility to get you "a fair deal," which translates to "the best possible deal": the most money, the most time with your children, and the least amount of interference from your ex-spouse. Lawyers are ethically bound to operate from this premise. It's their job. The problem is, your spouse's attorney is charged with the same responsibility. The end result is that the divorce process becomes extremely adversarial. It's you against your spouse.

> Divorces are part of our adversary process. By design, the system pits one party against the other. The theory is that the decision-maker (the judge) has the benefit of the most persuasive argument from each side and the attack by cross-examination reveals the weaknesses of each side's position. Though this may be an effective way to make decisions in commercial and criminal cases, it certainly is not appropriate for the troubled family. It pits husband against wife, mother against father and hostility escalates into the ultimate war, the trial.*

Although protecting oneself is important, sometimes the very things you do to protect your personal interests jeopardize the slightest hope that you and your partner will remain civil to one another, let alone consider reconciliation.

Consider Greg, a man who desperately wanted to save his marriage. His wife was having an affair, often flaunting her infidelity in Greg's face. Greg was trying really hard not to be reactive because he hoped that the affair would eventually die a natural death. Indeed, research shows that affairs often end and reconciliation is possible as long as the betrayed spouse doesn't become retaliatory.

Greg's attorney felt that he wasn't taking a strong enough stand. He suggested that they try to get an order to prevent the man from having any contact with Greg's children. He also suggested that the man's questionable financial history be made public in order to cast him in a negative light. Although I understood why such a suggestion would be appealing, I also knew that had Greg followed his attorney's advice, it would only have incited his wife, etching their divorce in stone. In this case, winning the legal battle would mean losing the marriage-saving war.

But divorce attorneys are hired to "win," rather than consider a particular legal act's implications on future relationship dynamics.

---

*Divorce-Without-War.com.

Divorce attorneys clearly understand that divorce is as much a psychological war, as it is a legal war. That part of the process called "discovery" gives attorneys the tools with which to attack the opponent and to gain psychological as well as legal advantage. Depositions (examinations before trial) of friends, family, and business associates . . . are all part of the tactics used to bring your opponent to their knees.*

If, for example, in your heated discussions about the possibility of divorce, it becomes clear that both you and your spouse want full custody of your children, you will be in for a battle sure to make whatever positive feelings you might have had about your spouse vanish. You will be asked to compile as much information as you possibly can that will not only portray you as the more fit parent, but portray your spouse as inept and unfit. To boost your case and comply with your attorney's requests, you scrutinize your memories for all of your partner's faults and failures both as a parent and as a coparent, which distorts your perception and robs you of any lingering feelings of appreciation for your shared history. And to make matters worse, once you learn of your partner's portrayal of *your* shortcomings as a parent, the outrage you feel reconfirms in your own mind why you have been considering divorce in the first place.

Concern about the long-term damage done to relationships and families because of the adversarial nature of the legal process has prompted an alternative for those considering divorce. Mediation is a nonadversarial process involving an impartial third party who helps couples problem-solve, communicate more effectively, and reach mutually agreed-upon resolutions that are in the best interests of the family.

Although the goal of mediation is not reconciliation (nor should it be confused with marriage counseling), because of the collaborative nature of the process and its focus on building communication skills, couples opting for mediation often decide to reconcile rather than divorce. Even if divorce is the end result, the spirit of cooperation gained through the mediation process greatly benefits the couple's post-divorce relationship, which is especially important when children are involved. Unfortunately, not enough people consider mediation when their marriage is on the brink. If they did, it's possible that more marriages could be saved.

*Divorce-Without-War.com.

Now that you know what drives the divorce machine, you might wonder whether certain people are more susceptible to its influence than others. And the answer is yes.

THE WALKAWAY-WIFE SYNDROME

Although divorce offers the illusion of happiness to people of all ages, races, and personality types, there is one group that is particularly susceptible to the sound of the divorce siren. It's women. Approximately two thirds of the divorces in our country are filed for by women. What's going on here? Why are so many women throwing in the towel?

In the early years of marriage, women are usually the primary caretakers of the relationship. They're the ones who are doing a daily temperature check: "Have we had enough closeness today?" "Are we spending enough time together?" "Do we feel connected emotionally?" If the answer to these questions is, "Yes," life goes on. If not, women press for more closeness. They tell their husbands, "You don't value our relationship anymore." "We never do anything together." "Why do you always put work ahead of me?" Often, instead of recognizing their wives' needs, men simply feel as though they are being nagged and withdraw, emotionally and sometimes physically.

Because of this lack of response or even hostility, women become frustrated. They try another approach: complaining about their partners' lack of involvement about *everything* else in their lives. "I feel like a single parent." "You are such a couch potato." "Why don't you ever lift a finger around the house? I do everything myself." Although they are still only trying to get their spouses' attention, men recoil big time. (I've never met a man who moves closer to his wife as a result of being "nagged," no matter what his wife's intentions!) After months or years of negative interaction, women finally give up. They tell themselves, "I've tried everything. Divorce has got to be better than this. I'll find somebody who cares about me. Even if I don't, I'm so alone in this marriage, I can't take it anymore. I know I'll be happier without him." And with that, they plan their escape.

The interesting thing about this plan is that it usually hinges on a particular event that may take years to materialize. For example, "I'll leave my husband when the kids leave home," or "I'll get a divorce when I go back to school and learn new skills so I can support myself," or "I'm going to meet another man and as soon as I do, I will be out of here." And now comes the tricky part.

In the months or years that follow her decision, the wife is no longer trying to fix the marriage. She stops complaining. To her, this surrender to the inevitable is definitely a bad thing. To him, well, you don't need to be a rocket scientist to figure out what the husband thinks. He's thrilled! She's off his back. She must be happy again, or so he thinks and he proceeds with business as usual. Business as usual, that is, until "D Day"—the day his wife turns to him and says, "I want a divorce," to which her absolutely devastated husband replies, "I had no idea you were unhappy! Why didn't you tell me?" With that response, the marital coffin is nailed shut.

The tragedy of this situation is that this is the point at which most men finally understand the depth of their wives' unhappiness. They are finally ready to do the kind of soul-searching that would make having a great marriage possible. They are willing to do back flips to keep their marriages/families together. But by that time, most women have built a wall around themselves, one that is impervious to men's efforts to change. It's divorce, full speed ahead.

I'm convinced if more women knew the truth about divorce, they might not be so quick to dismiss their husband's offers to become better people and partners. They might actually stick around long enough to find out that their husbands really mean what they say about changing.

THE ANYTIME MIDLIFE CRISIS

Don't get me wrong. Men are lured by the divorce trap too. They are fooled into believing that life would be better if only they were single, had more and better sex, more adoration, fewer responsibilities and obligations, more nights out with the guys, and less nagging. Many otherwise sane, moral, responsible men wake up one morning and scrutinize their lives. They feel something is missing. They're not happy. In fact, they're downright depressed and withdrawn. Sometimes there's just a gnawing sense that something is wrong and a growing urgency to do something about it. And though they really aren't sure what's ailing them, they convince themselves they need to leave their marriages to find out.

Other times, men think they know what's at the root of their unhappiness. "I hate all this responsibility. Life is short, I don't want to feel so burdened all the time." "I got married for the wrong reasons—she was pregnant, we were too young, I was desperate to get out of my house, I felt pressured by her." "She's always so rejecting and critical. I want to find someone who appreciates me." "Our sex life has been nonexistent, I don't want to live like this anymore." "My father died a few months ago and it made me realize that I don't want to be in a marriage where there is conflict."

Perhaps these rationales sound familiar. Can you say midlife crisis? If a man is between forty and fifty, and he's developed a recent interest in working out, eating healthfully, buying new clothes, and has been eyeing that proverbial red convertible (or some other, less expensive boy toy) you can suspect a midlife crisis. And you may be right! But it's been my experience that men can have what's been termed a "midlife" crisis at almost *any time* in their lives. In fact, even men in their twenties have been known to feel despondent about their lot in life and start fantasizing about greener pastures. Although they don't have balding heads, expanding waistlines, and wrinkles, these younger men are, nonetheless, acutely aware of the happiness clock ticking speedily away. Rather than confront or fix what's wrong in their lives or in their marriages, many of these men try to free themselves from their depression and anxiety by picking up and leaving.

Wives of these men try to talk sense into them. They give them books about midlife crises. They cut out magazine articles and leave them around the house. They recruit friends to talk to their husbands. They pull out wedding pictures to jar memories of happier times. When that doesn't work, they urge their husbands to see a therapist about depression. They suggest Prozac or St.-John's-wort. They leave pamphlets about clinical depression strewn on desks or beside toilet seats. But alas, none of these desperate attempts to defog their divorce-prone men seems to make a dent; in fact, the urge to escape becomes even stronger.

BEATING THE ODDS

If reading about the pervasiveness of the divorce trap has made you pessimistic or overwhelmed, don't be. I've got some good news for you. No matter how rough your situation might be, you *can* beat the odds! You really can. I've helped thousands of people teetering on the marital edge reverse the momentum to make their marriages more loving. I can say with confidence that *you can save your marriage!* In fact, the reason I am writing this book is to show you in a step-by-step fashion precisely how to do that.

If you're someone who is considering divorce, I want to congratulate you for even reading this far. It's tempting to avoid anything that challenges your thoughts about leaving. You just want to get on with your life. And now, you've got some marriage therapist who doesn't know you from a hole in the wall warning you to abandon your last hope for happiness. But still, you're reading. For this, I give you a world of credit. You must have a gnawing sense that divorce might not be the answer for you.

If you are considering divorce, I want you to know that I agree with you if you think that life is too short to be miserable. I am not suggesting you stay in an unhappy marriage and resign yourself to loneliness and misery. But in recent years, we've learned a ton about why some couples are able to keep their love alive while others aren't. And it all boils down to one thing—relationship skills. How you handle conflict, how you communicate, how you problem-solve—all determine how strong or fragile your love bond will be.

Unfortunately, most of us never learned these skills from our parents. So how in the world should we know what to do when things get rocky? If your partner hasn't been loving, affectionate, or communicative, it's probably because s/he doesn't know how. If you've been unsuccessful in getting through to your spouse and getting more love in your life, it's not because your spouse is a bad person, it's just because you need better tools to reach him/her. And that's easy. I can teach you new skills to make your marriage the marriage you've always wanted. All you need to do is to approach this book with half an open mind (maybe even a quarter of an open mind) and put my techniques into practice—I'll do the rest of the work.

Maybe you are saying to yourself, "I've tried everything, why should I invest myself only to be disappointed again?" I'm telling you, you haven't tried everything. And I'm not suggesting that you totally give up any thought of going your separate ways. All I'm suggesting is that you agree to give the methods in this book a few weeks or months to work. Then decide. You can always get divorced. But give your marriage the last try it really deserves. You'll sleep better at night if you do.

Or perhaps you are reading this because a divorce is the last thing on earth that you want. In the pages that follow, I am going to spell out for you exactly what you need to do to reverse the downward spiral in your marriage. I will share with you everything I know about saving marriages from the brink of divorce. If you follow the seven-step program in this book carefully, it will be just as if you are in my office with me. You'll learn what you need to do to turn things around, how to evaluate your partner's responses and reactions, and what to do next. I will give you lots of examples of people who were in your shoes and how they rejuvenated their love. I will offer you the building blocks for change. But I'm going to be completely honest with you.

First, you, not your spouse, are going to have to do the lion's share of the work here. Because your spouse is skeptical, at best, you are the one who is going to have to prove that life together can be different. You may not like the fact that this feels so one-sided, but for now, I say, "That's too bad." That's just how it is. Get used to this idea, swallow your pride, and push up your sleeves.

Second, in *Divorce Busting,* I gave people the impression that change could happen overnight. It can and sometimes does. But thanks to the feedback I've gotten from readers and clients, I now know that it usually doesn't. It probably took years for your marriage to reach this point and repairing the damage will take time. If you are an impatient person by nature—when you want something, you want it now—you are going to have to work on yourself to slow down. I can offer you some tips about keeping calm when things seem at a standstill, but in this case, patience is more than a virtue, it's a necessity.

Finally, there are no guarantees. Sometimes, you can seven-step until the cows come home and it might not save your marriage. But I can tell you that unless you follow the steps in this book, you will never know for sure whether or not your marriage could have been saved. Right now, you've got nothing to lose and everything to gain. People who followed the Divorce Remedy program felt better about themselves and more optimistic in general, no matter what.

Having said all that, I want you to know that if I didn't believe your marriage could be saved, I wouldn't have wasted my time writing this book. If we can put men on the moon, eliminate life-threatening diseases, develop a vast network of worldwide communication, surely we can figure out a way to keep love alive. I believe I know how and when you're done with this book, you will too.

In the next section of the book, I am going to take you by the hand and lead you through the seven steps you'll need to take to save your marriage. In "Start with a Beginner's Mind," I will help you free yourself from the change-defeating kind of thinking that plagues all of us from time to time and replace it with new ideas.

In "Know What You Want," I will help you identify your marriage-saving goals. Although you may think you already know what they are, you haven't been specific enough. I will help you make your goals crystal clear.

In "Ask for What You Want," I will encourage you to approach your spouse with your goals and I will suggest strategies to use if your spouse isn't as receptive as you would like.

In "Stop Going Down Cheeseless Tunnels," I will help you figure out which strategies you've been using that have been backfiring and help you redirect your energies to doing things that produce the results you want.

In "Experiment and Monitor Results," I will teach you field-tested techniques for getting through to the spouse you love. I will help you become more systematic and learn how to "read the results" after you've tried something new. By the time you put step five into practice, you will have a much higher marriage-saving IQ.

In "Take Stock," I will ask you to stand back for a moment and evaluate how much progress you've made since you've started the program. Once you're clearer about how far you've come, you'll know exactly what you need to do to reach your goals.

In "Keeping the Positive Changes Going," I will teach you how to make your changes permanent. You'll learn how to prevent minor setbacks from becoming a spiraling downward trend. In short, I will show you how to make being solution-oriented a way of life.

Once you have learned these new techniques, you'll be ready for "Pulling It All Together." You'll see how other people in your shoes have made the seven-step program work for them. I will walk you through the path they took, week by week, so you can see exactly how the program works from beginning to end.

In Part 3, "Common Dilemmas, Unique Solutions," you'll find answers to the commonly asked questions put to me by thousands of divorce busters on such topics as infidelity, Internet affairs, passion meltdown, depression, and last, but not least, the midlife crisis.

You will want to read Part 4 over and over and over. That's because it is full of success stories of people who feel as you do about the importance of making marriages work, people who used my proven seven-step program and managed to make their relationships more loving than ever. Their letters are truly a blessing!

So what are you waiting for? Let's get started!

Part 2

Seven Steps to Saving Your Marriage

It's time to push back your sleeves and begin the hard work of repairing your marriage. And I do mean hard work. Although I will take the mystery out of relationship change, you are going to have to do the heavy lifting. The hardest parts of this program are not the skills you will learn—they are amazingly simple—it's the *application* of those skills. Why? Because your emotions about your spouse and your marriage have the potential to make you say and do things that will derail you from achieving your goal. No matter how strong you are, or how determined you might be to save your marriage, I guarantee that your emotions will ambush you from time to time. I will help to manage these intense feelings but in the end, it will be your job to stop your negative feelings from having a life of their own. I want to warn you that this marriage-saving stuff isn't exactly a piece of cake because I believe that forewarned is forearmed.

Having said that, I also want you to know that with each small success, it will become easier and easier for you to stay on your marriage-saving track. You will get better at predicting and circumventing challenges. But developing the kind of focus you need to make a marriage miracle happen doesn't occur instantly. As with any other skill, learning how to repair a relationship takes time, practice, and patience.

CHAPTER TWO

Step Number 1—
Start with a Beginner's Mind

A teacher stood before a class of kindergartners and drew a big dot on the blackboard. She turned to the class and asked, "What do you see here?" One little boy shouted out, "I see a squashed bug." The girl seated beside him added, "No, it's the top of a telephone pole." Another student interrupted, "I see a piece of candy." A fourth child concluded, "That is a full moon."

The same teacher then went into a class of senior high school students and, again, drew the dot on the chalkboard and asked, "What do you see here?" Her question was followed by a minute of dead silence, after which one teenager blurted out, "I see a dot on the chalkboard," a comment that evoked a sea of laughter. Nothing more was said. On reflection the teacher concluded that we begin our lives as question marks and end as periods.

Buddhists believe that people should endeavor to approach their lives with a beginner's mind because in a beginner's mind there are many possibilities. While in an expert's mind, there are but a few. Although age and experience can bring wisdom in some areas of our lives, it can also bring narrow-mindedness and shortsightedness. We get set in our ways. Our creative juices stop flowing. We no longer question our assumptions and beliefs. We know what we know, and we know that we're right. Often, we're not even aware of our own blinders because we assume our way of seeing the world is the only possible perspective.

Since many of the concepts, strategies, and techniques upon which this seven-step program are based challenge mainstream thinking, it is *essential* that, *before you do anything else,* you empty out your expert mind. And because I know that you might not even be aware of your unique set of blinders, I will help you discover which parts of your thinking have placed having a great marriage slightly out of your reach. There are two primary areas in which people's "expertise" clouds their thinking when they're having relationship problems. The first involves dearly held fallacies about love and marriage. The second has more to do with faulty misconceptions about how to bring about change in their relationships. As I describe people's favorite solution-blockers, see which ones sound familiar to you. Then exorcise them.

LOVE'S ILLUSIONS

Did you know that of the marriages that end in divorce, 50 percent end during the first seven years? Only seven short years! How is it possible that two people can be so madly in love that they stand before all of their teary-eyed family and friends and promise to love and cherish each other until "death do us part," only to call it quits seven years later? I'm convinced that the primary cause for this swift change of heart is that people don't know what to expect when it comes to love and marriage. And, if you have unreasonable expectations, you are bound to be disappointed. Disappointment causes us to believe that our marriages are broken, or that our spouses are flawed. And once we start thinking that way, divorce becomes a logical solution.

But unreasonable expectations about love and marriage are not just problematic for those in their early years of marriage. For example, the only group for whom the divorce rate is still on the rise is folks whose marriages have lasted thirty years or more. Why? Because if you start a marriage with the wrong ideas about what it takes to make a relationship work, rather than abandon those ineffective beliefs over time, most people just grow more attached to them. They've had thirty years to say to themselves, "I'm right, s/he's wrong." Unfortunately, bad ideas are one of many things in life that don't improve with age.

Why are we often clueless about making marriages work? No one is born knowing how to have a happy marriage. It's not part of your DNA; you have to learn it. And, if you weren't fortunate enough to have learned how to have loving relationships from watching your own parents (or the people who raised you), you are left to your own devices for guidance. You make things up as you go. If you're lucky, your ideas have some merit, but more often than not, your approach to things doesn't always work out the way you might wish. Relationships can be rather complicated and it helps to have directions and an agreed-upon set of rules by which both partners play.

There are many common misconceptions about relationships. You undoubtedly have a few of your own. Perhaps you're wondering which of your many expectations about marriage need a little fine-tuning. Well, wonder no more. Take the following relationship IQ quiz and see for yourself.

THE RELATIONSHIP IQ QUIZ

Answer True or False to each of the following statements:

1. Conflict and anger are signs that your relationship is failing.

False. All marriages, even the best of marriages, have their ups and downs. It's impossible to live under the same roof with another human being for any length of time and *not* disagree now and then.

People in loving marriages understand that conflict goes with the marital territory. It's more than unavoidable, it's necessary. People need to let off steam and air their differences. When they don't, they're in for trouble. The fact is, the single best predictor of divorce is the constant avoidance of conflict!

In my work, I've encountered many people who dislike conflict so much that they do everything they can to avoid it. These people honestly believe that keeping their feelings to themselves is what's in the best interest of their marriages. This strategy always backfires. Bottled negative feelings become poison, making people physically ill, angry, resentful, and hateful. If people keep their negative thoughts and feelings to themselves, they don't give their partners the opportunity to correct/change their behavior. It's unrealistic to expect people to be mind readers.

Having said that, I'd like to point out that the worst possible advice anyone could give to a newlywed couple would be, "*Always* express your feelings. *Always* tell your partner when you are upset about something." In good relationships, you learn to distinguish between the important issues and the petty ones; one of the secrets to a good relationship is learning to choose your battles wisely.

2. You're more likely to divorce if there are differences in your backgrounds, likes and dislikes, and interests.

False. Research shows that people who stay together and are happily married are no more similar than those who divorce! They come from decidedly different backgrounds, hold different beliefs, and have sharply different interests. But what separates those who have successful relationships from those who don't is that they learn effective ways to deal with their differences and handle conflict. They nurture the interests they do share and try to develop new ones from time to time. Successful couples understand that their partners are not supposed to be their clones. They believe that life would be incredibly boring if their spouses were mirror images of themselves. Instead, happily married people learn to both appreciate their differences, find ways to grow from them or simply make peace with them.

3. In healthy relationships, major disagreements get resolved over time.

False. Research tells us that approximately 60 percent of what couples argue about is unresolvable! If you eavesdrop on couples' arguments as newlyweds and then again after they've been married for twenty-five years or more, you might be surprised to find that much of the content is the same. However, *the way* in which people discuss these heated issues *does* change over time. We tend to mellow a bit, which makes a huge difference in how our partners react to us and vice versa.

Too many people think that their marriages are in trouble because they continue to argue about the same things for years. Well, welcome to the club! If you have been thinking that in good marriages, people eventually find mutually satisfying solutions to all major problems, you've been fooling yourself. This just isn't the case.

4. In healthy marriages, spouses have the same definition of what it means to be loving.

False. Very false, I might add. No two people define love in exactly the same way. What it takes for you to feel loved is probably fairly different from what it takes for your spouse to feel loved. Why? Your definition of love springs from a number of factors: your upbringing, your culture, your gender, and your life experiences in general. Since you and your spouse have had different life experiences, you will undoubtedly view love differently as well. Although this, in and of itself, is not problematic, it will become a problem if you fail to honor and accommodate your partner's point of view.

Let's say you grew up in a family that thrived on intellectual arguments. You feel right at home with a good "debate" because you spent years doing that with the people you love the most. But you end up marrying someone whose family members were extremely polite and wouldn't dream of openly challenging each other.

Because you long for those intense debates, you prompt, prod, and push your partner, hoping he or she will take the bait. But it doesn't work. You feel empty, hurt, let down. "If my spouse loved me," you tell yourself, "s/he would want to share more openly." Too many people believe that if their spouses truly loved them, their spouses would feel exactly the same way they do, but this kind of thinking is all wrong. Why?

Real Giving

Having a good marriage doesn't depend on people having a shared definition of love. It involves understanding your *partner's* definition and showing your love based on *that* definition, not *yours*. That's what real giving is all about. Not enough people engage in real giving. Instead, we give to others that which we would like to receive.

For example, when I'm feeling down, I like Jim to pursue me and ask me what's wrong. To me, that's a loving act. In the early years of our marriage, when Jim was feeling down, I showed my love by encouraging him to talk. But the results weren't so hot. I didn't get it.

But as time went on, I learned more about Jim. If he's upset about something, he needs time and space to work things out alone. I figured out that, in our marriage, a *real* act of love would be for me to back off when he was subdued, no matter how unnatural it felt. Real giving is when we give to our spouses what's important to *them—whether we understand it, like it, agree with it, or not!*

If you and your spouse have spent years debating about love definitions ("If you loved me, you would want to spend more time with my family," versus "If you loved me, you would want to spend more time alone with me on weekends," and so on), stop wasting time. You're both right. To have a loving marriage, you have to put yourself out and love your partner the way s/he wants to be loved.

5. People just fall out of love.

False. Some people believe that they need to divorce their spouses because they've fallen out of love. To them, love is a feeling that is either there or it's not there. If it's there, you get married. If it's not there, you divorce. This is one of the silliest ideas I have ever heard.

First of all, people don't just *fall* out of love. If love dwindles, it's because the marriage wasn't a priority. Love is a living thing. If you nurture it, it grows. If you neglect it, it dies.

The number-one cause for the breakdown in marriages in our country is that people don't spend enough time together. They take their marriages and their spouses for granted. Work, the kids, soccer games, community activities, and family obligations become more important than spending time together and the marriage gets placed on the bottom of the priority list. When this happens, the little time people do spend together, they end up fighting. Then they grow apart. This distance and alienation sometimes fool people into thinking they've fallen out of love.

Second, love isn't just a feeling, it's a decision. Happily married people understand that if they engage in activities that bring love into the marriage, they will *feel* loving. There is no magic or mystery here. What you decide to do on a daily basis will determine how much love you and your partner feel for each other. You both decide whether you're going to spend time together regularly or do your own thing, forgive each other or hold grudges, accept each other's weaknesses or point fingers of blame, apologize when in error or smugly stand your ground, be generous and giving or put your own needs first.

Of course, we're human, and our ability to be loving and kind to each other ebbs and flows, as do our feelings for our partners. However, wise people don't allow negative feelings or the absence of loving feelings to make them question their commitment to their spouses. They just understand that they're going through a rough time and that soon, they will *decide* to do what it takes to evoke feelings of love again . . . in themselves and in their spouses.

If you're someone who has been considering divorce because you aren't feeling love for your partner, I know you will disagree with what you just read. You have undoubtedly tried to convince yourself that love is a romantic feeling that you either have for someone or you don't, as if the feeling has a life of its own. And since you aren't feeling close to your spouse right now, you've probably told yourself, "I love or care about him/her, I'm just not *in* love anymore." I want to tell you that, if you believe that you've lost that loving feeling, I have the compass that will let you find it again. If you give yourself half a chance and follow the steps outlined in this book, you will discover that you can fall *in* love again.

If you're still skeptical, consider this: When you got married, if someone would have told you that in x number of years, you would fall out of love, you would not have believed that person. Your positive feelings for your partner at the time would have prevented you from even entertaining the possibility that love would die. Well, the same is true in reverse. Your current negative feelings are blinding you to the possibility that you will ever feel different again.

Perhaps it's your spouse who has doubted his/her feelings, not you. You are the one who has heard those dreaded words, "I love you, I'm just not *in* love with you anymore," or even, "I never really loved you in the first place." I know how devastated you must feel. But rather than wallow in self-pity, be reassured by this. Your spouse isn't seeing things clearly now. When people are miserable, they view their lives through unhappy lenses and recall only unhappy events. In fact, miserable people will often swear the good times never even happened!

Although this might sound like an impossible task, don't get too bent out of shape if your partner has expressed doubt about loving you. Even if you do, don't argue, don't debate, and don't try to prove that your partner isn't thinking clearly. Whatever you do, don't drag out your wedding album and point to your smiling faces, offering proof that there once was love and adoration. This will only backfire: The more you try to convince your spouse that s/he is being biased, the more s/he will want to show you that you are wrong. The more you push, the more s/he will pull away. If your spouse reports falling out of love, just say nothing and remind yourself that nothing is permanent. If s/he fell out of love, s/he can fall into love again.

One more very important point: If your spouse has expressed doubt about loving you, as you go through this program you will feel tempted to do a status check fairly regularly. Again, you need to get a grip on yourself. Do not ask whether your spouse loves you. Don't ask whether his/her feelings have changed. And—this is the hardest thing to do—stop professing your love for your spouse. Believe me, your spouse knows your feelings. Each time you say, "I love you," and your spouse feels unable to reciprocate, you remind him/her that something is missing. You don't want to put your partner in that position. When you stop talking about your love, your spouse won't think you stopped loving him/her, you will simply be taking some pressure off your spouse. I know it's hard, but I told you that this wasn't going to be easy.

6. An affair doesn't have to ruin a marriage.

True. There is little that is more devastating than to discover your spouse has been unfaithful. Most people take to heart the promise they make to forsake all others. The connection, closeness and intimacy, and trust you feel with your mate is very personal, something that is meant just for the two of you. This is why infidelity feels like such a violation.

But affairs happen, and when they do, the repair of the marriage is no easy task. Sometimes those who have been hurt swear they will never recover. They're convinced that they will not be able to forgive and move forward in the marriage. And although I completely understand why people feel this way, I also know that the future doesn't have to be as bleak as they are anticipating. Most people survive infidelity and can, in fact, make their marriage stronger once they work through the issues infidelity has brought into their lives.

If you or your spouse has had an affair, I urge you to read chapter 10. It will offer you concrete information to help you get your marriage back on track.

7. Most people are much happier in their second marriages because they've learned from their mistakes.

False. Although it's true that some people learn from their mistakes in their first marriages and are able to develop happier second marriages, this is, by no means, the rule. You may remember reading in the last chapter that 60 percent of second marriages end in divorce!

I also told you that one of the reasons there are more divorces in second marriages is that people enter their second marriages with the bad relationship habits they learned the first time around. They simply find new partners with whom they can do that old familiar dance. Stepparenting issues make second and subsequent marriages challenging. But there is another reason second marriages aren't necessarily better than first ones.

Unless you understand that *marriage* doesn't make people happy, you will spend the rest of your life trading in marital partners for new ones. Happiness is a do-it-yourself job; you can't rely on another person to fulfill you. Unless you feel satisfied with *your own* life, you will not be able to determine whether your unhappiness stems from personal or relationship issues.

If you are someone who is considering divorce, I would strongly urge you to ask yourself whether you love what you do every day. Are you on a path that is satisfying to you as an individual? If not, don't blame your partner, even though you might be tempted. If you aren't doing what you want to be doing, you have no one to blame but yourself. Now I understand that sometimes we have to make sacrifices in our lives for others— our children, for example—but by and large, if you are off-course, you need to do something about it. And why not make those changes right now, while you're *still* in this marriage?

I once worked with a woman who announced, "I'm not even sure why

I'm here today. I probably should have gone to an attorney instead." She never worked outside her home and was positive that her husband would be vindictive and make her fight hard for a fair settlement. I asked her how she planned on supporting herself. She hadn't even thought about it. She told me that once their children had moved away from home several years ago, she had considered getting a job but never initiated the process. She felt that her self-esteem had suffered in her marriage and that she wouldn't be able to find work.

After talking with her for a while, I told her that she could always divorce, but why not get her ducks in a row first? I suggested she find work and then think some more about her future. Several days later, a friend of hers asked her to work at a preschool, and because she loved children, it was something she had always wanted to do. She agreed.

I checked on her a month later. She was feeling great about her job and her newfound skills. Her supervisor had nothing but nice things to say to her about her contribution to the school. For the first time in years, she felt good about herself and her direction in life. And you know what happened? Her husband, that critical old guy, started looking better to her. She couldn't help but get excited about her new achievements and she shared them with him. He was quite supportive and this was an eye-opener to her. The better she felt about herself, the better their relationship became. During my last contact with her, she told me that she and her husband were getting along much better and that she was no longer considering divorce.

Did any of the answers in this Relationship IQ Quiz catch you by surprise or make you disagree with me? If so, good. It reassures me that your expert mind is being challenged and I'm exercising your beginner's mind. Now I want to talk with you about the predictable places couples experience marital challenges.

THE MARRIAGE MAP

In the mid-seventies, author Gail Sheehy wrote a landmark book called *Passages*. Although studies on child development were exhaustive at that time (we knew about the "Terrible Twos" and the dreaded teenage years), no one really had a clue as to what happened to adults once they hit age eighteen. Did emotional, psychological, intellectual, and spiritual development cease after your eighteenth birthday? Gail Sheehy thought not. Sheehy showed us how people of *all* ages continue to grow, change, and develop and that they go through predictable life crises and transitional stages.

Her book was very comforting. In the same way that parents of two-year-olds are comforted by the knowledge that a toddler's rebelliousness is predictable and normal, soul-searching thirty-year-olds finally understood their angst and recognized the universality of their feelings. As we passed through each developmental stage, we appreciated the permission Sheehy granted us to feel okay about our internal and external struggles. We learned that we were not alone.

As a longtime observer of relationships, I can tell you that, like people, marriages also go through different developmental stages and predictable crises. Everyone is familiar with the infancy stage of marriage—the infamous "honeymoon period"—but what happens after that? Does marriage have its equivalent to the "Terrible Twos" or the stormy teenage years? In fact, it does. But because people are unfamiliar with the emotional terrain, the normal hills and valleys of marriage, these predictable transitional periods are often misunderstood, causing overreactions. Those who manage to weather these universal stormy periods usually come out the other side with greater love and commitment to their spouses. That's why I want to offer you a marriage map.

The marriage map is meant to give you a broad overview of the experiences most couples have when they negotiate the marital terrain. As you read through these stages and developmental passages, don't get too hung up on the timetable. Some couples move through these stages more quickly than others, and some bypass certain stages entirely. See if any of this sounds familiar to you as you think about your own marriage and that of friends and family.

STAGE 1—PASSION PREVAILS

Head over heels in love, you can't believe how lucky you are to have met your one and only star-crossed lover. Everything other than the relationship quickly fades into the background. Much to your amazement, you have so much in common: You enjoy the same hobbies, music, restaurants, and movies. You even like each other's friends. You can finish each other's sentences. When you pick up the phone to call your partner, s/he is already on the line calling you. You are completely in sync. Everything is perfect, just the way you imagined it would be. When little, annoying things pop up, they're dismissed and overlooked.

At no other time in your relationship is your feeling of well-being and physical desire for each other as intense as it is during this romantic period. The newness and excitement of the relationship stimulates the production of chemicals in your bodies that increase energy and positive attitudes, and heighten sexuality and sensuality. You feel good in your partner's presence and start to believe that s/he is bringing out the best in you. Depression sets in when you're apart. There aren't enough hours in the day to be together. You never run out of things to say. Never, never, have you felt this way before. "It must be love," you tell yourself. While in this naturally produced state of euphoria, you decide to commit to spending the rest of your lives together. "And why not," you reason, "we're perfect together." And marry, you do.

Unless you elope or opt for a simple, judge's chambers-style wedding, your euphoria takes a temporary nosedive as you plan and execute your wedding. Once you get past the superhuman challenges dealing with family politics and hosting a modern-day wedding, your starry-eyed obsession with each other reemerges and takes you through the honeymoon period. At last, you are one. You have committed your lives to each other forever—. soul mates in the eyes of God and the world. And for a period of time, nothing could be more glorious. But soon, your joy gives way to an inevitable earth-shattering awakening; marriage isn't at all what you expected it to be.

STAGE 2—WHAT WAS I THINKING?

In some ways, Stage 2 is the most difficult because it is here that you experience the biggest fall. After all, how many miles is it from bliss to disillusionment? Millions. What accounts for this drastic change in perspective? For starters, reality sets in. The little things start to bother you. You realize that your spouse has stinky breath in the morning, spends way too long on the toilet, leaves magazines and letters strewn on the kitchen counter, and never wraps food properly before it's put in the refrigerator, and to top things off, snoring has become a way of life. There are big things too.

Although you once thought you and your spouse were kindred spirits, you now realize that there are many, many differences between you. Although you share interests in hobbies, you disagree about how often you want to participate in them. You like the same kinds of restaurants, but you enjoy eating out often while your partner prefers staying home and saving money. Your tastes in music are compatible, but you prefer quiet time in the evening while your mate enjoys blasting the stereo. You have many common friends, but you can't agree on which nights to see them.

You're confused about what's going on. You wonder if an alien abducted your partner and left you with this strange and complicated being, a person with whom you can't agree on a single thing. You argue about everything. "Who is this obstinate person I married?" you ask yourself. "What was I thinking?" You knew life wouldn't always be a bed of roses, but you never thought all you'd get was a bed of thorns. You figured that love would carry you through the rough spots, but you didn't imagine there'd be times you didn't feel love. You feel disillusioned and you wonder if you made a mistake. When you remind yourself you made a lifelong commitment, you start to understand the real meaning of eternity.

Ironically, it is in the midst of feeling at odds with your once kindred spirit that you are faced with making all sorts of life-altering decisions. For example, it is now that you decide whether and when to have children, where to live, who will support the family, who will handle the bills, how your free time will be spent, how in-laws fit into your lives, and who will do the cooking. Just at the time when a team spirit would have come in mighty handy, spouses often start to feel like opponents. So they spend the next decade or so trying to "win" and get their partners to change, which triggers stage 3.

STAGE 3—EVERYTHING WOULD BE GREAT IF *YOU* CHANGED

In this stage of marriage, most people believe that there are two ways of looking at things, your spouse's way and your way, also known as the Right Way. Even if couples begin marriage with the enlightened view that there are many valid perspectives on any given situation, they tend to develop severe amnesia quickly. And rather than brainstorm creative solutions, couples often battle tenaciously to get their partners to admit they are wrong. That's because every point of disagreement is an opportunity to define the marriage. Do it my way, and the marriage will work, do it yours and it won't.

When people are in this state of mind, they have a hard time understanding why their spouses are so glued to their way of seeing things. They assume it must be out of stubbornness, spitefulness, or a need to control. What they don't realize is that their spouses are thinking the same thing about them! Over time, both partners dig in their heels deeper and deeper. Anger, hurt, and frustration fill the air. Little or no attempt is made to see the other person's point of view for fear of losing face or worse yet, losing a sense of self.

Now is the time when many people face a fork in the marital road. They're hurt and frustrated because their lives seem like an endless confrontation. They don't want to go on this way. Three choices become apparent. Convinced they've tried everything, some people give up. They tell themselves they've fallen out of love or married the wrong person. Divorce seems like the only logical solution. Other people resign themselves to the status quo and decide to lead separate lives. Ultimately, they live unhappily ever after. But there are still others who decide that it's time to end the cold war and begin to investigate healthier and more satisfying ways of interacting. Although the latter option requires a major leap of faith, those who take this leap are the fortunate ones because the best of marriage is yet to come.

STAGE 4—THAT'S JUST THE WAY MY PARTNER IS

In Stage 4, we finally come to terms with the fact that we are never going to see eye to eye with our partners about everything and we have to figure out what we must do to live more peaceably. We slowly accept that no amount of reasoning, begging, nagging, yelling, or threatening changes our partners' minds. We look to others for suggestions; we seek religious counsel, talk to close friends and family, attend marital therapy, read self-help books, or take a relationship seminar. Those of us who are more private look inward and seek solutions there.

We more readily forgive our spouse for his/her hardheadedness, and recognize that we aren't exactly easy to live with either. We dare to ask ourselves whether there's something about *our own behavior* that could use shaping up. When disagreements occur, we make more of an effort to put ourselves in our partner's shoes and, much to our surprise, we have a bit more compassion and understanding. We recognize that, as with everything in life, we have to accept the good with the bad. Fights happen less frequently and when they occur, they're not as intense or as emotional as in the earlier years of marriage. We know how to push our partner's buttons and we consciously decide not to. When we slip, we get better at making up because we remind ourselves that life is short and very little is worth the pain of disharmony. We learn that when you've wronged your spouse, love means always having to say you're sorry. We mellow. We let things roll off our back that might have caused us to go to battle before. We stop being opponents. We're teammates again. And because we're smart enough to have reached this stage, we reap the benefits of the fifth, and final, stage.

STAGE 5—TOGETHER, AT LAST

It is really a tragedy that half of all couples who wed never get to stage 5, when all the pain and hard work of the earlier stages really begins to pay off. Since you are no longer in a struggle to define who you are and what the marriage should be, there is more peace and harmony. Even if you always have loved your spouse, you start to notice how much you are really liking him or her again. And then the strangest thing starts to happen. You realize that the alien who abducted your spouse in stage 2 has been kind enough to return him/her to you. You are pleased to discover that the qualities you saw in your partner so very long ago never really vanished. They were just camouflaged. This renews your feelings of connection.

By the time you reach Stage 5, you have a shared history. And although you'd both agree that marriage hasn't been easy, you can feel proud that you've weathered the storms. You appreciate your partner's sense of commitment and dedication to making your marriage last. You also look back and feel good about your accomplishments as a couple, a family, and as individuals. You feel more secure about yourself as a person and you begin to appreciate the differences between you and your spouse. And what you don't appreciate, you find greater acceptance for. You feel closer and more connected. If you have children, they're older and more independent, allowing you to focus on your marriage again, like in the old days. And you start having "old day feelings" again. You have come full circle. The feeling you were longing for during those stormy periods is back, at last. You're home again.

ABOUT THE MARRIAGE MAP

I'm certain that if more couples realized that there really is a pot of gold at the end of the rainbow, they'd be more willing to tough it out through the downpour. The problem is, most people fool themselves into thinking that whatever stage they are in at the moment, is where they will be forever. That can be a depressing thought when you're in the midst of hard times. And in marriage, there are lots of hard times—unexpected problems with infertility, the births of children (marital satisfaction goes down with the birth of each child), the challenges of raising a family, children leaving home, infidelity, illnesses, deaths of close friends and family members. Even if there is lots of joy accompanying these transitional stages, it's stressful nonetheless. But it's important to remember that nothing lasts forever. There are seasons to everything in life, including marriage.

Also, it's important to remember that people generally don't go through these stages sequentially. It's three steps forward and two steps back. Just when you begin to feel more at peace with each other in stage 4, a crisis occurs and you find yourselves slipping back to stage 3—change your partner or bust! But if you've been fortunate enough to have visited stage 4, sanity sets in eventually, and you get back on track. The quality and quantity of love you feel for each other are never stagnant. Love is dynamic. So is marriage. The wiser and more mature you become, the more you realize this. The more you realize this, the more time you and your spouse spend hanging out in Stage 5. Together again, at last.

YOU CAN IF YOU THINK YOU CAN

In the beginning of this chapter I warned you about two places where your "expertise" might get in the way of your having a better relationship. The first had to do with unrealistic ideas you might have had about love and marriage. I hope in reading this far you have quieted your expert mind and put your beginner's mind to work. But you're not quite done just yet. You need to do more cerebral "spring cleaning."

Without knowing you personally, I know that you have some less-than-effective ideas about how to improve your relationship. Everyone does. In this section, I will introduce you to a new way of thinking—solution-oriented thinking—that will change the way you look at your marriage forever. Some of these ideas might seem odd at first if you haven't been exposed to them before. Lots of people tell me that they have to read or be told this information several times before they really "get it." It's not that these ideas are so difficult; they are, in fact, simply common sense. But it's been my experience that when it comes to emotionally charged relationship issues, common sense is the first thing to go.

If, on the other hand, you are a veteran solution-oriented thinker, the following principles will be familiar to you. As you read through them, allow yourself to feel good about how much this way of thinking has become part of your life. Consider this your refresher course.

THE BUILDING BLOCKS OF SOLUTION-ORIENTED THINKING

It takes one to tango

Florence knew her marriage was headed for trouble. She and Pete argued incessantly. She loved her husband and wanted things to improve between them. She asked him if he would go for counseling. He refused. She thought that seeing a female counselor was a problem for him, so she did some research and got the name of a male counselor who had a great reputation. She approached Pete with the idea of going to therapy again, only to have him say, "I told you that I'm not interested in going for therapy, not now, not ever. I don't believe in that stuff. Go yourself."

Florence felt hurt and frustrated. She went to the bookstore and bought a self-help book that she found inspiring. She asked Pete to read it and, although he agreed, she noticed he never picked it up.

Finally, out of desperation, she urged Pete to go to their pastor with her to discuss their problems. Pete told her that he had no need to talk about their personal lives with anyone and that she should quit nagging. That was the straw that broke the camel's back. Florence felt she had tried everything to improve their marriage and Pete wasn't interested. Since she was so unhappy and Pete obviously wasn't willing to work on their marriage, Florence decided there was nothing left for her to do other than get a divorce.

It's easy to understand why Florence felt so frustrated by Pete's lack of willingness to go to therapy or read a self-help book. But just because Pete wasn't willing to do these things didn't mean that he wanted a divorce or that he wasn't committed to their marriage. All it meant was that he wasn't willing to work on the marriage *Florence's way*. There are many people who are totally devoted to their spouses but wouldn't dream of seeking outside help. It's unfortunate that Florence didn't realize that she didn't require Pete's active participation in the activities she was considering in order to improve their relationship. Let me explain.

The only person necessary to start improving your marriage is *you*. You can effect change in your relationship singlehandedly. You're probably saying to yourself, "That's impossible. I've always been told that you can't change other people." Well, that's wrong. Need some proof? Consider the following situation.

If you were having a nice evening with your spouse and, for some strange reason, you wanted to effect a change and get your partner really angry, can you think of something you could say or do to trigger that response in him or her? I bet you anything you're chuckling right now, thinking, "All I need to do is to be a backseat driver and tell my husband how to drive, he gets furious immediately," or "If I don't call my wife when I have to work later than normal, she gets into a tizzy." In short, you know *precisely* what to do to push your spouse's buttons. We all do. Well, my friend, here's some good news: If you know how to push your partner's buttons in a negative way (i.e., effect a negative change), you can learn to push your partner's buttons in a positive way (i.e., effect a positive change). I am convinced that all people have within them positive change buttons. You simply have to learn what those buttons are and how to activate them.

Here is a letter from a woman who, after learning that "It Takes One to Tango," decided to stop pushing her husband's negative buttons and start pushing his positive buttons instead:

Just a few weeks ago I was ready to walk away from my marriage. My husband's attitude stunk. He thought *I* should do everything around the house and he could relax and do nothing. We fought every other day and started to not like being around each other. I have nagged and waited ten years for just a tad of help around the house. I never wanted him to be a maid and scrub toilets, just a little helping hand now and then. And today . . . it happened.

I came home for lunch . . . he had the day off, and the house was clean—dishes done, all the clutter picked up!!! I almost thought I walked into the wrong house. I about died. I am walking on air. Why the clean house? I've given this a lot of thought.

I know that I have been more patient with him and made extra efforts to be nice and not "bitchy." I've complimented him and let the small things ride. Last night I was gonna nag him and instead, I let it go.

Let me tell you, if these are the results I am going to get, I am never going to stop! I am so happy about this that I just want to burst. I am just so happy/thankful . . . I had to let you know.

Mary

Imagine. This woman had been nagging her husband for ten years to help more around the house to no avail. If you were to eavesdrop on a conversation she was having with one of her girlfriends back then, I bet she would have said that her situation was hopeless, that she had tried everything and nothing ever worked. And she would have been dead wrong.

You see, by changing the way in which Mary approached her husband, he changed his behavior toward her, rather dramatically, I might add. When she decided to stop nagging and start being kinder and more loving, he felt more inspired to be more loving toward her. She changed, he changed. Need another example?

Rob was scared that his wife, Ellen, was thinking about leaving their marriage. She seemed more and more withdrawn and spent increasing amounts of time going out in the evenings with single women friends. Rob realized that part of the reason Ellen was seeking a social life outside their marriage was that he had been focused on work for so many years. Ellen had often complained about his long hours, but Rob brushed aside her comments. To boost her spirits, she started getting together with her girl-friends on a regular basis.

At first, Rob felt relieved when the nagging stopped. But when Ellen's outings became more frequent and when she began returning home later and later, he grew concerned. To relieve his anxiety, Rob asked Ellen many questions regarding her whereabouts. He waited up for her and grilled her when she walked through the door. The more he pressed her for informa-tion, the more she resisted. Gradually, Rob began to wonder if Ellen was having an affair. He started to go through Ellen's personal letters, e-mail, notes, and phone records. Ellen caught wind of Rob's investigations and became furious and more private about her activities.

Rob confronted Ellen about her behavior. He urged her to stop social-izing with her single friends. He talked about his feelings of insecurity. Rob even asked her to go for counseling. Ellen not only refused to seek coun-seling, she completely withdrew from Rob. Even their "pass the salt" con-versations came to an abrupt halt.

Rob felt fairly certain that, without Ellen's cooperation, their marriage was about to end. But he decided to experiment by changing his own ac-tions. Rob reasoned that he didn't like the person he had become—suspi-cious, sneaky, prying, and clingy. That wasn't the "real Rob." He decided that even if his marriage were to end, he would have to work on himself to get back to the self-confident, independent man that he was.

He decided that from that day forward, he would stop interrogating Ellen. Instead of waiting up for her with twenty-one questions, he would do his best to go to sleep prior to her return. If he asked about her evening, it would only be to demonstrate his desire that she enjoy herself with her friends. In fact, although he had never done it before, he told her to have a good time before she went out one evening. Rob wasn't sure that his new plan would change Ellen's mind about going out or about their marriage, but he knew it would make him feel better about himself. And he was right. As soon as he put his plan into motion, he started to feel more in control of himself, which boosted his self-esteem enormously.

In the days that followed, Rob discovered that it was easier to stick to his game plan than he thought. He was so exhausted from the emotional stress that going to sleep early was not a problem. Ellen was surprised to find him sleeping each time she returned. She even woke him one night to see if he was okay. He resisted asking any questions about her evenings out and this also surprised Ellen. One morning she said, "Aren't you even going to ask me who was there last night?" Confidently, he responded, "Not really." Rob glanced over and noticed a puzzled look on Ellen's face.

A week later, something unusual happened. Ellen canceled her plans to be with her friends and asked Rob if he wanted to go to a movie. Rob was dumbfounded, but happy, and naturally accepted her invitation. Rob promised himself that he would not bring up any potentially unpleasant subject and he didn't. They had a very enjoyable evening together.

Over the next few weeks, Rob noticed that Ellen was spending less time with her friends and more time at home with him. He never asked her why and she never offered an explanation. Nor did he let Ellen in on his plan to change his own behavior instead of badgering her. They just gradually began to enjoy each other's company once again.

Despite the fact that Rob and Ellen never openly discussed the events that occurred between them, it was crystal clear to Rob what had happened and how he, singlehandedly, managed to turn things around. He changed, so she changed.

In my work with clients, I very often counsel just one partner. Even in great marriages, it's often the case that one spouse is more driven than the other to engage in marriage-enhancing activities. When I do marital therapy, I don't feel flustered if only one spouse attends. I don't consider it second-rate therapy. The truth is, I often prefer working with one partner or seeing spouses separately. When I help my clients approach their marital problems more productively, their spouses sit up and take notice and positive change buttons get pushed like crazy. I really don't need two people to create wonderful changes in a marriage, and neither do you. You just need you.

If you are someone who has requested, nagged, or begged your partner to become more involved in marriage-improving activities, quit it now. Although your spouse doesn't know it yet, s/he is about to join forces with you to make things better. When you tip over the first domino in your marriage, relationship change will be right around the corner.

Since I've written about and taught the "It Takes One to Tango" princi-ple for many years, I have a pretty good idea about the questions you might be asking yourself right now. Let me take a stab at answering some of them.

Q: If one person can trigger change in another, why do we spend so much time trying to convince our partners to change first?

Basically, there are two reasons we waste our energy trying to convince our partners to change. First, we're convinced they're wrong. And as such, it only stands to reason that they should recognize their faults, admit they are wrong, and start taking our advice. We've been brainwashed to believe that if we talk enough, explain our insights clearly enough, our spouses will finally get it. So, like the Energizer Bunny, we just keep going and go-ing and going. Never mind that what we're doing isn't working or that it's alienating our spouses and making our lives more miserable and lonely. If we're right, we're right, and we're not going to stop proving our points un-til we've made ourselves perfectly clear.

But there is another explanation for our behavior: We have a hard time actually believing that a change in our actions can affect or influence our spouses. We *know* that our spouses affect us. They make us angry. They hurt our feelings. They do things that prompt us to retaliate and hold grudges. This, we see very clearly. That's because we live inside ourselves. If our spouses say something that we feel is hurtful, our hurt radar goes off and we immediately take notice. In our minds, any of *our* negative responses are clearly a result of our *spouses'* actions.

But because we don't live inside our spouses, we are often clueless about the ways in which *our* actions affect *them.* When their anger or hurt radar goes off, it's not apparent to us. So, their rude and unloving actions seem to come from out of the blue. "Where is this coming from?" we ask. And of course, our conclusion is simple—our spouses are moody, nasty, and antagonistic people. Get the picture?

We fail to see or appreciate how *our* actions trigger emotional responses in our spouses. This is especially true when we did nothing intentional to set it off. There are two parts to communication, the message we intend to send and how it's received. Frequently, though our intentions are benign, our message is perceived negatively. For example, if a woman is unaware that her spouse was looking forward to spending time with her on Friday night, she might think she's being kind to suggest that he go out with friends. She would be very surprised by his unpleasant response and his shortness with her later in the evening. She will assume he's being a jerk or that he must have had a hard day at work. The last thing she will consider is that his unpleasantness had anything to do with *her* or something she said. And because she assumes he is just being a jerk, she won't be too nice to him, which will give him more cause to believe that she instigated the unpleasantness between them! A comedy of errors!

Here's an incident that actually happened between my husband, Jim, and me one day. We were sitting in the family room having a discussion when he said something that caught me a bit off guard. In order to collect myself, I momentarily turned my head to look at the television, take a deep breath, and resume our conversation. By the time I turned back, Jim was reading a magazine. I waited a moment, and when he didn't stop reading, I turned and watched television again. Several moments passed and I decided it was time to continue discussing the issue at hand.

Once again I turned to Jim, who was still reading. Annoyed, I glanced away, and when I did, he promptly stood up and started walking out of the room. I said, "Jim, where are you going? We are in the middle of having a conversation." He blurted back, "But you're watching television." I replied, "I'm watching television because you're reading a magazine," to which he responded, "I'm reading because you're watching television." I corrected him saying, "I am only watching television because . . ." Well, I won't bore you anymore. I think you know exactly what I said. I think you also know exactly how Jim responded. Thank goodness, I realized that I was doing what I advised others not to do and so I eventually silenced myself.

The point to remember is this: interactions in relationships are circular. You do something→your partner responds→you react→your partner responds, or, if it makes you feel better, you can view it the other way around. Your partner does something→you react→your partner responds→you react, and so on. Where the cycle begins is just a matter of perspective. And the good news about all of this is that when things are spiraling out of control, there is something you can do other than try to convince your partner to change. You can interrupt the cycle by changing *your* actions.

Q. Why do *I* have to be the one to change?

You don't. Either spouse can make that decision. But since you're the one reading this, I strongly suggest that you're the one to tip over the first domino. Look, in most relationships there is one person who takes the initiative to getting things back on track. If this is you, congratulations! You have an important job. Don't keep score. You won't be doing all the work, you will just be the one who starts the ball rolling. As soon as you see your efforts paying off, you will ask yourself why you waited so long.

If your spouse has half a foot out the door and you want to save your marriage, you will just have to accept the fact that, for now, *you* are in charge of setting your marriage on course. If all goes according to plan, you won't be alone in your efforts to improve your marriage for long.

Q. What if I push the wrong button?

Sometimes people hesitate making changes because they aren't sure if what they're about to do will work. I want you to know that there is only one wrong button and that's the one you push over and over that hasn't been working. Once you avoid that button, it's hard to go wrong. Later in this program, I will teach you how to read the new results you are getting and how to modify your approach if you are off the mark. Don't worry about screwing up. Only experts worry about mistakes.

Q. My spouse and I are barely speaking (or are separated). If I change my approach to things, will my spouse even notice?

If you are concerned that changes in your behavior will go unnoticed because there is so much emotional distance between you, don't be. If you were to do something vindictive, would he or she notice? You bet. Just because there is little discussion about your marriage doesn't mean that each action, each word, isn't being carefully weighed and considered. So, start changing, and even though your spouse might not say anything about it or even appreciate it at first, it doesn't mean s/he isn't noticing.

Sometimes the distance between spouses is more than emotional; they are living apart. To make matters worse, in some stormy marriages there is hardly any contact at all. If this is your situation, don't be discouraged. You have to make the most of the interactions you *do* have. Each phone call, brief encounter, e-mail, or face-to-face interaction has to feature you in the best possible light.

For example, perhaps you learn in this program that you need to be more upbeat in your partner's presence. If so, every phone call, no matter how brief or seemingly unimportant, should be an opportunity for you to show in your voice, intonation, and in the content of your discussion that you are feeling good about yourself and your life. You need to stop bemoaning the fact that you wish you had more time together. If you don't, you don't. Make the most of the time you do have.

Q. Isn't it manipulative to try to change someone?

I love this question! Manipulation carries with it a very negative connotation. Evil and conniving people manipulate, right? Wrong. *Everyone* manipulates. Manipulation simply means that you are attempting to influence other people's behavior toward your ends. We do this all the time. You try to convince your resistant spouse to spend more time at your parents' house. You urge your partner to be the one to get up with the baby in the middle of the night. You want your mate to get off your back for spending too much time at the computer. We attempt to convince our spouses to change for all sorts of reasons, all the time.

When the strategies we use to effect this change are ones that come naturally to us, our attempts at relationship change are considered genuine and benign, even if what we are doing is hurting our relationship in the long run. If we plan our strategies, however, if we think things through before we act, we wonder whether we're being manipulative, even if the methods we use effectively nip relationship problems in the bud.

From my perspective, it's a shame that we all don't think more about our actions before we act. We would cause our loved ones a lot less pain if we did. The more mindful we are about how we treat the people in our lives, the happier they will be.

Q. Why should I believe that anything I do will make a difference when it hasn't before?

No matter how hard you've convinced yourself that you've tried everything, you haven't. If you really believed that, you wouldn't be reading this right now. I know you've been feeling discouraged, and I don't blame you. But I've been in the people-changing business for years, and I've seen couples headed for disaster stave off divorce, as late as the eleventh hour. Even when one partner seems wholly convinced that real change isn't possible, it's not a lost cause. So, don't allow yourself to get into a negative frame of mind—you'll need all the energy and focus you can muster.

On the other hand, your discouragement might not be due to the fact your spouse wants out. *You* might be the one considering divorce. If so, your discouragement probably stems from the fact that you've finally convinced yourself that your marriage problems are due to your spouse's personality and that personalities just don't change.

Look, I won't lie to you. If you've been upset with your spouse because he is a recluse and doesn't like too much excitement in his life, I will not be able to help you turn him into a man who swings from chandeliers and is the life of every party. If your wife is driving you crazy because of her shopaholism and her inability to balance her checkbook, I won't be able to guide you to turning her into a spendthrifty, certified public accountant. However, I *can* help you turn a recluse into a man who is willing to go out more often and take more time to smell the roses. I can offer suggestions that will turn a person who is cavalier about the excessive expenditure of money into someone who is more frugal and organized about finances. In other words, although your spouse might not undergo a major personality overhaul, s/he will be able to make enough small changes that life can be substantially different for the both of you.

But you have to give your marriage another try. And you have to remember to have a beginner's mind when it comes to your spouse. Stop thinking you know everything there is to know about him/her. Stop believing that there's nothing in the world that could get your spouse to be different. I know there is. Just keep reading.

YOU DON'T NEED TO ANALYZE WHY YOU'RE STUCK IN ORDER TO SOLVE YOUR MARITAL PROBLEMS

I was taught that couples needed to understand the root cause of their problems before they could find solutions. During therapy sessions, I spent a great deal of time helping my clients examine how the past had shaped their personalities and behavior. All of this introspection was fine and dandy, but the truth is, it rarely helped people solve their marital problems. Knowing that you're overreacting because your father was critical or that you hate conflict because your parents never fought doesn't help you respond more rationally to criticism or more calmly when conflict is in the air. It just makes you more clear about why you feel the way you do. You get smarter about why you're stuck!

Luckily for me, I had some brave clients who finally mustered up the nerve to tell me, "Michele, now we *understand* why we're not getting along. When do we get to the part of therapy where you help us figure out what to *do* about it?" I learned that insight doesn't necessarily lead to change. Insight leads to insight.

Perhaps you've never been to a therapist but you've been diagnosing your problems on your own. Maybe you've been reading self-help books or taken quizzes in magazines that are designed to help you figure out whether your spouse is passive-aggressive, verbally abusive, controlling, over/under-sexed, or if s/he is in the throes of a midlife or PMS crisis.

Maybe you've shared your findings with your mate: "The problems in our marriage are due to the way *you* were raised," or "If you weren't so depressed all the time, we wouldn't be having this problem." And if your marriage is like most, your research into the causes of your relationship problems is a big waste of time.

For one thing, in all likelihood, your spouse won't agree with your diagnosis. No matter how many articles you leave around the house, or how many different ways you try to convince him/her of your view on things, it won't matter. Even if you're right on the money, if your partner doesn't agree, it will only cause more dissension between you to push it.

Second, "cause-hunting" triggers a cycle of blame and counterblame. You think the problem is your partner and your partner thinks the problem is you. Because you both become defensive, you aren't likely to take to heart anything your spouse has to say. You just get angry and so does s/he.

This leads to the most important reason you shouldn't waste your time "cause-hunting." Once you ascertain that the problems in your marriage reside in your spouse, there is nothing you can do but sit and wait for him/her to change. That takes away all of your power. In essence, you're saying, "Until you see things my way, and change, I will just sit here in the corner and suffer." Not too flattering a picture, eh?

So what can you do about all of this? Instead of focusing on how the problems in your life came into being, why not focus on how to create solutions, like Walter and Mary, who are prime examples of people who gave up their search for causes and headed straight for solutions.

Walter and Mary argued about finances for years. When I met with them they admitted to having spent much of their time together trying to figure out why money was such a problematic subject. Mary thought it was because Walter was irresponsible and liked having toys more than saving for a future, a tendency he picked up from his father. Walter thought that Mary acted too much like a parent, always telling him what to do and denying him any joy in life. When I asked them what they had done to try to resolve the differences between them, they told me that they just argued about who's right and who's wrong. In other words, not much.

Rather than understand *why* they were at war about money, I simply asked a few questions to get them pointed in the right direction. I laid the groundwork by telling them that in a sense, they were both right. Mary's philosophy made it possible for the family to feel secure about their financial future, whereas Walter understood the importance of enjoying each day. I suggested they had something valuable to teach each other about life. Then I asked Walter, "What would Mary have to do for you to feel that she understood your need to enjoy life?" He responded,

> It would be great if, just once in a while, she would encourage me to buy something for myself or the family, without my having to bring it up. I always feel like the little kid, asking "mom" if it's okay to spend some money. Probably one of the reasons I'm always thinking about what I can buy next is that she holds on to the reins so tightly. If she'd loosen up a bit, I probably would stop fantasizing about accumulating things.

I then asked Mary, "What would Walter have to do for you to feel he understood your need to be responsible and feel financially secure?" She replied,

He said he feels like the little kid, but he should only know what it feels like to be the parent. I hate it! I would love it if he would be willing to sit down with me and take a close look at our financial situation. Maybe he should take over paying bills. Then he would see where we stand.

After our session, I sent them home with a homework assignment, "Pay attention to what your partner does that helps you feel more optimistic about how you handle your finances."

Two weeks later, they returned. Mary started the session by telling me that Walter actually paid the bills for the first time in their marriage. Besides being surprised at how long the process took him, she said that he commented he was also surprised at the amount of money going out that month. When Mary told him that this month's expenses were actually lower than usual, Walter became noticeably quiet. Mary assumed he was really beginning to understand what she had been worrying about all along. She appreciated his effort to take responsibility and his apparent thoughtfulness about their situation.

Walter had good news too. About a week after our last session, Mary suggested that Walter get tickets for a basketball game because she knew he loved going with his buddies to watch basketball. Walter said he was astonished because the only seats available were expensive ones. Mary interrupted Walter and told me, "Here I was, being nice to him and he started to try to talk me out of it! He told me, 'I really don't need to get tickets, I can watch the game on television.' I had to laugh. I tell him to splurge and he becomes me!" They both laughed.

Once Walter and Mary stopped trying to pinpoint the reasons they were fighting and focused on what they needed to do to stop, solutions became obvious. And since it worked so well, they decided to be more solution-oriented in the future, a decision with which I wholeheartedly agreed.

SMALL CHANGES MATTER

After reading about Walter and Mary you might feel that your problems are monumental compared to theirs and that you don't even know where to begin chipping away at the years of resentment. When it comes to solving problems, it really doesn't matter where you start. That's because when you start changing one small thing, anything, it will lead to other changes. In the same way that one person changing his/her behavior will lead to changes in others, a positive change in one situation will lead to positive changes in other areas of life. Like Walter and Mary.

When Walter and Mary met with me, their primary interest was to find a way to stop fighting about money, but it became quickly apparent that the benefits of cooperating about finances were far-reaching. When Walter and Mary became more understanding of each other's attitude toward money, they started feeling more loving toward each other in general. Although they used to go out together once a week, they had stopped doing that because of the tension. After a couple of weeks of better teamwork around the money issue, Walter asked Mary if she wanted to go out for dinner on the weekend. She was pleased about the invitation.

They started spending more time together in general and doing little thoughtful things for each other. Mary knew how much Walter enjoyed watching sports on television, so rather than give him a hard time about certain marathon TV-watching days, she made him snacks and even joined him. Because he so appreciated her thoughtfulness, Walter started doing kind things for Mary. Every day before she left for work, he would rush outside in their cold winter and start her car for her and scrape the ice off her windows, a job she detested. She loved getting into her warm, ready-to-go car. It gave a good start to her day.

All these little loving gestures started to add up and when a thorny situation would arise, they found themselves being more compassionate and forgiving. They even reported an improvement in their sex life. The positive changes in their marriage spilled over to their family life. There was less tension, more playfulness, and less arguing between the kids. So, you see, one small change can be the beginning of a solution avalanche.

Mary and Walter's case isn't unusual. I see it happen this way all the time. In fact, I count on it happening this way. I ask my clients, "What will be the *very first sign* that things are starting to move in the right direction?" and I feel confident that once they get there, the rest is history, as they say. That's because one small change begets another and another and another.

THINK SMALL

So, what does this mean for you? It's time for you to start thinking small. It is said that the journey of a thousand miles begins with a single step, and it is true. Any positive change in your partner or your marriage, no matter how small, is something worth celebrating. When you think about how far you have to go for your marriage to be where you want it to be, you may have the tendency to overlook or underestimate the importance of baby steps forward, but this would be a big mistake. You have to train yourself to notice baby steps and allow yourself to feel positive when they occur, no matter how far you might be from your marital goals. If you pat yourself on the back when you see positive movement, you will feel inspired to keep going. It will help you develop patience, without which you will not be successful. But what do I mean by "baby steps"?

If you and your spouse are separated and s/he wants little to do with you, consider it a baby step forward if your mate asks you for a favor, or the tone in his/her voice sounds somewhat more pleasant, or s/he asks you how you're doing, or seems to linger a few minutes longer when picking up the mail. All of these may seem insignificant to you, but they may be a sign that your spouse is beginning to soften. Keep your eyes open for anything that is slightly different than before. Different is good. It doesn't mean you will be out of the woods, but it may mean that you have located your compass.

Are you ready to start with your beginner's mind? That's great. Now that you're thinking about solutions and change, you need to know exactly what your goals are for your marriage. It's time to move on to Step 2.

CHAPTER THREE

Step Number 2—
Know What You Want

I t is said that if you aim at nothing, you'll hit it every time. Most successful people will tell you that having a vision of your desired outcome is one of the most, if not the most essential step to making good things happen in life. And when it comes to making *personal* changes—losing weight, becoming richer or healthier—we believe them. But when we think about improving our love lives, people bypass this goal-setting stage entirely and dive headfirst into relationship oblivion. It's not that we don't long for better times. We wish things would be better, we pray that things will improve, we hope tomorrow will be a brighter day, but we fail to sit down and apply the same rigor to our marital improvement project that we might to improving any other aspect of our lives. But why?

There are lots of reasons. We don't take our goals seriously enough. We are doubtful that people can change. We don't believe that our relationships will ever really improve. We incorrectly believe that relationship goal-setting must be a two-person activity. Yet, despite all of our reservations and doubts about the viability of relationship goal-setting, we spend much of our lives trying to get through to our partners, to get them to be more understanding, compassionate, and loving. In other words, we try to influence our mates without the benefit of a compass to help us know when we're on track.

That's why I want you to stop what you're doing right now and get yourself a pen and a piece of paper. You are going to write down your relationship goals. I know you think you already have your goals figured out, but for the purposes of this program, they are not specific enough. Specific goals contain within them seeds for solution, and you're not quite there yet.

But why write down your goals? First of all, by writing things down, you are taking an action. Although Step Number 1 was geared toward challenging your thinking, the rest of the program is about taking action. It's time to get out of your head and start moving your body. Second, when you see your thoughts in black and white, it makes them more real. Third, writing your goals down will offer you a baseline to which you can refer in days to come. You will be able to chart your progress and identify areas needing more of your attention. It's time to start writing.

A word of warning: If you're longing for a better relationship, you might be tempted to scan through the chapters looking for specific techniques aimed at bringing you and your partner closer. Don't give in to that temptation. Before you experiment with the techniques outlined in this book, you need to have a very clear picture of your ultimate goals and of the signposts along the way. If you don't, you won't know if you're headed in the right direction. The more you're hurting right now, the more likely you are to think I'm overstating the importance of goal-setting, but I've been in the marriage-saving business for years and you will just have to trust me on this one. ***Don't skip this step!***

> *List two or three things you are hoping to change*
> *or improve about your marriage.*

Finished? Then we're ready to talk about solution-oriented goal-setting. Not all goals are created equal. As I describe the guidelines for setting solution-oriented goals, I want you to look at the goals you just listed and see whether they include the following criteria.

GOAL-SETTING RULE NUMBER 1
Think about what you want *in your marriage,*
not what's missing

It never fails. When I ask troubled couples, "What is it about your marriage that you are hoping to change?" they rarely answer the question. Instead, they either discuss their partner's faults—"He's way too critical," or "I wish she weren't so controlling," or they start telling me about what's missing in their marriages—"Our sex life isn't very good," or "We never socialize with our friends." I would classify these comments as complaints rather than goals. Complaints describe what you're unhappy about rather than what needs to change.

The trouble with complaints is that you are focused on the problems in your marriage rather than what you can do about them. You need to translate your complaints into goals. For instance, if you think your marriage would be better if your spouse didn't have such a bad temper, you need to ask yourself, "When my spouse has more of a handle on his emotions, what will he be doing that will clue me in that things have improved?" Perhaps your answer might be, "When I talk about something the kids did wrong, he will ask me questions about it rather than raise his voice immediately," or "When she gets frustrated with how things are going at home, rather than bark orders at everyone, she will calmly ask people to do their jobs." In other words, when the negative parts of your marriage improve, what exactly will be happening that isn't happening now? Let me give you a few more examples.

Instead of thinking:	**Think:**
I don't want to be separated → any longer	I would like her to be home by May.
I hate it when he avoids me →	I'd like him to be in the same room with me after dinner.
I wish she weren't so negative →	It would be nice if she would admit there were a few positive times between us.
He's so nasty →	I would like him to compliment me once in a while and let me know he appreciates the things I do for him.

Get the idea? Now, go back to the goals you've written above and see if you described *what you want* as opposed to what you are unhappy about. Talk about the future rather than the past. You can translate your complaints into positive goals right now by asking yourself the following question:

"When my spouse stops doing _____, what will s/he be doing instead?"

Now, if necessary, rewrite the things you hope to change about your marriage, making sure they are requests for change rather than complaints.

GOAL-SETTING RULE NUMBER 2
Think action

You may think that statements such as, "I'd like my wife to be more understanding," or "I wish my husband would lighten up sometimes," or "I would love it if my husband were more sensitive," classify as goals, but they don't. They are way too vague. In order for goals to be solution-oriented, they must describe the *specific actions* people will take to improve things. Let me give you an example.

I worked with an "empty nester" couple whose marriage was in deep trouble by the time we met. George was the breadwinner in the family, while Ellen was a stay-at-home mom. He worked hard to support his wife and four children and she was a very devoted mother.

Although they were both good at their respective jobs, it was clear that their marriage had suffered. They hardly spent any time together as a couple. All of their joint activities were family-oriented. They grew apart and rarely talked about anything other than the children. They began to wonder if their distance was a sign that they had fallen out of love with each other.

When I asked them what they were hoping to change, George said, "We are strangers to each other. I don't even know where to begin connecting again. I sometimes wonder if it will ever be possible to feel like a couple. Yes, that's my goal, to feel like a couple again." Ellen quickly agreed. She said, "I've felt so alone for so long, I don't even think I know what it would feel like to be a couple anymore. But if our marriage is going to last, we need to be more connected."

George and Ellen thought they had answered my question, but I knew that my work with them had just begun. They knew they wanted to improve their marriage, but they didn't know what their improved marriage would look like. So I asked, "When the two of you feel more like a couple and are more connected, what will you both *be doing differently* then?"

After a little persistence, George and Ellen came up with a list of specific actions they could take. George said:

- We will start dating again. It's been years since we went for dinner just the two of us.
- We will start being more intimate. We've been making love once every four to six weeks. If we made love once or twice a week, I'd feel closer to Ellen.
- We'd develop a common interest such as golfing together or playing bridge with other couples.

Ellen's list was different:

- We would talk about something other than the children. Anything else will do. I want to hear about his day and I want him to hear about mine. It would be wonderful if he would talk more about his feelings.
- I want the two of us to talk about the future. We've been so busy raising children, we've stopped dreaming about the future.
- I want him to be romantic, like in the old days. He can buy me flowers once in a while, leave me thoughtful notes, or plan a surprise date for us.

Here's another example.

Les and Kelly were separated for three months. Les wanted to work on the marriage but Kelly wasn't so sure. She had been thinking about divorce for many years and wanted some space to think things through. Kelly refused to come for counseling, so I worked with Les. When I asked him about his goals, he said, "I want to stay married. I want Kelly to recognize that our marriage is salvageable. We had good times in the past and I know we can have good times in the future." I then asked Les, "If Kelly starts to believe that your marriage is salvageable, what will she start *doing* differently?" Here are some of the behavioral signs Les thought he would see if Kelly were to have a change of heart.

- Kelly would call Les once in a while to see how he was feeling.
- Kelly would agree to going out to dinner with Les at least once a month.
- When Les called Kelly, instead of saying she was busy or too tired to talk, she would spend at least ten or fifteen minutes on the phone.
- Kelly would occasionally discuss a future plan that included Les.
- Kelly would invite Les to her family reunion, scheduled for the following summer.

If you don't translate all of your vague, unspecific goals into action-oriented formulas for change, you won't be able to spot an improvement when it happens. It will sneak right by you because you haven't been clear enough in your own mind as to what you and your partner need to do to make things better. And if you're fuzzy about the specifics, how can you expect your partner to get it right? S/he won't. Believe me. Vague goals lead to misunderstanding and hurt.

Now go back and review your goals. Are they action-oriented? Do they describe the *actual behavior* you are hoping to see when your marriage improves rather than listing adjectives? If not, you should grab your pen or pencil and fine-tune your goals. Leave nothing to the imagination. *Now, rewrite any of your three goals that weren't action-oriented or specific enough.*

GOAL-SETTING RULE NUMBER 3
Think small

If you are having trouble with your marriage, I know you're in a lot of pain. And if you're hurting, I also know that you want the pain to end as quickly as possible . . . like yesterday. You want what you want and you want it *now*. You can't fathom why your spouse just doesn't get with the program and start loving you completely, immediately. Life, you tell yourself, would be so much easier if s/he did.

It's completely understandable if you are thinking this way. However, this sort of impatience will work against you. For one thing, it will prevent you from recognizing the small signs of improvement along the way. Change in relationships is usually a gradual process. You don't go from being miserably at odds with one another to being intensely in love again overnight. There are hundreds of baby steps along the way. It's really important to identify these baby steps in advance of moving forward so you'll know if you're headed in the right direction.

I once watched a well-known woman golfer sink a long, thirty-foot putt with ease. The interviewer on television later said to her, "That was a tough shot, what were you thinking? What helped you to make that shot?" Without hesitation, she replied, "When I have to make a long putt, I never aim at the hole. I pick a spot that is in line with the hole, but closer to me and aim at that instead." That's excellent advice. Let me give you an example.

Barb just found out that her husband, Cal, had had an affair with his secretary. She was absolutely devastated. Never in their fourteen years of marriage would she have thought that Cal would have done something like that; he was such an honorable man with strong family values and morals. She began to feel herself fall apart at the seams.

At first, she felt the need to get away from Cal and left to visit her mother. When she was away, she realized that her pain was no less intense than when she was home. She decided to return home and came for a counseling session with me. When I asked her goals, she said she had done some soul-searching while she was away and, although she felt devastated, she sensed that Cal felt bad about what happened and that she really didn't want to end her marriage. I asked her what she was hoping to change and she replied, "I want to feel complete faith and trust in him again."

I hope that as you read Barb's goal, you were thinking, "While that's understandable, given her immediate situation, it's pretty unrealistic." No one in his/her right mind goes from discovering a spouse was unfaithful to having complete faith and trust in that person without there being a lot of steps in between, right?

So I said, "I know you want to have faith and trust in Cal again, but in light of what just happened, let me ask you another question. What will be the *very first sign* that you and he are starting to move in that direction?" After a moment's thought, she replied, "Although he seems remorseful, he hasn't actually apologized yet. Therefore, he would have to tell me he's sorry about what happened. He would take steps to replace her so that she wasn't working around him anymore. He would call me if he has to be late coming home from work." These were all reasonable, doable signposts of change toward her ultimate goal of achieving more faith and trust in her husband.

In addition to being positively stated and action-oriented, your goals have to be broken down into small chunks, actions that can be accomplished within a week or two. If your goals are too ambitious and therefore out of your reach, you might incorrectly think your marriage is doomed when in fact, it is not doomed at all. The problem may simply be that you haven't set your sights on something a bit more obtainable. Consider Jack and Georgia.

After six months of separation, Jack decided to return home to his wife, Georgia, and their three children. Georgia was thrilled he was coming home, but she was somewhat apprehensive about whether Jack would remain at home this time. She feared that he might leave again if there were too many arguments.

At first, everything appeared to be going okay. The children were relieved to have their father back home. Jack and Georgia were talking more and spending lots of time together as a family. But Georgia felt insecure and anxious about their future together. The more she pressed Jack for reassurances, the more he withdrew. Georgia decided to come for a few sessions of counseling by herself to discuss these issues.

During our conversations, I asked Georgia what would help her feel less anxious and worried about their marriage. She said, "We used to have a great sex life and Jack was very affectionate. He told me that he loved me daily. None of this is happening now; that's why I feel so insecure. It's hard to be relaxed about the future when he expresses or shows no feelings of love. I think he just came home because of the kids."

I realized that Georgia's impatience was getting in the way of her seeing and appreciating small signs of change in her marriage. I acknowledged her feelings and then said, "Perhaps Jack is slowly coming around to the point of being able to tell you of his love and being more sexual with you. But before those things happen, what might be some signs that your marriage is moving in the right direction?" After some more thought, Georgia said, "I would settle for his holding my hand once in a while or touching my shoulder gently as he passes me in the hall. I would even consider it progress if he just told me he was happy that he came home. He doesn't have to say, 'I love you,' he just has to say something positive about the fact that we're a family again."

I sent Georgia home asking her to look for small signs that their marriage was improving. The next time I saw her, although their sex life hadn't improved much, she felt more confident that their marriage was headed in the right direction. "Jack's been talking about wanting to rent a house on a lake next summer with the kids. It's the first time in a year that he has included me in a future plan. Plus, he's been calling me more from work just to say hi. He even stopped on his way home from work the other day to pick up my favorite dessert." Although Georgia and Jack had a ways to go before they were completely out of the woods, Georgia felt that Jack seemed much happier and she believed that passion was right around the corner. Georgia learned an important lesson: Change happens one small step at a time.

Speaking of small steps, it's now your turn to make sure that the goals you've identified are not too unreachable within a relatively short period of time. When I see people in my practice, I try to help them establish goals that can be achieved in between sessions, usually a week or two. That's because nothing breeds success like success. Once you feel a bit of momentum, you just want to keep going and going and going.

Look at each of your goals and ask yourself, "What will be the very first sign that things are moving in the right direction?" Adjust any goals that are aimed too far into the future.

Now that your goals for your relationship are positively stated, action-oriented, and broken down into manageable pieces, you are to ask for what you want.

CHAPTER FOUR

Step Number 3—
Ask for What You Want

Now that you know exactly what you want in your marriage, it's time to share your thoughts with your spouse. Although you might be thinking, "I've told him/her a million times what I want/need; it won't do me any good," you may have been asking the wrong way. In fact, lots of times people think that they are requesting a change from their partners when they are doing nothing more than complaining. Complaints turn people off and build resistance. They don't spark a spirit of cooperation. I learned this firsthand in my own marriage.

My husband, Jim, works very hard and often likes to "veg out" on weekends and relax. I, on the other hand, am a fairly active person who likes going places and doing things. This has always been a major difference between us. Early in our marriage, I sat Jim down and told him I wanted to talk to him about something. I said, "You never want to do anything on weekends. It seems that all you enjoy doing is sitting around, watching TV, and hanging around the house. Yes, you'll go out to dinner occasionally, but that's it. It's not terribly exciting."

Sure enough, Jim got defensive and told me that I should do whatever I wanted but that I should stop bugging him. I got really upset; after all, I was just trying to make our marriage more enjoyable for both of us. Therefore, I defended my actions and wondered why *he* was being so defensive. The more I defended myself, the more he attacked.

Out of pure frustration, I finally said in a loud voice, "I don't know why you're getting so upset! All I really want us to do is to go into the city once every four to six weeks and do something out of the ordinary!" To which he replied, "Well, that's fine! Why don't you just say *that* then?" He caught me by surprise. Why, I wondered, if he's so willing to go into the city with me, did he put up such a fight when I approached him about it? The answer was simple. It was *how* I approached him that made all the difference.

In the beginning of our conversation, although my *intention* was simply to state the facts in an attempt to justify my asking him to change, I was actually condemning him for being who he is. Naturally, this strategy bombed. When I simply asked for what I wanted without complaining, he was much more ready to oblige. Funny how that works! From that point forward in our marriage, I worked hard at simply asking for what I wanted rather than telling Jim about all the reasons I was miserable.

Although you may feel convinced that you've already asked for what you want without good results, you may have inadvertently been doing what I had been doing—complaining. I was certain that I was being clear and concrete about my wishes when, in fact, the only thing I was being clear and concrete about was how Jim was disappointing me.

Perhaps your requests have been positively stated, but you've been breaking goal-setting Rule Number 2—your requests haven't been action-oriented. You may have been asking for things like better communication, more closeness, less tension at home. By now, you know your partner had to be a mind reader to figure out what you really wanted. So try asking again, this time using action-oriented behavioral descriptions.

If you need an example, let me tell you specifically how we resolved our differences in how we spend our time on weekends. Instead of saying that I wanted him to be more adventurous or more involved in our relationship, I told him that I would like him to go with me into the city once every four weeks and try a new restaurant or go to a show. I also told him that I would appreciate it if he would take a hike with me or go to a movie on Friday or Saturday evening. Stating my requests in action-oriented terms helped enormously.

And finally, maybe you failed to break your goals down into small steps and you frustrated yourself or your partner by expecting too much too soon. For example, if, after having being separated for three months and not seeing very much of each other, your reluctant spouse returns home and you think, "Since she's decided to come home, I need to hear her say, 'I love you,' right away," you're bound to be disappointed. Look for smaller, more realistic signs of progress.

If your goals aren't broken down into small steps, here's your chance to get it right and see what happens. There are a few things you should keep in mind though before you approach your partner with your requests for change.

One—timing is very important. Although choosing a good time of day or week won't necessarily guarantee success, choosing a bad time will guarantee failure. If I want to guarantee that Jim will respond negatively to a request, I know exactly when to ask him.

- Just before he leaves for work
- When the kids are around
- When he is preoccupied or doing something
- When he is at work
- When he is very tired and wants to go to sleep

As you read what I've just written, you're probably thinking that Jim has a very long list of times that he is unapproachable. I'd have to agree. But there are lots of other times when he is more receptive: on weekends before the kids wake up, over dinner when we go out together, on his car phone when he is returning from work.

If you sit down and really think about it, you know *exactly* when your spouse is approachable and when s/he isn't. In fact, that's what I'm going to ask you to do right now. Even if you can't think of times you feel confident that your spouse is going to be responsive, I know you can think of times when s/he won't be. Pick up your pen again and answer the following questions.

1. When is my spouse least likely to pay attention, be conciliatory, or be patient with my requests?
2. When is my spouse most likely to pay attention, be conciliatory, or be

patient with my requests? (Think back to a time when you got a positive reaction from your partner when you asked for something. Identify what was going on then.)

3. Now, commit to writing when, in the next few days, you will tell your partner what you want to improve about your marriage.

ASKING FOR WHAT YOU WANT MAY MAKE ALL THE DIFFERENCE IN THE WORLD

You may be pleasantly surprised to find that setting solution-oriented goals and then asking for what you want in a more constructive way are extremely productive. But even though you've moved in a positive direction, you are only beginning to scratch the surface when it comes to keeping your marriage on track. So enjoy the moment, but don't get too comfy because you have a lot more work ahead of you. In the meantime, let your spouse know how much you appreciate his/her efforts and keep reading.

ASKING MAY NOT MATTER AT ALL

Sometimes, no matter how well you make or time a request, your partner may not respond the way you had hoped. There are lots of reasons this might be so. There may be so much tension between you that your partner is not about to do anything you ask. Or, your spouse may be so uncertain about staying married, s/he may not be receptive to requests for change right now. You may have talked so much about your marriage that everything you say at this point goes in one ear and out the other.

If your marriage is dangling by a thread and your spouse has made it perfectly clear that s/he is not interested in working on your marriage, don't ask him/her for *anything* right now. You have very little bargaining power at the moment. Your first task is to get your spouse to realize what a good thing s/he would be missing out on if s/he were to leave your marriage. Chances are, prior to beginning this program, you have asked your reluctant spouse for things that pushed him/her farther away. So don't ask your partner to change a thing right now if your marriage is extremely shaky. Instead, fast forward to the next step, Step Number 4.

If your marriage is on the brink of divorce, you may be asking yourself why I had you read this step if you weren't going to use it. The answer is simple. What you will learn as you go through this program is that everything is about timing. Now's not a good time for you to ask for anything. But hopefully, as you go through this program, your spouse will decide to reinvest in your marriage, and there will be a time in the not-too-distant future that you will be able to apply all the information you are learning here.

CHAPTER FIVE

Step Number 4—Stop Going Down Cheeseless Tunnels

As a psychology student, I had the opportunity (if that's what you want to call it) to observe how quickly rats learn by observing them as they searched through mazes looking for a piece of hidden cheese. We can take a lesson from these rats.

You have a maze that contains five tunnels. Take a piece of cheese and place it down tunnel number four. Release a hungry rat and initially the rat will explore the tunnels looking for the cheese. As soon as it discovers the cheese is down tunnel number four, it will begin its search there each time. As long as you continue placing the cheese down tunnel number four, it will ignore all the other tunnels and only go down tunnel number four.

If you change the experiment and place the cheese down tunnel number one, at first, the rat will go down tunnel number four several times, looking for that piece of cheese. But in a relatively short time, the rat will stop going down tunnel number four and begin to explore the other tunnels.

Now, it is said that the only difference between rats and human beings is that human beings will go down tunnel number four for the rest of their lives because they will tell themselves, "I know this is the right tunnel. It's got to be here. I know I'm right." People will go down cheeseless tunnels forever because they're more intent on proving to themselves that they're right than they are in finding and eating the cheese! A friend of mine says that human beings will even set up lawn chairs outside of tunnel number four waiting for the cheese to arrive! Funny, isn't it?

When it comes to pursuing the cheeseless tunnels in our lives, it isn't very funny at all. It makes our lives miserable and weakens our marriages. Why? Because when you do more of what hasn't been working, you not only fail to eliminate the problems in your life, you actually make things worse.

When we're unhappy in our marriages, we do something to try to fix the situation. If we're successful, life goes on. If we're not successful, instead of telling ourselves, "*That* didn't work, better try something new," we simply keep doing more of the same. Often, because we assume that we weren't emphatic enough, we even step up our efforts, and try it "one more time with feeling." That's when real trouble begins.

The wife who wants her husband to be more communicative sits him down and tells him she's unhappy with his aloofness. He acknowledges her concern and goes about his business. The next morning at the breakfast table, he picks up the newspaper and starts reading. She tells herself that she probably didn't make herself clear so, once again, she tells him of her dissatisfaction. Now, he feels she's nagging so he withdraws even more—but it prompts her to lecture him again. Feeling badgered, he leaves the room and she follows him, crying. The more she pursues, the more he withdraws. The more he withdraws, the more she pursues.

Consider Sue and Sam. They had major disagreements about how to handle their teenage son, Larry. Sue thought Sam was too strict, whereas Sam thought Sue was too lenient. Every time Sam laid down the law, Sue would intervene and undermine his plan. This enraged Sam, and he became even harsher with Larry. Seeing Sam scold Larry prompted Sue to defend Larry more emphatically, which, in turn, triggered an even harsher response in Sam. Sue didn't realize how her intervention brought out the worst in Sam. Sam didn't realize how his hotheaded approach with Larry triggered Sue's interfering behavior. They were both doing more of the same, and their family life deteriorated.

Sometimes the very thing you do to *solve* a problem—the strategy you use or the coping mechanism that comes naturally to you—is what's actually prompting your partner to persist and escalate the annoying behavior. I've seen this happen in my practice all the time.

Consider the wife who consults with me about her depressed husband. She tells me that the more she's tried to be upbeat and give him pep talks, the more depressed he's become. But not once, in all the years she's been his cheerleader, has she ever questioned whether she should stop trying to talk him out of his depression and do something completely different instead. Because it's logical to attempt to cheer up a depressed person, she keeps going down cheeseless tunnels rather than begin to explore uncharted territory. She complains that *he's* stubborn and resistant but what about her?

The first thing you need to know here is that everybody in the world engages in "more of the same" behavior. We all do it. I do it. You do it. Your spouse does it. Your neighbors do it. Everyone does it. In fact, I would say that the reason you do what you do to solve problems is because it's the most logical thing to do. You may have done a lot of research and you're convinced it's the "best" thing to do. But just because your plan of attack is logical, doesn't mean it is going to be effective. I can't tell you how many couples I see who stay stuck in the same marital problems for years because each spouse is convinced that s/he is right, and therefore, is unwilling to try a new approach. Never mind that it isn't working!

Have you and your partner had arguments where you say and do the same exact things each time the disagreement pops up? You make your argument, your spouse defends him or herself, you do the same, and you're off and running. You can predict with great accuracy every expression on your partner's face and the precise words s/he will use. Your partner can do the same thing about you. You've had these arguments so many times, you've memorized the entire scene. You know your spouse's lines so well, if s/he got sick, you could be the understudy. I sometimes jokingly think that instead of doing the same old argument over and over, couples should just say to each other, "Honey, we haven't done argument number 7 for a long time, why don't we do it tonight?"

Here are a few of the topics that prompt "more of the same behavior" in couples:

Money matters
Children/stepchildren

Sex
How free time is spent
Extended family issues (mothers-in-law, sisters, brothers, etc.)
Household chores
Communication

Get the picture? Sometimes, it's not the topic that pushes your "more of the same" buttons, it's the time of day, week, month, or year. For example, lots of couples find themselves doing "more of the same" during the "bewitching hour," in the evening when people take off their career hats and put on their family hats. That's when the phone rings, the doorbell sounds, the kids are fighting, and the grilled cheese sandwich starts burning on the stove top. Couples tell me that even though they can and do anticipate the tension during the bewitching hour, they always approach it in exactly the same way, a way that adds to the chaos. Sound familiar? Here are some other time-related triggers.

Bill payment time
Holidays
Mornings as everyone is rushing out the door
Visits from out-of-towners
Winters when the sun doesn't shine
PMS time (sorry, women)
During an extra-heavy workload period
Every Sunday night before the work/school week

I imagine that you can conjure some images of the scenes that have taken place in your house that have been instant replays. I also imagine that you have told yourself time and time again, "I can't believe how stubborn s/he is." Right? Well, my friend, the more stubborn you think your spouse is, the more stubbornly you have adhered to doing more of the same. It's time to be honest with yourself and identify your own cheeseless tunnel. Get out your pencil and answer the following questions. Don't fudge.

Think of a troublesome situation or argument that arises on a regular basis. What is it about? If you can think of more than one, write that down too.

What is your usual way of handling it? What do you say? What do you do?

What's your partner's usual way of handling it? What does s/he say and do?

When your partner stubbornly makes his/her point or acts a certain way, what do you typically do in return?

If you are having any difficulty answering the questions above, answer the following question. Although you may not agree with your partner on this point, what would s/he say you do that drives him/her nuts in regards to this problem? Don't be defensive, just answer the question.

By now you should have a pretty good idea about the strategies you've been using that are worth abandoning. Even though you may believe in what you were doing, or that they came naturally to you, they're not worth doing if they aren't bringing you closer to your spouse and helping you to feel more love in your life. It's time to change the way you think about the process of change in relationships. It's not just a matter of acting on your feelings and doing what seems right, it's a matter of approaching your spouse in such a way that a loving relationship is the end result.

In every situation that arises in your marriage, it would be great if you could take a deep breath before you do anything and ask yourself, "What is my goal here?" Are you hoping to feel closer to your spouse? Are you expecting to spend the evening together peacefully? Once your goal is in sight, ask yourself another question. "Is what I'm about to do going to bring me closer or move me farther away from my goal?" If the answer is, "closer," then, by all means, stick with your plan. If the answer is, "farther away," stop. Do not proceed. Do something different instead.

Now that you've had a chance to think about what you do that is unproductive, you can no longer pretend you don't know how you have been contributing to the problems you've been experiencing. I want you to make a commitment to becoming more conscious of the times when you are only making matters worse by stubbornly sticking to what you know isn't working. More important, I want you to promise that you will try your very best to become solution-oriented and quit falling in love with your ineffective problem-solving strategies. It's unrequited love at best. Many people start seeing improvements in their marriages without the benefit of working through the remainder of the program because they simply committed to stop doing what hasn't been working!

I know that some people get really nervous when I tell them to switch gears because they're afraid they might inadvertently make matters worse. But the truth is the only real failure is to keep doing what hasn't been working, and, if your marriage is teetering on the edge, doing more of the same is downright dangerous.

Lena had been unhappy in her marriage for a long time. She and Garth had been married for ten years and had no children. Lena finally told Garth that she wanted a separation to see how she felt about staying married to him. She wanted to know whether she missed him when they were apart.

Panicked at the thought of separating, Garth begged her to reconsider. Although Lena felt sorry for the pain she was inflicting on her husband, she said she was going to move out next month when a friend's apartment became available. Garth askd her to go for counseling. She was firm in her response. "I have no interest in working on our marriage right now." He tried to get her to talk about her feelings. She said nothing positive about their lives together. To refute her, he pulled out old love letters and photographs, pointing to good times they had had together. She responded by saying she had been acting and that she should have received an Oscar for her performance. The more he tried to point out the positives in their marriage, the more she showed him her discontent. Clearly, his efforts to approach her logically and lovingly weren't working. But this didn't stop Garth. In fact, it scared him to think he was going to lose Lena, so he pursued her even more.

Rather than talk more about their relationship, he thought it might help to buy her gifts. Every four or five days there were flowers. Then came the Hallmark cards placed strategically all over the house, in the refrigerator, the microwave, by her dresser, and on her nightstand. Lena simply said, "Garth, please stop. This isn't working." But Garth did not heed her words. He called her at work five or six times a day and despite a cold reception, begged her to talk to him. She finally found herself hanging up on him angrily and eventually refusing to take his calls. He wrote letters and sent her e-mails. And the sad part was Lena's reaction. By the end of the four weeks, she could no longer stand the sight of him. Although she originally considered her leaving to be a trial separation, now she was certain that she never wanted to see him again. Garth's "more of the same" behavior pushed Lena out the door, out of their marriage, and into another life.

In Garth's defense, it's a natural reaction to clutch someone you love and want to hold on forever when you feel love slipping away. But this illustrates the point I've been trying to make all along. Just because something is logical or natural doesn't mean it's the right thing to do.

So are you convinced yet? I hope so. Ready to discover new ideas to help you find the cheese? Then proceed to step number 5.

CHAPTER SIX

Step Number 5—Experiment and Monitor Results

L et's review the steps you've taken so far. You've uncluttered your mind from your old problem-saturated thoughts. You've determined exactly what you want to change about your marriage. You've asked your partner for what you want. And finally, you've identified your "more of the same" behavior and promised yourself that you would no longer do what doesn't work. You've already come a very long way! Good for you. If you've skipped any of these steps, it's time to go back and do your homework.

My guess is that you are now really ready to try something new. That's good, because I'm going to teach you a slew of specific techniques, methods, strategies to get your spouse's attention and quickly lay the groundwork for more positive interactions. The interventions run the gamut from straightforward to those that defy common sense and are, therefore, more challenging to implement. Which strategies you use depend on your particular taste, what seems appealing, and the severity of your marital problems. It's my belief that you should always begin with the simplest techniques and work your way up to more complicated methods only if necessary. Why use a stick of dynamite when a gentle nudge will do?

In addition to becoming armed with new ideas and techniques to improve your relationship, I am going to teach you how to assess if what you're doing is working. Sometimes what you try works, sometimes it doesn't, and sometimes, the results are ambiguous. I will tell you what to look for if change is imminent, how quickly you can expect positive changes, how to tell if the method you're using is backfiring, and how long you should stick with one method before trying something new. You see, no matter what other relationship experts might have told you, improving one's marriage (just like anything else in life for that matter) is a trial and error process. You experiment and watch the results. If it works, you keep doing it. If it doesn't work, you try something different.

The bottom line is that you need to become more systematic; better at noticing how your approach to things creates subtle changes, both positive and negative, in your partner's responses and reactions. And this is considerably easier to do if you have a plan in hand and a concrete method for evaluating how it's working.

Because I know you are eager to improve your relationship, you might be tempted to start experimenting before you read this entire chapter. That's okay. But I want to tell you something important before you begin. Many people find it useful to keep a Solution Journal. The purpose of a Solution Journal is to keep track of what you do that works. You can do this in a free style version to your liking, or you can follow the guidelines below. Either way, you should pay close attention to what you do that prompts even a small positive response in your spouse. Here are some things you might want to include:

Date_____

Describe the challenging situation:
  Write down in specific terms what happened that troubled you.

Describe in action-oriented terms how you handled the situation:
  Write down your solution-oriented approach.

Describe your partner's immediate reaction:

What did s/he say or do? In what ways was his/her response different/more positive than usual?

Describe your partner's reaction several days following the situation:

Sometimes change takes time. Note positive changes over the next few days.

Although I recommend that you do keep a Solution Journal, I know that some people are not note takers or writers. If you are averse to writing things down, I strongly suggest you keep detailed mental notes about the things you do that seem effective. Now on to strategies that work.

A COOKBOOK OF MARRIAGE-SAVING STRATEGIES

Choose Your Battles Wisely

Before you choose from the marriage-saving "weapons" below, you should make sure the battle you're fighting is worth fighting for. Some issues are worth going to bat for, while others, as irritating as they might be, should be overlooked, ignored, or accepted as unchangeable. (Remember, 60 percent of what couples argue about is not resolvable!) Make sure that the changes you're after are things you simply can't live without.

Although it's true that you shouldn't let feelings of resentment and anger brew inside you, sometimes counting to ten, taking a cold shower, or going for a run is the best way to deal with life's small annoyances.

Strike When the Iron Is Cold

When it comes to relationships, the old adage, "You should always strike when the iron is hot" is lousy advice. Probably some of the most unproductive things we do, we do in the heat of passion. We do "more of the same," we say hurtful things, and we end up pushing our partners farther away. So here's my advice to you:

Even though you might be tempted to respond to a situation on the spur of the moment, especially if you're angry about something, don't. Take a deep breath. Count to ten. Take a walk around the block. Go for a drive. Tell yourself that you will deal with things later that evening. Do what you must to put a beat in between an anxiety-producing event and your handling of it. It's amazing how much more clearheaded you will be if you don't respond right away. Taking a time-out before you react will give you the opportunity to ask yourself those two important solution-oriented questions, "What's my goal here?" and "Is what I'm about to do or say going to bring me closer or move me farther away from my goal?" Then, when you're not quite so emotional, you can decide what actions will be in your best interests, what is more likely to make your marriage more loving. This is precisely what you should strive for in this program . . . becoming more mindful of how you approach all the issues in your marriage. Plus, sometimes when you put some distance in between an event and your reaction, you may find yourself mellowing a bit and deciding that it's not a battle worth fighting after all.

Cheerleading

I want you to answer the following question very candidly: Do you think your spouse perceives you to be complimentary or critical? If you're honest, your response will probably be, "My spouse would say that I'm more critical." Whether we like to admit it or not, we are pretty good at telling the people in our lives what we don't like about them. We're good at letting them know when they've let us down—when they've done something wrong, hurt our feelings, misspoken, or when they're sloppy, lazy, or inconsiderate.

However, we're amazingly slow on the draw when it comes to letting them know about the good stuff. We think they look good in their new clothes, but fail to tell them so. We enjoyed the meal they made but forget to comment on it. When they come home early to spend time with us, instead of thanking them, we complain about how much time we spend apart. One very honest woman told me that, in an effort to please her highly sexed husband, she decided to have sex every day rather than twice a week. Rather than let her know he was pleased, the only thing he said was, "I wish you were more experimental. You always want to make love in the same way." Instead of appreciating the things our partners do, we nail them for the things they don't do.

Sometimes people confuse criticism with assertiveness. We feel proud of ourselves when we muster up the courage to let people know they have disappointed us. And certainly, there's a time and place for criticism. But if we really want to stand our ground and influence people around us to be kinder and more loving, there's another, more effective way to do it.

Research shows beyond a shadow of a doubt that the most effective way to modify someone's behavior—to get him/her to do more or less of something—is to reinforce or positively reward that person when that individual is doing what we want him/her to do! In other words, catch your spouse in the act of getting it right and bring on the fanfare! A well-timed compliment, hug, or note of appreciation goes a lot farther than a heart-to-heart about marital dissatisfaction. Punishment-criticism (even kindly worded criticism), icy glances, silent treatments—are much less effective ways of influencing others. Yet, we somehow believe that when we complain, or discuss what we're unhappy about, it will prompt our spouses to change. It's this kind of thinking that gets us into trouble.

Beth was very unhappy about the fact that her husband, George, showed little interest in her life. He rarely asked her about her day and seemed disinterested when she talked about most things. Beth decided to tell George about her unhappiness. Much to her dismay, George appeared impatient with her complaints about him and he became angry.

It was Beth's plan to confront George again about his insensitivity to her feelings during their drive to work the next morning (they worked in the same building). Just when she was about to let him know how she felt, he asked her, "What's on your agenda today? What do you have planned?" Beth felt tempted to ignore his question and share her negative feelings about their marriage but took a deep breath and started telling him about the tasks she planned on accomplishing that day. After a moment's silence, she said, "George, I really appreciate your asking me what I'm doing today. It means a lot to me." Although little was said during the remainder of their drive to work, when they arrived at the office, they kissed briefly and told each other to have a nice day, something they hadn't done for months.

In the weeks that followed, George put more effort into connecting with Beth. And because Beth realized the value of cheerleading, she continued to let George know how much she appreciated his interest in her. Apparently, this was all George needed to stay on track.

Jenny was frustrated with how little energy Wes put into the care of their year-old baby girl. After Jenny's repeated discussions about his lack of involvement, Wes begrudgingly promised to help more with the baby's daily needs. He began diapering her more often, getting up with her at night, and giving her a bottle a few times a day. Although Jenny noticed Wes's efforts, she felt compelled to let him know when he wasn't doing something the same way she would. After a few weeks of hearing about his fathering shortcomings, Wes told Jenny, "Since you know everything about parenting and I know nothing, why don't you just do it yourself?" and he stopped caring for the baby. Jenny was miserable.

Jenny sought counseling with me. I wondered whether she believed that Wes was putting the baby in imminent danger by his actions. She said, "No." That being the case, I suggested she start out by apologizing to Wes for her critical behavior, and from that point forward, find as many reasons as possible to compliment him. Jenny admitted that she failed to say anything positive to him about his new behavior because she was so focused on making sure Wes was "doing it the right way." After our talk, she understood the importance of encouraging him, even if his style of parenting wasn't "perfect" in her eyes.

In the weeks that followed, Jenny trained herself to zip up her lips when she felt tempted to comment about the small differences in their parenting styles. In addition, every time Wes took the initiative to care for their baby and share in their parenting responsibilities, Jenny responded positively. Sometimes she complimented him, sometimes she smiled, and sometimes she just did something she knew would please him in return. Jenny was delighted with the results. The more Jenny encouraged Wes, the more adept he became at fathering. The more adept he became at fathering, the more involved he became with their little girl. He couldn't wait to come home at night to be with her. This, of course, pleased Jenny no end and their relationship improved as well.

There are important morals to the two stories you just read. The first: You can focus on what's missing in your life and be miserable and make everyone around you miserable, or you can focus on what you have and feel pleased and help everyone around you feel good about themselves and about you.

Second, even if your spouse isn't doing exactly what you had hoped for, don't withhold praise and positive feedback. When you encourage small steps along the way, your spouse will see you as an ally rather than an enemy and be much more likely to want to please you. With any luck, s/he might eventually get it "right."

Focus on the Problem-Free Times

Since you and your spouse are experiencing problems right now, you probably feel that your relationship has been this way forever. But you're wrong. I know that there have been times in the past when things were more loving, times when you argued less, were more intimate, and felt more compatible. It's human nature to focus on what goes wrong and pay little attention to what goes right, especially when you're hurting.

When I work with couples, it's not unusual for them to have several good weeks in between sessions. However, if they have one or two small arguments during the month, they will report that they fight *all the time*. They fail to notice or acknowledge the peaceful interludes. I realize that it is most people's expectation to tell their therapists about their tough times, but I see this tendency to focus on problems rather than solutions everywhere I go. We analyze to death interactions that are uncomfortable but we overlook or downplay the significance of more pleasurable times. If we happen to notice positive things happening, we consider them to be flukes or accidents, and never ask ourselves, "How did we get that to happen?" After all, we don't want to look a gift horse in the mouth.

This is unfortunate because the answer to many of our relationship problems lies in what we do differently when things are going *well* with our partners. Good times don't just happen, we make them happen. We talk, think, feel, and arrange our lives differently when we're getting along with our partners. You need to become a solution detective and figure out how you and your partner act, think, and feel differently when you like each other so that you know what makes your relationship work. I'll give you an example.

Mindy began counseling because her husband, Victor, was thinking of divorce. They co-owned a business and their management styles varied greatly. She was compulsive about getting things done in a timely fashion, whereas he was more laid back, a difference that caused them to fight frequently and bring their disagreements home with them. They were both concerned that their children observed them fighting with greater frequency, but felt at a loss to find solutions and stop fighting.

I asked Mindy what was different about her marriage when they got along better. Although at first she had a difficult time answering the question, she eventually recalled a time two years earlier when their marriage was going quite well. "Lots of things were different. We divided our tasks so that he was responsible for his things and I was responsible for mine. If he moved more slowly than me, it was his problem, not mine. That seemed to work better. Plus, I was more patient with him. I didn't snap at him as much as I do now."

I asked her, "When you were more patient, how was he different with you?" She smiled and said, "He was nicer. We spent more time together. Our lives are so busy now that all we do is work and take care of our family. We never go out anymore as a couple. Occasionally, he will go out with his friends and that really bothers me because I think that if we have extra time on our hands, he should be with me. So I get angry."

Mindy also figured out that during peaceful times, she's better at letting the small things slide. Given her fiery nature, I was intrigued about how she managed to do that. They lived on a farm and she told me that she liked to go to the barn and work around their farm animals because that calmed her down. In other words, she took a time-out. Lately, she hadn't been doing that. Instead, she let every little annoyance get under her skin.

She realized, too, that in times past, she had allowed herself to be more vulnerable with Victor. She talked more about her love for him, and about the things she appreciated in him. Lately, because of the tension, the only time she talked to him, she was nasty.

By the end of our discussion, Mindy had a blueprint for change that was based on what worked in their relationship in the past:

- Divide our responsibilities at work.
- Spend more time together as a couple.
- Be more patient with Victor.
- Let the small things drop.
- Take a time-out when things get tense.
- Express positive feelings more openly.

Many couples tell me that their relationships go more smoothly when they spend more time together. When things are rocky, the last thing they feel like doing is being together. So, they spend increasing amounts of time apart. Despite the fact that they know that their good times revolve around being together, they just aren't in the mood to make it happen. What they don't know is that research demonstrates that the quickest and most effective way to change how you think or feel about your life is to take an action. When you do, it triggers different feelings and perspectives. Taking an action is much more expedient than sitting around waiting for your attitude to change.

So, the long and short of it is this. Even if it's difficult, even if you're not in the mood, even if it seems artificial or unnatural, once you identify what has worked for you in the past, get yourself moving and do it. Do it today. Don't waste another day.

Finally, another reason people don't put their knowledge about what works into action is because they feel self-righteous. I knew a man whose wife was very jealous. He complained that every time he went out with his buddies, his wife would get angry with him. I asked him, "What's different about the times that she doesn't get angry?" He realized there had been a few occasions where she seemed to be more accepting of his choice to be with his friends. "I guess those were the times when I called her while I was out and let her know what I was doing and when I'd be home." Thinking that he had just solved his own problem, I said, "Well, great. Now you know exactly what you need to do." However, he replied, "Yeah, I know calling her works, but I just don't think I should have to do that. Why should I have to call her?" It always amazes me how many people would rather put up with conflict and hard feelings arising from unpleasant interactions with their spouses rather than take a very simple action that would nip things right in the bud. Learn from these people's mistakes, would you? Do what works, even if you think it's unfair or unreasonable. It will simplify your life immensely.

Here are some questions that will help you identify what works in your marriage. In regards to the problem(s) you are having right now, think back to a time in your marriage when it wasn't a problem and ask yourself:

What was I doing differently back then?

How was I treating my spouse differently?

What was different about my life during that time?

What was my spouse doing differently?

How was my spouse treating me differently then?

What was different about our lives together?

What was different about our family?

What would close friends and family say about how our lives were different back then?

If something on the list is no longer doable, ask:

What need did that fulfill in us?

And then:

What else could we do that might fulfill that very same need?

One last thing to keep in mind: Besides helping you identify solutions, focusing on the exceptions to the problem will make you feel better. You and your spouse have solved thousands of problems over the course of your marriage. This will help you remember that you have those resources. Plus, instead of immersing yourself in problems, you'll be focusing on solutions. And remember, *what you focus on expands.*

ACT AS IF

Problems often arise in relationships because people think they can predict the future. "I just know how my wife will respond when I tell her I'm going out," or "Steve will undoubtedly fly off the handle when my parents come for dinner." The problem with predicting dire outcomes in the future is that, whether we know it or not, we begin acting in certain ways that broadcast our expectations to our partners, and these subtle signals often bring about the very results we fear.

When you expect failure and feel defeated before you approach a challenging situation, it's helpful to ask yourself how you would handle the situation differently if you were expecting a positive outcome. How might your approach to your partner differ if you thought s/he would respond lovingly? Once you identify how your actions would differ under these circumstances, "act as if"; pretend you are expecting good things to happen and watch what happens. I'll give you an example of a time I used the "act as if" technique in my own life.

Years ago, I had been away from home at a conference. I was gone for about five days. During that period, I called home every day to check on my husband, Jim, and my children. By day three, I could tell that Jim was getting tired of playing Mr. Mom. He grew less than friendly with each passing call.

Upon arriving home, I was sitting next to a friend on the plane and as we pulled into the gate, I told my friend that I had a knot in my stomach. I assumed Jim—who was picking us up at the airport—wouldn't be too happy to see me. Because I was expecting an icy reception, I told my friend

I would cautiously allow Jim to set the tone for our greeting. I would keep a low profile, not be too effervescent, and certainly not let on that I had had a good time with my friends.

My friend, who happens to be a therapist, asked, "How would you greet Jim differently if you were expecting him to be happy to see you?" That was a no-brainer. I would get off the plane excited to see him, throw my arms around him, kiss him, and start telling him about the conference and what happened there. I also would want to know about his time at home and how he was feeling. Now, contrast in your mind's eye how differently Jim might have felt about these two different receptions!

I decided to "act as if." Even though I wasn't confident that Jim was elated about my homecoming, I acted as if I thought he were. I greeted him exuberantly. And happily, within about ten seconds, I was sure I made the right decision. He was thrilled to see me and we had a great ride home together.

The next time you find yourself thinking negatively about how a situation may turn out, stop for a moment and ask yourself:

How was I going to approach this situation given my pessimism?

How would I like the situation to turn out instead?

How would I handle this situation differently if I were expecting good things to happen?

Then, regardless of how skeptical you might be about the possibilities of good things happening, "act as if." Do all the things you would do if you were convinced of a positive outcome. Then watch the results.

DO SOMETHING DIFFERENT

Human beings are creatures of habit. Most of the time, we're on automatic pilot. We sleep on the same side of the bed every night. We sit in the same chair at our dining room table. We take the same route to work each day.

Being on automatic pilot is not necessarily a bad thing. Habitual responses are economical. They allow us to go through our lives without having to concentrate on what we're doing. But being on automatic pilot is a problem when relationship difficulties arise. If you act like a robot when you and your partner are at odds with each other, it could really be disastrous and most of the time it is.

As you learned in the last chapter, during stressful times, spouses argue about the same old subjects, in the same way, often at the same time of day. We do it unconsciously. But novelty is a wake-up call; any change in routine—a change in your actions, your approach, the setting, the timing of your disputes—can get people out of their hypnotic trance and has the potential of yielding different results. Here's an example.

Cathy was someone who, any time her husband was quiet, assumed he was angry or upset with her. She would frequently ask him, "What's wrong?" Each time she did, he would respond, "Nothing's wrong." She would say, "I know something is wrong, tell me what it is." He would tell her, "Nothing is wrong, please stop asking me that question." She would insist that she was right about her perception of him, and he would finally explode angrily and their day would then be ruined.

One day, she decided to do something different. They were getting into their car to go see a movie together when Cathy noticed her husband seemed sullen. As usual, she asked, "What's wrong?" but when he replied, "Nothing," she decided to try something new. She turned on the radio and started to sing along with the music. Within a few minutes, he said, "Hon, do you mind if I turn down the radio? There's something I'd like to discuss with you." He proceeded to share his feelings about something that had happened earlier that day. It was the first time in the history of their marriage that he'd opened up to her voluntarily. She changed, he changed!

Janet and Jonathan argued about money every Friday night when they returned home from work. Because they started out their weekend with an argument, the rest of the weekend was miserable. This had been going on for months. Jonathan finally decided to do something different in the hopes of having a pleasant weekend for a change.

Friday night rolled around and Janet initiated the usual conversation about money. Jonathan said, "I want to talk to you about this, but I would prefer waiting until Sunday. Is that all right with you?" Surprised by his response, Janet simply said, "Okay, whatever."

They decided to go out for dinner together on Friday night and, for the first time in months, had a really good time as a couple. On Saturday, they decided to go shopping together for furniture and again had an enjoyable time. By Sunday, they were feeling better about each other than they had for a long time, which probably explains why, when Janet brought up the money issue on Sunday night, they were able to resolve their differences. A simple change in the time they discussed their heated issue allowed them to find a solution.

I received a letter from a man who decided to be creative about frequent arguments he was having with his wife.

Last week when Sue arrived we talked about how we could better resolve our conflicts. I took your "do something different" suggestion and told my wife that if we are determined to fight, we would have to do it without our clothes on. This would eliminate fighting in shopping malls, family gatherings, while walking down the street or any place outside in our winters. Since our five children are no longer at home, we agreed to try it.

The inevitable happened and we started an argument. I decided to go for it. Now, if we were younger and trim, then shedding our clothes could be a pleasant distraction that would make us forget what we were arguing about. On the other hand, lumpy, saggy bodies can be quite funny, but what happened was better than either.

I got right into the argument and at the same time began peeling off clothes and throwing them emphatically on the floor of the laundry room to punctuate the very serious points I was making in my case. Meanwhile, Sue was taken aback. "You are serious!" she said. I agreed and continued making my case as socks, shirt, pants and underwear hit the floor. Sue started to laugh. She laughed until tears ran down her cheeks. I laughed too, but I continued discussing the issue. We soon found ourselves in complete agreement!

In the past few days, we have laughed again and again about the hilarious image. Sue said she will never be able to keep a straight face in an argument again. I cannot even remember what the argument was about now. I just know it was the best one we ever had.

Now I want *you* to go back to the last chapter and review what you learned about your "more of the same" behavior. For each "more of the same" behavior that you identified, figure out what you'd have to do to get your spouse's attention. To jump-start your imagination, let me give you a few examples.

If you've been talking a lot about your feelings lately, stop talking about them completely. If you've been holding things in, let your feelings be known. If you've been apologetic and soft-spoken, take a strong stand. If you've been fiery, start being patient. If you've been clingy, start being more independent. If you've been ultra-independent, start showing your spouse you need him/her more. In order to make your spouse react differently, you have to do something completely out of the ordinary.

On a piece of paper, list each of your "more of the same" behaviors. Then describe in specific terms what you could do differently next time the problem occurs. Make sure you are concrete and action-oriented. For example, if you're someone who has been suspicious because your spouse is spending more time away from home and your "more of the same" behavior has been to grill him/her every time s/he returns home, here are some things you could do differently:

Don't be home when your spouse arrives.
Don't ask any questions about his/her whereabouts.
Instead of being angry as usual, act pleased to see your spouse.
Make your spouse wonder about *you*. Be less accessible and predictable.
Instead of grilling your spouse, seduce him/her upon arrival.

Now it's your turn.
My "more of the same" behavior is:

Here are some things I could do that would really surprise my spouse:

Do this for every "more of the same" behavior you've identified in the last chapter.

If you are having trouble thinking of something that might be different, you might consider using humor. It's often the case that we get so darn serious about our marital problems that our humor goes right out the window. In fact, a friend of mine told me that once in the midst of a heated argument, her husband said something really funny, but she absolutely and positively refused to laugh. She feared that her laughter would make her husband think that "he won." Nonsense. Laughter is great marital medicine. Here's an example of how I ended a difficult situation with Jim by using humor.

One morning Jim was making me breakfast and I was reading the mail. We belong to a golf club and we had received a roster of the members of the club. I found myself feeling mildly annoyed at the fact that the men were listed as members and their wives' names were listed in parentheses. I commented to Jim about my irritation. At first, although he understood, he thought I might be overreacting. The more he defended the policy of the club, the more irate I became. Finally, I said to him, "Maybe I should just write a letter to the club about how unfair I think this really is," at which point, he brusquely left the room and went to our bedroom. Our wonderful Sunday morning had come to an abrupt halt.

I felt tempted to march upstairs and defend my position, but I knew that Jim would have gotten even angrier at me and we would have fought more intensely. In all honesty, although I felt irked about the golf club's policy, it really wasn't a burning issue for me. So I decided to do something different. I wrote him a note and walked into our bedroom to deliver it to him.

When I entered the room, he was lying on our bed and refused to make eye contact with me because he was expecting me to argue with him. Nonetheless, I walked over to him and handed him my note. It read,

I love you. (Michele)

Although he tried hard not to laugh, I could see it wasn't working. He started to chuckle. I laughed. Then he laughed even louder. We hugged, went downstairs, resumed making breakfast and resurrected our pleasant Sunday together.

THE MEDIUM IS THE MESSAGE

When you are trying to get through to your partner, there are many ways to do it. You can have a face-to-face discussion, write a heartfelt letter, talk about things over the phone, or send a greeting card. Lately, with the popularity of the Internet, I hear more and more about couples who use e-mail to make peace and find solutions when talking things out doesn't work. Many couples (including Jim and me) admit to having some of their most productive conversations over the telephone. (I tell couples who have two telephone lines to call each other, even if they're in the same house!) The point is, just because you might not be able to get through to your partner during a face-to-face conversation, doesn't mean you should give up. Simply try a different medium.

I know a woman who had been begging her husband for months to be more forthcoming about his out-of-town trips or his late nights at work so that she could make her own plans. Despite what seemed like several thousand reminders, he never did what she asked. This enraged her and they fought constantly. One day, instead of doing the same old thing, she left a calendar and a Magic Marker on the kitchen counter along with a note suggesting that her husband mark his schedule for the following week. When she came downstairs, she discovered her calendar marked with his plans for the next three months.

Another woman I know unintentionally hurt her husband's feelings. She tried apologizing, but he wasn't quite ready to accept. She gave him a day or two to pout, and still, he was holding his grudge. Again, she tried talking to him about the situation, but he wasn't receptive. Then she became creative. Right before his morning shower, she got out her lipstick and wrote, "I love you and I am very sorry" on the shower wall. Then, after putting the lipstick on her lips, she kissed the wall, leaving "smaks" all over the shower. And then she waited quietly for him to begin his morning routine.

Her husband shaved and stepped into their shower. He turned on the water and simultaneously started to laugh. Though words failed to break the ice, lipstick worked well.

Stu was very concerned about Resa's drinking. For years, he talked of his concerns about her health and about the example she was setting for their two children. Stu's mother was an alcoholic and he was extremely worried that Resa was going down the same path. Every time he discussed his fears with her, they ended up arguing and her behavior never changed. Out of desperation, he decided to write her a heartfelt letter, telling her how much he loved her and how scared he was about losing her. He left the letter on her dresser right before he went on a business trip.

When he returned, he feared that she would be extremely angry at him, but much to his surprise, she greeted him with tears in her eyes and, for the first time in their marriage, admitted that she had a drinking problem. She also said that she was willing to talk to an addictions counselor to help her quit drinking. Resa told Stu that the letter gave her a chance to think about what he was saying without feeling that she needed to defend herself or react in any way. Although the feelings Stu expressed in the letter were very similar to discussions they had had in the past, she felt profoundly affected by seeing his words in black and white.

EASIER DONE THAN SAID

A variation of the "medium is the message" technique, this intervention suggests that you stop using words entirely to get your messages across. No talking on the phone, no letter writing, no e-mails, you just take action! Women really benefit from using this technique because we now know that men are less verbally-oriented and more action-oriented than women. Men sometimes get overloaded with words and they stop listening. When that happens, it doesn't matter *how* their wives say things, they're not going to be able to get through to their husbands with words. It's in one ear and out the other. Actions, on the other hand, get their attention.

I was once interviewed on the radio by a husband and wife team. Knowing about my experience in helping couples improve their marriages, the woman jokingly said to me, "If you're so smart, tell me what I can do to get my husband to repair the steps leading to our back porch." Before I could respond, she said, "I know exactly what I need to do. I need to stop nagging and I need to take action. If I want him to fix the steps, all I have to do is grab some tools and start doing it myself. The moment he notices me doing this, he'll come right over to me, look over my shoulder, grab the tools out of my hand because I'll be doing it the wrong way, and he'll take over. It works that way every time." That's exactly what she did. It worked!

Sharon spent years talking, even begging her husband, Pat, to be more adventurous and start doing fun things with her on weekends. It seemed to her that most of her friends had very active social lives and she felt deprived. But nothing she said to Pat about her unhappiness ever seemed to make a difference. He simply preferred staying home.

Out of complete frustration, Sharon decided that she had to begin to do things that were fun either alone or with friends. After several such outings, her husband became curious about what she was up to. He realized that he disliked spending weekends alone. After three weeks of her becoming more independent, Pat told her that he would like to join her the following weekend on a trip to the city's art museum. Sharon practically fell out of her chair. Nonetheless, she was happy that Pat wanted to join in.

They had a great time together and instead of returning home after being at the museum, Pat suggested that they go out for dinner at a new restaurant. Sharon had wondered whether an alien had abducted her husband and exchanged him for this stranger, but she approved of the trade-in. In the weeks that followed, Sharon continued making plans for herself and at least half the time, Pat asked if she wanted company.

If words have failed to produce positive results in your marriage, if you've said to yourself, "I talk until I'm blue in the face," then stop talking and start doing. It's easier done than said.

DO NOTHING

Some people are fix-it addicts. Fixing their marriages becomes the main focus of their lives. The problem with this is that relationships are like seesaws: the more one person does of something, the less the other one will do. If one person takes out the garbage all the time, the other partner won't even think about garbage day. If one person remembers family members' birthdays all the time, the other partner doesn't have to think about birthdays. If one partner is the marriage handyman or woman, the other partner can put the marriage on the back burner.

Sometimes the very best thing a fix-it addict can do is to back off and do nothing, because by doing so, it gives their partner the opportunity to step in and rise to the problem-solving occasion. Being a fix-it addict myself, I know about the importance of backing off firsthand.

My most deeply entrenched "more of the same" behavior had to do with the raising of our daughter, Danielle. I felt Jim was too harsh with her and too rule-bound. I felt that kids need a lot more TLC. He, on the other hand, felt that I was a pushover and that I wasn't doing Danielle any favors by not having clear expectations of her in every aspect of her life. Because of these basic differences in perspective, we argued a great deal, especially when Danielle was a pre-teenager.

The typical pattern was this. Danielle would do something, I would correct her mildly, and Jim would come down on her harder. In order to soften the blow, I would step in and reassure her in some way. This would infuriate Jim and he would lash out verbally at me and then at Danielle as well. When I asked myself what my goal was, it was twofold: one, to help Danielle feel good about herself and two, for Jim and Danielle to have a more loving relationship. Although I knew that my actions were bringing about the exact opposite of what I was hoping for, I continued to do "more of the same" for years. I had become a fix-it addict.

Then one day I decided to practice what I preach. I was out of town doing a seminar and I received an SOS call from Danielle. She said, "Mom, Dad is being mean. He's yelling and saying mean things." Well, that's all I really needed to hear. I told her to go and get her dad because I wanted to talk with him. In the minute or so that it took for Jim to get on the phone, I realized that if I lectured him about his actions as I had done a thousand times before, he'd get mad at me and even madder at Danielle. So, in an instant, I decided to reverse a marriage-long habit. I decided to say nothing. Jim got on the phone expecting a lecture and instead, I told him that I just wanted to say good night to him. "Good night," he told me, and then we hung up.

The next day at the airport, on my way home, I called in the late afternoon to see how Danielle was doing. Surprisingly, Jim answered the phone. I said, "Jim, it's only three-thirty in the afternoon, what are you doing home?" He replied, "I felt really bad about what happened between Danielle and me last night so I decided to leave work early, buy a dozen roses [she loves flowers], pick her up at school, and take her out to dinner." We were both silent for a moment. Then he said, "Do you feel better?" to which I replied, "Yes, definitely. Do you?" "Yeah, much better," he said.

You see, this whole wonderful thing never would have happened if I hadn't butted out. If I complained, Jim would have gotten mad *at me* instead of *himself*. Without me pointing fingers, he only had himself to look at in the mirror that night. And what he saw, he didn't like a whole lot. So, he fixed it. And he did a damn good job, if I do say so myself.

I learned a lot that day. I realized that I didn't need to be in the middle anymore. In fact, I learned that by doing nothing, I had really done something, probably the most important something I had ever done in the history of our parenting together. Call me a slow learner, but I caught on, and rarely intervened again. Their relationship is so incredibly close now that I wonder why it took me so long to do nothing.

If you're someone who is always assuming responsibility for making things better in your marriage, it may be time for you to take a sabbatical. Relax. Give your spouse the opportunity to notice you're not fixing things anymore. Like me, you may be surprised with the way in which your spouse will step up to the plate.

DO A 180

Just as its name implies, if what you're doing doesn't work, do the exact opposite. As counterintuitive as this might be, it often works.

Janice was a woman who liked peace in her house and would get upset each time her husband got angry. Unfortunately, her husband, Cameron, had a low tolerance for frustration and would anger easily. Every time he started to grumble, she would try to pacify him. The more she tried to calm him down, the angrier he would become.

One day, Cameron was working in their family room and started to complain loudly about having to complete a computer task for which he had received no training. Instead of reassuring him, Janice stormed into the family room, banged her fist on the table, and shouted, "What was your boss thinking? You weren't at the training. How in the world are you supposed to know what to do? Now you're going to get angry and our evening will be ruined. Your boss is really something!"

There was dead silence. Shortly thereafter, her husband composed himself and said, "Will you settle down, please? I know I can figure this stuff out if you just give me a little more time. Relax." I'm not certain who was more surprised by this interaction!

Brett wanted his marriage to work more than anything in the world. However, Stella, his wife, was fairly certain she wanted out. Brett was heartbroken. In an effort to get Stella to change her mind, Brett did everything he could to please her. He did all the housework, the lion's share of taking care of their children, encouraged her to go out with her friends, and do other enjoyable activities without him or their family. When they were home together, he was extremely cautious about how he acted and what he said for fear that he might make her angry. His lifelong friends were telling him that he'd turned into a doormat. Although he understood what they were saying and why they were saying it, he felt he had to keep a low profile or Stella would just take off. Although he didn't like the man he had become, he felt paralyzed by fear. Stella simply went about her business without paying a whole lot of attention to Brett. He hoped that if he could be careful about his actions long enough, Stella might appreciate the changes in him. So far, it hadn't been working. The nicer he was, the crueler she seemed to be to him.

One evening Stella told Brett that she was going to work out and that she would be home around 9:30 P.M. He said, "Fine, see you then." Although he would have preferred that she spend the evening with their family, he was trying to be supportive. Nine-thirty came rolling around and no Stella. Brett assumed she was running a little late from aerobics class. But when the clock struck 11 P.M., he found himself growing incredibly angry. By midnight, he was furious with her. Stella finally walked through the door at 12:30 A.M., at which time, Brett's emotions got the better of him.

In a loud voice, he insisted that she sit down because they needed to talk. At first, she resisted, but Brett would not accept "no" for an answer. He called her on her irresponsible behavior and let her know, in no uncertain terms, that he was tired of being the nice guy and that he couldn't believe how incredibly inconsiderate she had been for months. Brett told her that he was through with her shenanigans and that as far as he was concerned, if she wanted out, she should leave.

Stella was stunned by Brett's reaction. Instead of getting furious and threatening to leave, as Brett had anticipated, Stella sat quietly and listened to everything Brett had to say. In fact, she asked him if they could talk about this whole thing more calmly. She apologized for staying out late and said that she should have called him to let him know about her plans. Brett was so wrapped up in getting things off his chest that he almost didn't hear the apology. It was the first time in six months that Stella said anything kind to him. Instead of being "Mr. Nice Guy" and letting her off the hook, Brett agreed with her saying, "That's exactly right. You should have called," and promptly went to bed.

In the days that followed, Brett realized that over the course of their marriage, Stella had often told him that what she loved about him was his strength, his manliness, and his ability to be decisive. Brett realized that their crisis had turned him into a different person. Many of the qualities Stella loved about him were gone. Although their argument that night was not going to win them the couple of the year award, it sure made an impression in Stella's mind. The old Brett was back. Brett decided that from now on, he had to be himself, regardless of what happened with their marriage. Luckily for him, the real Brett— the less cautious, more spontaneous, somewhat fiery and opinionated guy—was much more appealing to Stella than the timid, lonely man who made himself invisible for fear he would alienate the person he loved most. Although Brett's 180 was spontaneous rather than planned, the lesson he learned from switching gears had a profound impact on the choices he made about his life from that day forward.

One important reminder here that bears repeating. When you do a 180, it's scary. It feels unnatural. It flies in the face of what's logical. If I had suggested to Brett that he take a strong stand and let Stella know exactly what he was willing to put up with and what he was not, Brett would have told me to go fly a kite. My suggestion would have sounded downright ludicrous or even dangerous. But almost all 180s feel that way.

So if you are considering doing a 180, don't let your fear that it will backfire stop you. You can always retrace your steps. The important thing to remember is that the worst thing you can do is to keep doing what hasn't been working. And, if you're considering this technique, I'd venture a guess that your problem-solving strategies thus far haven't been anything to write home about. Go slowly, but try doing a 180 and watch what happens.

THE LAST-RESORT TECHNIQUE

The last-resort technique is exactly what it says it is. You use it as a last resort. In theory, this technique is identical to doing a 180, but you put it to use when your situation is extreme. What do I mean by extreme? It's imperative that you begin doing the last-resort technique immediately if:

- Your spouse has said to you in no uncertain terms that s/he wants to get a divorce and it appears as if s/he really means it. It wasn't just said in the heat of battle.
- You and your spouse are separated physically.
- You and your spouse still live together but have very little to do with each other. You may be sleeping in separate rooms, have virtually no communication, and little or no sexual contact.
- Your spouse has filed for divorce.

Although it's true that many marriages do end in divorce, just because your marriage is really fragile right now doesn't mean you have to become a statistic. There are many people who beat the odds. Don't feel hopeless. I will give you specific instructions about what you should do to try to get things back on track. Although the last-resort technique doesn't always work, it works often enough for you to be eager to give it a shot. I have worked with many clients and have received many letters, phone calls, and e-mails from people whose relationships were on their marital deathbeds but were successful at turning things around by using the last-resort technique.

Typically, when marriage nears its end, only one spouse is in favor of divorce while the other desperately wants to stay together. The spouse eager to hold the marriage together often engages in behavior that pushes the other partner farther away. S/he pursues, reasons, chases, begs, pleads, and implores. There may be lots of phone calls, letters, heartfelt pleas for sympathy, even suicide threats. It doesn't take long before the departing spouse gets fed up with the pressure and insists the marriage is over, prompting the other spouse to chase even more. The effects of this chasing behavior are deadly to a marriage.

I am not an expert on what works, but I am an expert on what doesn't work. If you keep pushing your spouse, you will push him or her right out the door. You might as well file for divorce yourself because your actions are moving things in that direction. I know how bad you feel and I also know that it's human nature to try to hold on to important things in your life that seem to be evaporating into thin air. But I also know that it's human nature to want to escape when you feel coerced or pressured. So you have to stop pursuing your spouse immediately, even if you don't feel like it. It's the only chance you have of saving your marriage.

One of the things that happens when you chase your spouse is that you take the focus off your failing marriage and crumbling family and put the spotlight right on you. Your spouse gets so annoyed at you that getting rid of you is the only thing s/he thinks about. Your persistence is robbing your spouse of the opportunity to reflect on what is really happening in your lives right now. Because anger is the only emotion your spouse is feeling, it prevents him/her from having feelings of sadness, grief, guilt, remorse, or any other emotions that might help your cause. Your spouse is so busy glaring at *you*, s/he doesn't have time to look in the mirror and accept some responsibility for your marital problems. You need to quit supplying your spouse with a reason to leave.

Now, I know that asking you not to pursue your mate feels as if I'm asking you to stop breathing. But I am going to give you very specific instructions to help you reverse the destructive momentum. When you follow my advice, you may join the ranks of people who have been able to get their reluctant spouses to reconsider their decision to divorce and begin working on their marriages. Here's a letter from one such person.

I am writing this letter to you to let you know how doing the last-resort technique helped save my marriage of twenty-nine years. Four weeks ago my husband and I separated. In the beginning of our separation, my sister told me to give up on my marriage because it was too late. My husband had moved out already, and worst of all, he moved in with a woman he had been seeing for the past year. He had already told me that I should get on with my life and find someone who could "take care" of me. Begging him to stay obviously wasn't working. Through my tears, I finally got to the last-resort technique. I knew I could not afford to waste any time. I decided to stop fighting *with* him and start fighting *for* him.

So I did stop chasing him. I decided to act as if I were going on with my life. I went out dancing—which is part of our business—three nights in a row and had my ego boosted by other men who danced with me, complimented me, and offered me dates. Fortunately, we had to see or talk to each other each day because of our business. I was probably glowing when I saw him Monday morning at work. And when he asked me how my weekend was, I told him. I could tell by his facial expression that something within him changed. That night, he called me and agreed to talk the next day.

That was Tuesday, October 16, my fiftieth birthday, and he came home that night. We've done more talking this past week since we've been back together than we had all last year. We talked about how this happened and blamed nobody. We decided to drastically cut the hours I worked at our second shop so we would have time together. We intend to rediscover the fun we have together and never let the pressures of life fool us into thinking there is anything more important than the people we love.

The last-resort technique didn't cure the fundamental problems in their marriage and isn't designed to do so. It's simply a method of putting a halt to a dynamic that is sure to end a marriage. Once reconciliation is considered, you need to begin to deal with the underlying issues, either in therapy, or your own. Are you ready to do the last-resort technique? Good. Then this is what you have to do.

STEP 1—STOP THE CHASE

First, you need to stop doing anything that your spouse might look at as pursuing behavior. Here are some examples of behavior that I would consider "pursuing."

- Frequent phone calls
- Begging your spouse to reconsider
- Pointing out all the good in your marriage
- Writing letters
- Following your mate around the house

- Encouraging talk about the future
- Soliciting help from family members
- Asking for reassurances
- Buying gifts/ flowers
- Trying to schedule dates together
- Spying on your spouse

In addition, it is essential that you stop saying, "I love you." I know this will be hard. But remember what I told you. Each time you say, "I love you," you remind your spouse that the feelings of love aren't reciprocal at the moment. My guess is that every time you say, "I love you," your spouse says, "I know," or remains silent. Not exactly reassuring, is it?

STEP 2—GET A LIFE

I've worked with enough couples in this situation to know that when you feel desperate, you get clingy and depressed. You cry a lot, mope around, lose interest in things, and basically become a blob. Understand that this is perfectly normal. Losing someone you love and watching your family fall apart are definitely the most painful things you can ever experience. However, the end result—your desperateness—is not exactly attractive. In fact, it's very unattractive. And when you consider that you are competing with your spouse's fantasy of an ideal life without problems, or perhaps even a real-life affair, you'd better pick yourself up by the bootstraps and get yourself together! You need to act as if you are moving on with your life. Otherwise, you don't stand a fighting chance.

You're probably asking yourself, "How do I become more cheerful, strong, outgoing, or attractive when I feel like crap?" That's a good question. The reason you are feeling as crappy as you are right now is because you are living through some really tough circumstances. You are reacting as any normal person would. But, and this is the big but, this isn't the *real you*. You are much stronger and more confident deep down inside, aren't you?

Stop for a minute and ask yourself, "What was it about me that attracted my spouse to me in the first place?" Think of all your wonderful traits. Well, the person your spouse fell in love with is the "real you." You're acting differently right now because you're going through hell, not because you've changed radically as a person. Don't forget that.

I'm not asking you to put on an act. I'm just asking you to remember *who you really are*. You need to stop acting as if you're a victim because if you act the victim, you'll become the victim. Any self-defense instructor will tell you that the worst possible thing to do in a tense situation is to signal to a potential attacker that you believe you are helpless.

You need to immediately start doing things that are out of character for the way you've been acting lately. You need to become more upbeat in your partner's presence. You need to appear pleased with yourself and your own life. If you have phone conversations, sound content, even bubbly. Don't sit around waiting for your spouse to call. Go do things. Be with friends. Start a new hobby. Keep yourself busy. Start being less predictable. Let the answering machine pick up your calls. If you've always tried to engage your spouse in conversation when s/he calls, comes over, or is at home, be scarce and short on words. If you have been in the habit of grilling your spouse about his/her whereabouts, ask nothing. Simply wish your partner a good time. In short, you need to make your partner think that you have had an awakening and, as far as you are concerned, you are going to move on with your life, with or without your spouse. This doesn't mean that you should be nasty or angry or even cold. It just means that you should pull back and wait to see if your spouse notices and, more important, realizes what s/he will be missing.

One more point you should consider. Besides increasing the chances that your spouse will be more interested in you if you back off and start doing your own thing, there is another important reason you should "get a life." You've stopped doing things that give you pleasure. Chances are, you even think you've forgotten how to have pleasure. The best thing you can do is take care of yourself for a while.

Focus on making yourself a better person. If you've stopped going to church or synagogue, go back. If you've been wanting to take a new class, go for it. Think about some old friends you haven't contacted in a while. Pick up the phone and connect. Go visit a family member. Watch a sunset. Read poetry. Count leaves. Play golf. Go fishing. Do something that will put you back in touch with you, not just because your spouse might like you more if you do, but because it's important to feel centered and love yourself. You deserve it. I know you do.

STEP 3—WAIT AND WATCH

One of three things happens when you use the last-resort technique. The first is, nothing. Unfortunately, there are times when, no matter what you do, your spouse has firmly shut the door on your marriage. I tell you this because I don't want you to think that this is a magic bullet. It isn't. However, even if your marriage doesn't improve when you do the last-resort technique, your mental health will. I promise you. So many people have thanked me for suggesting this technique because it gave them back their dignity. They felt so lost and out of control prior to employing this method. With your self-esteem in place, you will feel more prepared to take on whatever comes your way. I know this isn't what you want to hear, but since it is a possibility, you should know about it. Having said that, you should also know that there are two other responses you might observe in your spouse.

The second possible response from your mate is that s/he becomes curious. S/he might start showing more interest in you, your whereabouts, and what you are up to in your life. Your spouse might even suggest you spend some time together to talk or do something enjoyable. It's also possible that your spouse might start asking you a lot of questions about your sudden changes. If any of these things begin to happen, here's my advice:

- Be loving in return, *but not overly excited or enthusiastic.*
- Accept some invitations to spend time together, but not all.
- Do not ask any questions about your future together.
- Be vague when asked questions about the changes in you. Say that you are just thinking things through.
- Continue to be upbeat.
- Do not say, "I love you."
- Resist getting into conversations about your marriage.
- Beat your spouse to the punch when it comes time to leave or separate from each other at the end of an activity. You set the tone for going your separate ways.

The general rule of thumb here is to be responsive to your partner's new interest, but not too responsive. If you go overboard, your partner will get cold feet. I've seen it happen many times before. If you are excited that the last-resort technique is working, share it with a friend, write it in your Solution Journal, go for a run around the block, but don't wear your emotions on your sleeve.

You need to stay interested, but cool, until you are absolutely convinced that your spouse's renewed interest in saving your marriage has taken hold. Once you feel absolutely sure that this is so, you can test the waters by becoming more obvious about your desire to stay together. You can try discussing your future together and see what happens. If your spouse is receptive, you can continue to move forward slowly and begin to tackle the issues that drove you apart in the first place. If, on the other hand, you're met with reluctance, backpedal just as quickly as you can. Resume your interested but distant stance until things move in a more positive direction. This might take a whole lot longer than you would like, weeks, even many months. However, you must be patient. As long as your spouse seems to be somewhat interested rather than pulling away, it's okay for your marriage to be in a holding pattern. It will try your patience, but what else do you have to do right now that could be as important as trying to save your marriage? Be patient.

The third possibility is the least likely, but it does happen occasionally, so it's worth mentioning. Once you pull back, your spouse may have an overnight change of heart, that is, s/he might want to abandon any thought of divorce and jump right back into things as if nothing had ever happened. This is rare, but I've seen it happen and I have some advice for you if it does. Don't move too quickly! It's really important to pace yourselves. If you act as if nothing had happened between you, it's only a matter of time before your spouse will have second thoughts about the decision. You didn't get to this place of disharmony overnight and, as much as you'd like to forget that it had ever happened, you probably won't get things back on track overnight. So, if you've been separated, don't jump right into being together again. If you've been emotionally miles apart, don't spend every waking minute at each other's sides and don't abandon all of your other interests. You have to back into your marriage cautiously. If you don't, and really deal with the problematic issues before you recommit, you might find yourselves in the same situation a few weeks or months down the road.

Once you have your partner's attention and you sense a real commitment to working things out, you can follow the steps in this program to make your marriage a healthier and happier place to be. You also can seek the help of a therapist who is solution-oriented. Here are some suggestions about choosing a therapist:

• Make sure your therapist has received specific training and is experienced in marital therapy. Too often, therapists say they do couples therapy or marital therapy if they have two people sitting in the office. This is incorrect. Marital therapy requires very different skills than doing individual therapy. Individual therapists usually help people identify and process feelings. They assist them in achieving personal goals. "How do you *feel* about that," is their mantra.

Couples therapists, on the other hand, need to be skilled in helping people overcome the differences that naturally occur when two people live under the same roof. They need to know what makes marriage tick. A therapist can be very skilled as an individual therapist and be clueless about helping couples change. For this reason, don't be shy. Ask your therapist about his or her training and experience.

• Make sure your therapist is biased in the direction of helping you find solutions to your marital problems rather than helping you leave your marriage when things get rocky. Feel free to ask him/her to give you a ballpark figure about the percentage of couples he or she works with who leave with their marriages intact and are happier as a result of therapy. Although your therapist may not have a specific answer, his/her reaction to your question will speak volumes.

• You should feel comfortable and respected by your therapist. You should feel that s/he understands your perspective and feelings. If your therapist sides with you or your spouse, that's not good. No one should feel ganged up on. If you aren't comfortable with something your therapist is suggesting—like setting a deadline to make a decision about your marriage—say so. If your therapist honors your feedback, that's a good sign. If not, leave.

• As I told you in the first chapter, although some people think that their therapists are able to tell when a person should stop trying to work on their marriage, therapists really don't have this sort of knowledge. If they say things like, "It seems that you are incompatible," or "Why are you willing to put up with this?" or "It is time to move on with your life," they are simply laying their own values on you. In my opinion, this is an unethical act.

• Make sure you (and your partner) and your therapist set concrete goals early on. If you don't, you will probably meet each week with no clear direction. Once you set goals, you should never lose sight of them. If you don't begin to see some progress within two or three sessions, you should address your concern with your therapist.

• It's my belief that couples in crisis don't have the luxury to analyze how they were raised in order to find solutions to their marital problems. If your therapist is focusing on the past, suggest a future-orientation. If s/he isn't willing to take your lead, find a therapist who will. Solution-oriented therapists can be counted on to help you set goals and focus on the future rather than on the past.

• Don't let your therapist tell you that change is impossible. Human beings are amazing and they are capable of doing great things—especially for people they love.

• Most of all, trust your instincts. If your therapist is helping, you'll know it. If s/he isn't, you'll know that too. Don't stay with a therapist who is just helping you tread water. Find one who will help you swim.

• Finally, the best way to find a good therapist is word of mouth. Satisfied customers say a lot about the kind of therapy you will receive. Although you might feel embarrassed to ask friends or family for a referral, you should consider doing it anyway. It increases the odds you'll find a therapist who will really help you and your spouse.

Relationship skill-building classes are also very helpful. They are often offered through churches and synagogues, schools, colleges, and mental health centers. Many of them are excellent and you should consider taking a course. They are educational and inspirational.

Whatever you do, don't take your renewed commitment to be together for granted. Beyond loving each other, you need skills to deal with the problems you've had in the past. If all you do is get back together without addressing your trying issues, your chances for success will be minimal.

On a brighter note though, many couples report having the best marriage in their lives once they've weathered the storm and have chosen to be together after all. It's like divorcing your old marriage and starting a new one without leaving your partner. You can have a wonderful affair with your spouse. Sounds great, doesn't it?

WATCH WHAT HAPPENS NEXT

Now that you have an arsenal of many different techniques that you can use to spark a change in your marriage, I want to offer you a method for figuring out whether or not what you are doing is working. The most important thing to remember is that you have to keep your eyes open. You have to commit to doing something different and watching your spouse very carefully to see how well your new approach works. Sometimes the effect is immediate. Other times, you have to wait a few days or even a few weeks. I'll help you sort through all this. But you have to keep up your end of the bargain, which is to watch, watch, watch. Don't put your head in the sand, hoping something is working when it's not. Conversely, don't become pessimistic prematurely. You have to be patient.

Here are some guidelines for reading the results of your divorce-busting efforts.

HOW LONG DOES IT TAKE TO IMPROVE/SAVE A MARRIAGE?

Although my book, *Divorce Busting,* has been a big hit with the marriage-saving crowd, one of my regrets is that I gave readers the impression that they could expect their marriages to improve practically overnight. While it is true that some people do experience immediate changes in their relationships, it's also true that, in most marriages, change takes much longer. How much longer? It depends on many factors: the severity of the problems, personalities of the spouses, length of time people have been experiencing difficulties, each spouse's level of motivation to do what it takes to make a marriage work, outside influences from extended family and friends, and the level of both partners' problem-solving skills. Every marriage is different.

But the consistent message I've gotten from those in the trenches is that patience is not only a virtue, it's an absolute necessity. Resign yourself to the fact that improving your marriage might take weeks rather than days, or months rather than weeks. This will help you avoid becoming disappointed if results aren't as immediate as you had hoped. Furthermore, you need to know that you can expect your good days and your bad days, good weeks and bad weeks. Sometimes, you'll feel as if you are really out of the woods, and then a day later, you'll feel as though you are back to square one. That's how change happens. You must expect these hills and valleys and teach yourself not to get despondent. Resist feeling sorry for yourself. Just remember that, chances are, tomorrow will be a better day.

You also need to keep in mind that even if you've been doing everything right, your spouse is likely to be suspicious if you've changed a great deal. S/he might think that you are just putting on an act to try to win him/her over. This is natural, and if your spouse expresses this doubt, don't be reactive. Just quietly tell your partner that this is the new you, and that you plan on remaining this new person no matter what happens to your marriage. Reassure your spouse that you can fully understand his/her skepticism. As long as you keep on track, your spouse will eventually see that this is the "new you," and not some impostor.

The bottom line is that you should take comfort in the fact that you are being proactive about improving your marriage. Even if you have a ways to go, at least you've started the journey, and that's more than a lot of people can say.

HOW CAN I TELL IF WHAT I'M DOING IS WORKING?

This one is very simple. Refer back to your goals. Recall what you said would be the first thing that would happen to signal things are moving in the right direction. You should set your sights on *that* change. It could be something as simple as, "I would like to be able to go an entire day without an argument." As soon as you've hit your mark—an argument-free day—you know that whatever you've been doing has been helpful.

It's essential that you train yourself to look for baby steps forward because that's how change in relationships usually happens. Don't expect your marriage to go from distant or tense to passionate overnight. As long as you are seeing mild progress, you can assure yourself that your new strategy has some merit. Keep doing it.

WHAT MIGHT BE A SIGN THAT THE METHOD I'VE USED IS BACKFIRING?

Before you approach your spouse, you will have a picture in your mind's eye of the kind of reaction for which you are hoping. If your spouse responds negatively to your new approach, stop what you are doing immediately. It means you miscalculated the usefulness of the strategy. Even if you've followed the advice in this book to a "T," if it didn't work, it didn't work. Always remember that the proof is in the pudding.

Having said that, there is one thing you might keep in mind. Sometimes, an angry reaction is not a bad thing. For example, if you've been extremely cautious and walking on eggshells with your spouse and you've noticed that nothing is changing, you might decide to take a stronger stand. When you change directions, it's entirely possible that your spouse's *initial* reaction might be one of anger. However, it's also possible that a day later you might notice some improvement—s/he might be kinder and more considerate to you. So, occasionally, you have to continue to observe beyond your spouse's immediate reaction to see if anything you're doing is beginning to sink in. The one thing to keep in mind though is that you should proceed cautiously with any new approach until you feel fairly confident that you've gotten a green light. If in doubt, wait.

HOW LONG SHOULD I STICK WITH ONE METHOD BEFORE DECIDING IT ISN'T WORKING?

You should see a small positive response within a week or two if you've hit on something that is beneficial. However, your marriage will not be transformed in that period of time. That will take longer. But there should be some telltale signs—more friendliness, less combativeness, more inter-action, a few more thoughtful gestures, an occasional sign of interest, and so on—within a two-week period. If nothing changes within two weeks, there is no harm in continuing to experiment with that method, especially if you sense change is imminent. However, if you find things backsliding at all, time to abandon ship.

In addition to the advice I've offered here, I want to share some posts on my Web site from folks who have put these techniques to use in some extremely tough situations. Their marriages were teetering on the edge of divorce. Their pointers are excellent, so you should heed them. They know what they're talking about. They've been there, done that.

> I sure hope you can avoid the mistakes I made while my husband and I were separated. We were separated for over a year; I filed for the big D after about ten months hoping that would shake/wake my husband up—'cuz he wasn't making any moves to come home and I just couldn't take it anymore. I was in such pain, but most of all just wanted to get on with my life—with or without husband (but, hopefully, with).
>
> Anyway, I tried to tell him how much I hurt, how much our divorce hurt, all the usual stuff. But you know what? He didn't hear it. He heard instead that I was pleading. He said later that he'd been thinking about coming home just before those episodes, but when I started in on the pain, our divorce, etc., he decided he just couldn't do it. So, my words of advice??? NO MATTER WHAT YOU'RE FEEL-ING TODAY, only show him happiness and contentment. Show him someone he will want to return to.

Go out, take a walk, exercise, scream, cry hysterically, or whatever, BEFORE he comes over. Work those feelings out the best you can. Then, when he arrives, be pulled together, "serene," and happy. I know this sucks. I know how hard it is. But I also know that it was only when I stopped showing my husband how much I cared, how much pain I was in, etc., that my husband decided to come home. So, please, use my experience to shorten your own.

1. No matter what, don't spend too much time alone. Your mind will fixate on the pain. Get involved with something that you always wanted to try, but never got around to when you two were together; try to make it something that she would find surprising.
2. The more they dislike us, the easier we are to forget about. So be prepared for a spouse who has programmed his/her memory to ERASE ALL GOOD MEMORIES!
3. All questions and issues that deal with your failing marriage or your broken heart must be put on hold until she wants to talk about them, which can take a long time. I know how hard this one was for me. Of course, issues concerning children should not wait, they are a priority over EVERYTHING!

I only briefly saw my wife two or three times a week as we exchanged visitation, which usually involved a hi, or hello. I wanted her to hang out for a bit. So, I started being more polite and relaxed every time I saw her. After a couple of weeks of this, these one syllable conversations started getting longer and more enjoyable, because she was no longer worried that I would ruin the day by complaining. THIS IS NOT EASY, but this was where I first noticed that my wife started warming up to me.
4. Her guilt is a time bomb, be careful. I think most women, especially my wife, CANNOT handle the guilt of breaking up their family, so they avoid anything that may remind them. Sometimes they'll start crying if you tell her how much you love her, or how miserable you've been since she left. But BE CAREFUL, these tears most often come from guilt, not true love.
5. NEVER LOSE YOUR COOL!! I had to always remind myself that my estranged wife and I were "casual neighbors" (it works). NEVER,

NEVER, NEVER let her drag you into a "fight." If you are upset, excuse yourself from the conversation, stating that you'll return when you can talk, not yell. Show her how cooperative you can be.

6. Don't ever expect an apology or an admission of guilt for leaving you. I know how hard this was for me, but I quickly realized that waiting for her to say "sorry" only made it harder for me to think of anything else. Eventually, she might surprise you.

7. Seek counseling to learn how to coparent your children. You both will learn a lot about what you're doing to your kids if you're being careless in your conflicts. It will also help you to strengthen your general concern for getting along for the sake of the kids. Without a doubt, this allowed my wife to remember how committed I am to being a wonderful father and husband. When you choose a new therapist, make sure she is involved in the selection process, so she won't suspect hidden agendas.

8. If she ever hints that there is a small chance that you could work things out, treat the situation with extreme care. Show genuine gratitude for their bravery in telling you this, comfort them by letting them know that you're scared too. DON'T GET OVERLY ENTHUSIASTIC.

9. DO NOT EVER ARGUE ABOUT HOW SHE FEELS, because it will only make her feelings stronger. You have to let your partner know that you respect her feelings, even if you don't agree with them. A great example of how I changed is this: My wife used to complain that I was never affectionate toward her, which made her feel unattractive. I used to say "well that's silly to feel that way. I tell you all the time how beautiful I think you are. You just need to pay more attention and give me some credit." WRONG! Now I say: "Tell me what I need to do more of, because I think you're extremely attractive."

10. No gifts, I love you's, special occasions, or anything other than being a very helpful father and kind friend.

I have been participating at this Web site for about seven months. I discovered Michele's techniques and was immediately taken by her sensible, get-the-job-done approach. The basics of her principles are very straightforward and easy to understand but not so easy to deliver correctly. I have been working on my 180 for about seven months now and can report that it has made a difference. The biggest problems for me are a lack of patience and a failure to recognize that letting my needs creep into my efforts only slows the whole process down and frustrates me even more.

I have speculated about how long it might take someone trying to save their marriage before experiencing success. I do believe that a good rule of thumb is that one month of genuine change is necessary for every year of marriage. In other words, if it took fifteen years (as in my case) of getting it wrong, it probably will take fifteen to eighteen months of hard work to have a chance of getting it right. Every setback in my situation was directly related to my impatience. When I saw a small positive change in my wife, I was ready for full reconciliation. It just doesn't work that way.

I never imagined how much effort and time would be necessary to create a chance to succeed. No wonder the divorce rate is 50 percent plus! This is easily the most difficult challenge of my life. I pray every day that I can find the strength to continue. For what it's worth I have compiled my personal summary of the mandatory do's and don'ts of this process.

MANDATORY DO'S WHEN DIVORCE BUSTING

1. Be patient. Time is an asset even when it seems to be killing you.
2. Listen carefully to what your spouse is *really* saying to you.
3. Learn quickly that anger is your enemy.
4. Learn quickly to back off, shut up, and walk away when you want to speak out.
5. Take care of yourself. Exercise, sleep, laugh, and focus on all the other parts of your life that are not in turmoil.
6. Be cool, strong, confident, and speak softly.
7. Know that if you can do a 180, your smallest consistent actions will be noticed much more than *any* words you can say or write.
8. Read as much as you can on this subject.

MANDATORY DON'TS WHEN DIVORCE BUSTING

1. Do not be openly desperate or needy even when you are hurting more than ever in your whole life and are desperate and needy.
2. Do not focus on yourself when communicating with your spouse.

3. Do not believe any of what you hear and less then 50 percent of what you see. Your spouse will speak in absolute negatives because s/he is hurting and scared.
4. Do not give up no matter how dark it is or how bad you feel.
5. Do not backslide from your hard-earned changes.

Now that you know some new things you can try to make your marriage more loving, I'm sure you're eager to get started. Remember, this will be a trial-and-error process. You'll have some successes and you will also stumble and fall. Pay close attention to your successes and figure out why they happen.

If you are still somewhat uncertain how to implement these ideas, don't worry. When you get to the end of Chapter 8, which concludes all seven steps, I'll show you how to pull all of the information together.

Now on to Step Number 6. The information in the next step will be useful to you *after* you've implemented Steps Numbers 1 to 5 and a bit of time has passed. This next step will show you how to take stock of how far you've come and help you figure out what you still might need to do to accomplish your long-range goals.

CHAPTER SEVEN

Step Number 6—Take Stock

At this point you've been involved in this marriage-saving program for some time now and one of three things has happened. One—things have changed dramatically. Two—things have improved slightly. Three—everything is exactly the same, or worse. I am certainly hoping that you fall neatly into categories one or two, and that you and your spouse are feeling better about each other than you have in a very long time. In any case, it's time to take an honest look at how far you've come and determine what's next on your marriage-saving agenda.

First, I want you to know how much I respect you for the amount of time, effort, and love you are putting into making your relationship work. In a society prone to disposable marriages, instant gratification, and self-centeredness, you are an oasis in the desert. You should feel proud of yourself. You should be able to go to sleep at night knowing that you are doing everything humanly possible to make your marriage work. That's worth a lot in my book.

Step Number 6 is where you will sit down and really examine the progress you've made since you've started this program. I know you've had your good days and your bad days, and that it's hard to appreciate how far you've come because you've been so acutely aware of day-to-day fluctuations, but it's important to see the bigger picture. The following questions will help you clarify where you are:

On a one-to-ten scale, with one being "the pits," and ten being "great," where on the scale would you say your marriage was prior to starting the program?

Where on the scale would you say you are right now?
(Average things out, please.)

Are you satisfied?

If not, given that things are never perfect in a marriage, where on the scale would you need to be in order to feel satisfied?

What might be one or two things you could do or that could happen that would bring your marriage up a half step (from a seven to a seven and a half) on that scale?
(Make sure your responses here are action-oriented.)

Your responses to these questions will indicate whether you've accomplished your goals, improved your marriage but aren't satisfied yet, or remained stagnant. What you do next depends in part on the status of things so far. Read the section below that applies to you.

I'VE ACCOMPLISHED MY GOALS

Congratulations! You must be feeling great about the fact that you have invested yourself in improving your relationship and it's paid off handsomely. You and your spouse are getting along better and you're feeling closer and more connected to each other. Your children, if you have them, are undoubtedly feeling happier and more secure. You've got to be feeling so much better!

While you're in the midst of relishing the moment, I want you to appreciate the role your partner has played in turning things too. Even if you were the one who purchased this book and has taken the initiative to make things better, you still have to give credit to your partner for being open-minded and responsive to you. It is much more difficult to sustain positive efforts when you're not met with some encouragement. So while you are busy patting yourself on your back, pat your partner too. You both deserve appreciation for a job well done.

But the truth is, the job is not yet done. Until you die, it is never done. The thing you have to concentrate on now is how to keep your wonderful changes going. In order to do that, you can go directly to the last step in the program, Step Number 7, and find out what you need to do to make being solution-oriented a way of life. Proceed to Step Number 7, I'll catch up with you there!

Better, but not quite there yet

The fact that things are improved is wonderful! Even if you've only come a short way, every improvement counts. You should feel quite encouraged, but you still have a ways to go before you feel that things are where they should be. Before you do anything else, you have to identify as clearly as possible what must happen so that in a few weeks or months from now, when you ask yourself the questions above, your rating will have improved significantly. Let me help you do that.

Go back to your response to the question:

What might be one or two things you could do or that could happen that would bring your marriage up a half step (from a seven to a seven and a half) on that scale?

This is a very important question. Your response to this question will provide direction as to what you need to do next. If you had trouble answering the question, let me give you a hand. When I ask couples what needs to change in order for them to feel a bit more satisfied with their marriages, some folks point to their spouses' behavior. For example, they say, "In order for us to move up a half step on the scale:

"my wife will have to tell me she loves me again."
"my husband will have to agree to spend more time in the evening away from his computer."
"my wife will have to initiate lovemaking."

If you are doing this program as a couple, once you identify what you want your spouse to do (and make sure it is positively stated, action-oriented, and doable in the next few weeks), talk to your spouse about what you are thinking and feeling. But don't stop there. You need to ask yourself:

What could *I* do that would make it more likely that s/he is going to *want* to make those changes?

Remember, you can trigger positive change by behaving positively toward your spouse. What do you need to do that will make your spouse feel more loving toward you and, therefore, want to go out of his/her way to please you?

If you are doing this program alone, rather than ask your spouse to make the change, ask yourself the question above, *"What could I do that would make it more likely that s/he is going to want to make those changes?"* Now, start doing that.

Other people tell me that in order to take a baby step forward, they have to continue to *change their own behavior.* For example, they tell me, "In order for us to move up a half step on the scale:

"I need to keep a better lid on my anger when the kids are noisy."
"I need to appreciate the small things she does."
"I have to be more patient when she's late."

Again, if you've identified a change that is necessary in you, make sure it's positively stated, action-oriented, and doable in the next few weeks. Then, surprise, surprise, become more diligent about doing it.

As with the response above, you might also ask yourself, "What could my spouse do that would make it more likely that I will stick to my plan?" Once you figure this out, you might discuss this with your spouse if you think s/he might be amenable to it.

Still others tell me that the only thing that must change in order for them to feel better about their marriages is their level of confidence that their improvements are permanent. They need to feel more certain. For example, they say, "In order for us to move up a half step on the scale:

"I need to feel more relaxed about the changes. I still feel that we are walking on eggshells."

"More time has to pass. This is so new. I'll feel better about us when I'm more convinced the changes are going to stick."

If this is how you responded, you should ask yourself, *"How much longer would these positive changes have to stick in order for you to feel that this improvement isn't a fluke?"*

When you respond to this, you should definitely keep in mind that, even in the best of marriages, there are ups and downs. Even if your changes are genuine, lasting changes, it doesn't mean that you won't have a bad day or week now and then. It's important for you to make a distinction between an occasional bad day and the beginning of a downward spiral. In fact, while I'm on the subject, you should answer this question. *"What would have to happen in order for you to feel that a bad day was just an isolated incident and not the beginning of a downward spiral?"* (As usual, be as specific as possible. I want you to get to the point where you start to believe that your bad days are flukes and your good days are the rule.)

Reevaluate your progress weekly. Keep doing this until you reach your goals, no matter how long it takes. Just keep recording your successes in your Solution Journal as you go, pat yourself on the back for small improvements, and be patient. You are heading in the right direction, just keep going.

Once you have accomplished your goals, you should turn to the next chapter and read about Step Number 7. You'll learn how to make being solution-oriented in your marriage a way of life!

I'm discouraged

If you have failed to see any progress by the time you are reading this, you undoubtedly feel discouraged. I completely understand why you are feeling this way. You've read many success stories in this book and you're wondering why you aren't one of them. My heart really goes out to you. I know how hard you're trying.

Look, there are lots of reasons things may not have improved in your marriage. And without knowing you personally, it's hard to pigeonhole the precise reason. However, I am going to tell you about the most common reasons people's marriages remain stagnant. Read through the explanations below and see what might fit in your case. Then, once you've "diagnosed" the problem, you will have a better idea about what you can do about it.

WHY NOTHING CHANGES

You haven't given a method sufficient time to work before trying something else

It is often the case that, if a technique doesn't yield immediate results, people scan the book for another strategy in the hopes it will work better or more quickly. Although this is completely understandable, it's unproductive. It's my experience that you should probably stick with something for at least a couple of weeks unless it is clear that you are getting negative results. Then, of course, you should quit immediately. But don't let your impatience get in the way of your being systematic about improving your marriage. You need to give things a chance to work.

This is especially true if you and your spouse are separated and you don't have much contact. In that case, even if the method you're using is going to be effective, it will definitely take longer to show positive results than it would if the two of you were together. Your spouse simply doesn't have enough opportunities to witness you changing. So, don't get discouraged and start trying a little of this and a little of that. If you do, you won't really get a true reading about the effectiveness of any technique.

One more reminder—unless things are deteriorating, there is no harm in sticking with a technique until you are absolutely positive about its potential to help you and your spouse feel happier together.

The strategy chosen isn't different enough from your usual approach

When people are stuck, I ask them what they've tried and they tell me, "I've tried everything." No one has ever tried everything. It only feels that way.

But what people *have* done, is that they've tried many, many variations of the same technique. For example, a woman tried asking her husband nicely to change and when that didn't work, she pleaded, begged, threatened, and cried. Nothing she said ever made a difference. So she decided to take a communication class where she learned how to express herself more effectively. She did well in class and mastered the skills. But when she went home and tried them out on her husband, he still responded the same old way. She felt frustrated and at her wit's end.

If you asked her, this woman would tell you that she tried everything. But if you look at what she did very carefully, what you'll notice is that all of her efforts fall under the same general category. Despite the subtle differences in her approach, her husband knew one thing and one thing only. "My wife is constantly harping on me when she talks." It didn't matter how she said what she said, or the level of emotion that she said it with—to her husband, words were words.

Although your pet strategy may not be words, I want you to mull over this example and see if you are making the same kind of mistake. When you try something new, is it *really* new or is it merely a variation of something you've just tried that hasn't worked? If you're uncertain, go back to Step Number 5—Experiment and Monitor Results—and review the techniques. Find one that is radically different from what you've been doing. Even if it seems a little odd for you to try it out, do it anyway. Give yourself permission to be creative. Ask yourself, *"Have I had any zany ideas about what might work but have held myself back from trying them?"* What are they?

Don't hold back a moment longer. Go for it. Remember, when I say, "Do something different," I mean *different*.

You're overlooking the small signs of change

One of the reasons you may not be noting any improvement in your marriage is that you are overlooking the small signs of change. I know how easy this is to do. You want to feel so much closer to your spouse and you're looking for those blatant telltale signs that your marriage is headed for higher ground. You're hoping for obvious expressions of love and tenderness. But in your eagerness to feel that your marriage is healed, it's entirely possible that you have been oblivious to the small positive things that have happened that are really harbingers of things to come. You fail to notice the less obvious, small acts of kindness, which are really the building blocks for what comes next.

If you've failed to notice these mini-steps, it's like missing a street sign when you're going to a party. You won't realize that you've been going in the right direction and you will feel lost. Without recognizing and appreciating that you're moving in the right direction, you won't feel encouraged to keep going.

Or perhaps you *have* noticed a few small things have improved but you've told yourself, "No big deal." In other words, since the changes weren't monumental, they weren't worth getting excited about. That kind of attitude will prevent you from moving farther. Every little step is a big deal and you should think about it that way. It will help you keep your stamina up. If you're guilty of downplaying the significance of small changes, here's your new mantra: "Little steps are big deals." Got that?

If you're a real goal-setter and go-getter, I know it's hard for you to jump up and down about small steps. If the world operated according to your standards, people would just identify the problem and do something to fix it. They would stop wallowing in the past or bad feelings and just pull themselves up by the bootstraps. They would get on with things. But not everyone is like you; we all move at different paces. So whether you like it or not, it's really important that you slow down and be patient.

Finally, you may have been telling yourself not to get too excited about small steps forward because you don't want to feel a false sense of hope. I know you are trying to protect yourself from a fall if things don't go the way you are hoping in the end. If I were in your shoes, I'd probably feel exactly the same way, but it's unproductive. Allow yourself to notice and feel encouraged by the small signs. You need to feel hope. While it's true that there are no guarantees about the future, if things don't work out the way you hope, you'll deal with it then. For now, think positively. Remember the self-fulfilling prophecy is a very powerful phenomenon.

Your attempts at change were halfhearted

Sometimes when there is a lack of improvement, it is because when you've experimented with a technique, you only did it halfheartedly. If your heart isn't in it when you approach your spouse, your spouse will think you are acting and will immediately see through what you're trying to do. S/he might feel manipulated, and therefore, not respond in a positive manner.

If doing things halfheartedly fails to bring about good results, why do people do it? Sometimes it's because the technique they choose doesn't feel right to them. They're just doing it because they think they should. That's not a good reason to do anything. You need to feel comfortable with what you're doing. It must make sense to you. You have to get behind what you're doing. If a particular technique feels artificial, choose something else.

Another reason people do things halfheartedly is that, although they might not be admitting it to themselves, they are still playing the blame game. They don't really want to accept responsibility for tipping over the first domino. They still want their spouses to change first. So, they go through the motions of change but don't allow themselves to fully get into their new solution-oriented modes.

If you have been feeling lukewarm about the strategies you've been using, I want you to be totally honest and ask yourself, "Am I still holding out hope that my spouse will see the light and change first?" If the answer is yes, go back to Step Number 1 and reread the part about the blame game. Don't fool yourself into thinking that you are really working on your marriage if that little inner voice is shouting, "S/he's wrong, let him/her change first." You are only wasting time. You first need to rid yourself of that distraction before you can do anything constructive about your marriage. Unless you put your heart and soul into changing your marriage and stop keeping score, your marriage will be in exactly the same place five years from now that it is now, or you will have no marriage at all.

You reverted to your old ways

In this case, it is clear that the technique you're using has some merit, but you accidentally slid back into your old ways, thereby prompting your spouse to do the same. Then, when you observe both of you doing the same old thing, you incorrectly assume that what you are doing isn't working and you get discouraged. In reality, it's not that the technique you are using isn't working, it's just that it doesn't work when you don't use it! Here's an example.

Through using this program, Andrea and Wally figured out that they got along a lot better when they used a budget to guide their financial expenditures. For a long time they were doing just that. Their finances improved and they were getting along famously. As a result, with each passing week, they found themselves becoming more and more lax about doing and sticking to their budget. After all, they told themselves, "How will this one little extravagant purchase hurt?" So they started splurging a little. One small purchase turned into another small purchase, and before they knew it, their spending was out of control again. Their fighting resumed with a vengeance.

Andrea and Wally felt discouraged and assumed that their budget wasn't working until they realized that the real problem wasn't that their budget hadn't worked, but that they had become lax in their efforts to stick to it. With a little reminder, they were up and running again, and they got back on track.

Back to you for a moment. If at any time during your participation in this program you noticed even slight improvements, it means you were doing something worthwhile. If the progress has slowed or even halted, it means you've probably stopped doing what works. Force yourself to resume doing what was working and see if that makes a difference. It probably will.

Your spouse is involved with someone else

I don't consider it a marital death sentence if one spouse is having either an emotional or physical affair with someone else. I have seen countless marriages survive infidelity and even become stronger after the healing begins. However, it is also true that positive change in marriage is harder to achieve when one spouse is emotionally or physically interested or attached to someone else. In my practice, when I see couples, who on the surface are saying, "We want our marriage to work," but as time progresses and nothing changes, it's often the case that one spouse has a "special friend" waiting in the wings. There are some key phrases I've heard over the years in marriages where this is happening. See if any of this sounds familiar to you.

"I admit that my spouse is changing, but it doesn't change how I feel about him/her."

"It's not about my spouse, it's about me. There's nothing s/he can do to make things better. It's all inside my head."

"Yes, my spouse is changing, but I think it's too little, too late."

"I feel like we're brother and sister." (Referring to the fact that there are no longer feelings of attraction.)

And last, but not least, the all-time favorite:

"I love you, but I'm not *in* love with you."

Because infidelity is so rampant and such a complex subject, I will devote an entire section to it in Chapter 10. If you suspect that your spouse's lack of responsiveness may be due to his/her outside interests, you will want to read that chapter immediately. Rather than repeat here what I discuss in that chapter, suffice it to say that you are not to blame for the lack of progress in your marriage. It's likely that you are doing everything right but you are hitting up against a brick wall. If your partner's extramarital interests are secretive, it's especially difficult because it prevents you from confronting the real issues in your marriage. And it prevents your spouse from seeing things clearly and from putting his/her soul into making your marriage work.

But the bottom line is that you shouldn't feel defeated. I will give you lots of ideas about how to approach your spouse even in this most challenging of circumstances. I know you're feeling as if you're swimming upstream, but suffice it to say that most affairs end within six months. More about that later. Just hang in there.

Your spouse has decided your marriage is over

One of the reasons nothing you do seems to be working is because it isn't. As cold and cruel as it seems, when some people announce the death of their marriages, they really mean it. For them, over means over. Once this happens, there is absolutely nothing anyone can say or do to change that person's mind. The only thing you can do is make matters worse.

But here's the problem for someone like you who desperately wants to make things better and keep your marriage thriving. There is no clear way to tell when "over" means "over" and when it means "over, maybe."

Sometimes people say, "It's over," in the heat of passion, and it means nothing. Sometimes people say, "It's over," after thinking things out, but the next day they wake up and they aren't quite as sure about ending their marriages as they were the day before. Even though they might give an unbending appearance, the divorce is far from etched in stone. And then there are the diehards, the immovable ones who rarely retract a decision once it's made. When these folks say it's over, only a miracle could change things.

Since it's hard to know whether your spouse is truly done with your marriage or just needs some more time to come to his/her senses, if I were you, I would err on the side of caution. Why not assume that this is going to take much longer than you anticipated, but that, in the end, things will work out. "Act as if" you believe that your marriage still has possibilities. Do the things you would do if you envisioned a positive outcome to all of your efforts. Don't allow friends, relatives, lawyers, or therapists to tell you that you should move forward in your life if that's not your heart's desire. If you are still hopeful that your spouse will eventually reconsider, keep practicing the techniques I've taught you. Don't stop until you are absolutely convinced that it's over. Surround yourself with people who will support you in this endeavor.

Sometimes people ask me how they will know when to stop trying to save their marriage. I don't have a clue. The only person who knows when you should stop working on your marriage is you. You are the expert here, not your mother, father, spouse, rabbi, pastor . . . just you. Only you, in the privacy of your own thoughts at night, can tell whether you've left no stone unturned, whether you still have energy to give. If you do, then continue. If, after lots of soul-searching, you decide that you can no longer continue feeling the intense hurt and pain that stem from the rejection you are experiencing, then, and only then, should you consider other options.

Start by focusing on your own life. When you let go, you will go through a mourning period that is natural. Even if you are at peace with your decision to refocus, you will probably feel intense pain. In some ways, it's very much like a death. It's the death of a dream that you had for yourself and your family. It's the death of a relationship. Allow yourself to feel the pain. And at the same time, begin to think about what you can do to fill the void. Spend time with loved ones. Do nice things for yourself. Keep yourself busy. Although it's hard to believe when you're going through it, know that your life will go on. You will find happiness again. Many of the people with whom I work who go through a divorce, go on to find new partners and blend families and have new children. Their lives don't end just because their marriages do. They join support groups in their churches or through their mental health centers. They double their efforts to spend time with their children. They learn everything they can about coparenting after a divorce. They find new interests. But all of this happens slowly. Healing takes a lot of time. You need to reach out to others. There is life after divorce.

I know that many of my divorce-busting fans might be surprised by my words here. I've never before talked about life after divorce. I feared that by discussing the D word, I might actually be encouraging people to throw in the towel prematurely. This is the very last thing I would ever want to do. I hate divorce. I believe you must know that by now. I write about the possibility of letting go for only one reason. I don't want people who have been in excruciating pain because of unrequited love to feel judged when they eventually decide to move on with their lives. In truth, we only have one go-around. We are all entitled to happiness. If, after you have tried everything humanly possible to win back your spouse's love to no avail, you can't torture yourself forever. Just make darn sure before you move forward with your life that you can honestly say, "I've given it my all." Then make peace with your decision.

It is my sincere hope that you had no reason to be reading this last section, that your marriage is moving along in a positive direction. But if not, skip the next chapter and proceed on to Chapter 9—"Pulling It All Together." Maybe a bit more specific information about how to apply these strategies might just make a difference.

CHAPTER EIGHT

Step Number 7—Keeping the Positive Changes Going

I f you are reading this chapter, it means that you've managed to make substantial changes in your marriage. Good for you. Now, if you're like most people, you're probably a bit worried about your good times lasting. In fact, you might be downright nervous about sliding back into your old ways. It might surprise you to hear me say this, but I'm really glad you are cautious. If you take your positive changes for granted, you might stop putting the kind of effort into your relationship that has been crucial to turning things around. I wouldn't want that to happen. You see, it's not magic that you and your spouse are doing better together. You took some very specific actions to achieve those goals. Nor is it magic that keeps the positive changes going. If you want to maintain your changes, you have to *keep doing* what has been working. It's as simple as that.

Since you have to continue doing what has been working in your marriage, you need to be clear about what you and your spouse have done recently to improve things. By now, this should be fairly obvious to you. If not, review your Solution Journal and/or ask yourself the following questions:

What have I been doing that has triggered positive changes in my marriage?

What has my spouse been doing that has triggered positive changes in my marriage?

What do I need to continue to do to assure that my spouse will stay invested in keeping the good things going?

The bottom line is that you can't sit back and take your changes for granted. If you want to stay in love with your spouse, you have to continue to do loving things every day. You never get to the point where you can stop being careful or thoughtful about how you treat your spouse. Every day is another opportunity to be solution-oriented and to keep your marriage on track.

Having said that, you should also know that everyone, and I mean everyone, gets off track from time to time. It's impossible to get along all the time. Since conflict is inevitable in marriage, you will continue to have ample opportunities to practice your solution-oriented skills. And I promise you that sometimes you will screw up royally. I do it myself.

I love telling people about the time my wonderful daughter was a preteenager. Like most kids that age, she had her good days and her bad days. I remember when she did something that bothered me and, at first, I tried to be the perfect parent. I reasoned with her, talked calmly, and tried to negotiate sensibly. When that didn't work, I lost it and started to rant and rave around the house. Crazed, I was yelling and walking past my bedroom door where my husband was sitting watching television. As he saw me rush past our door like a madwoman, he calmly pointed to me and said, "And there she goes, world-renowned solution-oriented therapist." Even I had to laugh.

Look, sometimes your emotions are going to get the best of you and you are going to develop a severe case of "solution-oriented marriage-saving" amnesia. This is to be expected. In fact, most people tell me that in certain situations, they knew exactly what they *should have* done, but they were so mad at their spouses, they just had to let them have it. And, they tell me, their outburst felt absolutely delicious. Granted, their spouses didn't respond positively at those times, but on rare occasions, letting 'er rip seemed like a more important thing to do. So expect those days and don't become disheartened. Research shows that people who have been successful at making major life changes all go through this zigzag process.

I always tell people that what separates the winners from the losers in this game of life isn't the amount of failure people experience. It's the way in which winners handle the failure. They just pick themselves up, dust themselves off, and get back on track quickly. They don't sit around playing the blame game, holding grudges, feeling sorry for themselves, or indulging themselves in feelings of self-reproach. They just say to themselves, "Oh well, guess I [my spouse] didn't handle things so well, I'll have to do better later." And later doesn't mean a week or two later, it means five minutes later.

The long and the short of it is this: Don't allow too much time to pass after a solution-oriented transgression. It doesn't matter who is at fault. All that matters is that you take responsibility for getting things back on track. Just remember that every day you and your spouse are distant and at odds is another day lost from your life. Even if you feel wronged, pouting or storming around won't make you feel better. Make up. But how?

TRUCE TRIGGERS

In Chapter 5, I taught you about the concept of "more of the same." I talked about the idea that couples argue about the same things, in the same way, in the same location, at the same time. But what I *didn't* tell you is that couples are equally ritualistic about how they make up. We have "make-up patterns" with our partners; things that you and your partner regularly do to melt the ice after an argument. I call them truce triggers. See if any of this sounds familiar to you.

Sometimes couples discuss what happened and resolve their differences before moving on. Others don't talk about the heated issue again. Sometimes there's an apology. Other times, the truce triggers might be more subtle. One spouse might bring the other a cup of coffee without saying anything at all. There might be a hug or a light touch in passing. There may be a phone call from work, "just to say hi." One spouse might do something kind or loving for the other. S/he might leave a note saying, "I love you," or "Do you want to go out to dinner tonight?" Some couples who have been keeping their distance from each other after conflict find themselves in the same room watching television together or reading. Although they aren't talking much, their nonverbal behavior is saying, "Let's be friends."

Timing is another factor to consider when you are thinking about truce triggers. Some couples refuse to go to bed angry and will make up before bedtime no matter what. Other people need a definite cooling-off period before reconciling and any attempt to make up before tempers have properly cooled down will only add fuel to the fire.

I've given the idea of truce triggers a lot of thought in my own marriage to Jim. I've learned that when there's conflict, Jim needs time alone to deescalate and calm himself down. I don't. I'd rather battle things out until we come to a solution or until he softens a bit toward me. In the early years of our marriage, I would pursue him and pursue him in the hopes we would find some resolution or he would show signs of softening. The more I would pursue, the more he would want to be by himself. The more he withdrew, the more I kept talking. Sometimes he would even leave the room. When he did, I promptly followed him. With a horrified look on his face, he would often say in exasperation, "Michele, what are you doing here?" and I would respond, "I want to resolve things. I want you to be more understanding." Then he'd say, "If you want to resolve things, why don't you just leave me alone?" to which I would respond, "How will leaving you alone resolve anything?" Anger would flare, hurtful things would be said, we'd go from bad to worse.

But eventually we both got smart. I figured out that if I want Jim to be nicer to me, I need to give him some space temporarily for him to come to his senses. Jim figured out that if he wants me to give him space, he needs to be kinder and more loving, even in the midst of our conflict. When I give Jim space, he eventually comes to find me and is pretty good at making up. He's discovered that when he is more careful and understanding during our arguments, I am more inclined to leave him alone sooner rather than later. So we both make more of a conscious effort to do what the other person needs in order to bring about peace at earlier junctures.

On the surface, this sounds like a simple thing to do, but it really isn't simple at all. To me, it feels unnatural to stop discussing things midstream and take a time-out. I hate it. To Jim, it feels unnatural to be conciliatory or empathetic when he's really angry at me. Yet, we both do the unnatural in order to bring peace to our lives. When I do what he needs to feel better, he reciprocates, and vice versa.

Years ago, I used to think that my way of making up was right; it was "healthier" to talk things out on the spot. Conversely, Jim used to think his way of making up was right; it makes more sense to give people the room they need to work things out internally. We'd argue about how we argued, that is, until we both finally figured out that we're both right. There really isn't a single correct way to get things back on track, there are many. The trick is that you need to identify your (and your partner's) preferred style of making up and then you have to accommodate each other's needs. When you do, you will get back on track more quickly and there will be less fighting in general.

In order to get back on track more quickly after conflict, you need to identify the signs that you and your spouse are ready to melt the ice. What are your "truce triggers"?

**How can you tell when your spouse is ready to make up? What is
s/he doing or saying?**

What makes it more likely that you will be ready to make up?

**Under what circumstances are you likely to *initiate* reconciliation?
Under what circumstances is your partner likely to do the
same?**

**What do you do? (talk in person, speak on the phone, write a note,
offer your spouse a cup of coffee, give your partner a kiss,
crack a joke)**

What does your spouse do?

**When is the best time to approach your partner? When is s/he most
approachable?**

When are you most approachable?

**Is there a location where you and your partner make up
frequently? If so, where is it?**

Once you are able to identify the usual steps you and your partner take to make up, discuss your patterns with your spouse. Then be more proactive about doing what it takes to reduce the times in your relationship where you and your spouse are really on the warpath. In my estimation, the couples who have the hardest time staying on track are the ones who think being right is more important than being happy together. If feelings of self-righteousness override your desire to be close, you'll be right but miserable. Don't get hung up on keeping score about who makes up first most of the time. This is a silly argument and I'll tell you why.

You might feel as if you're always the one to initiate making up and you might feel resentment because of this. The truth is, you are aware of the actions *you* take to make peace, but up until now, you probably haven't been as aware of the subtle signs *your partner* sends out about his/her readiness to reconcile. Think about it. Though your spouse might not say, "Do you want to make up?" or "I'm sorry," s/he might have made you a good meal, picked up your clothes from the cleaner, or called from work earlier in the day, using the kids as an excuse to talk.

Yes, it would be nice if s/he were more obvious about his/her efforts to reconcile, but don't let your pride stand in the way of getting more love in your life. The more you consciously take steps to get your marriage back on track when it gets derailed, the more you are modeling this behavior for your spouse. And I guarantee that if you do it often enough without keeping score or feeling resentment, your partner will eventually take the lead more often to set things on course.

In addition to just accepting the fact that you and your spouse will have your ups and downs, you should also do what you can to minimize the impact the downs have on your relationship. You can do this by developing a plan to handle predictable relationship challenges before they happen. If you have a plan to deal with the tough times, there is more likelihood that you will do something productive when they happen. Here are some questions that will help you strategize about the hills and valleys ahead.

Is there anything that might pop up within the next few weeks that could present a challenge to your sticking to these changes? If so, what is it?

This question is asking you to predict events or circumstances that, in the past, have triggered you and/or your spouse to behave in a less-than-solution-oriented manner. Let me give you a few examples. Let's say that every time you have houseguests, all hell breaks loose and you and your spouse fight a lot. If so, you might be a bit concerned about the visit you are expecting from your in-laws next week. Or, perhaps you know that you have a project that needs to be completed this week and that you get really tense when you are under pressure. Or, maybe your spouse gets really moody during certain times during the month/year and you just looked at your calendar only to find that his/her blue days are right around the corner. These are the kinds of situations I want you to be thinking about. List any potential challenging times or events.

How will you handle this situation differently this time?

Think about everything you've learned in this program so far. Identify at least one thing you could do differently if or when that situation occurs. Imagine what you might say or that would be different enough that your spouse would take notice. Record your response.

What would be a sign that you or your partner is slipping back into your old ways?

What specifically would you, your spouse, or both of you as a couple be doing that would make you think, "Oh, oh, here we go . . . doing the same old thing again"? Remember, describe these behaviors in action-oriented terms.

If you notice this happening, what will you do to nip it in the bud?

Again, be specific and action-oriented.

Now you know what you need to do to get your marriage on track and keep it that way. The more time that passes, the more positive experiences you and your spouse have, the more practice you have restoring after setbacks, the more confident you will become that your loving feelings are here to stay. It takes time, patience, and practice, practice, practice. But I promise you that if you are diligent about staying on track and don't allow relapses to frazzle you too much, eventually, you will become convinced that you and your spouse can conquer any challenge that comes your way. Being solution-oriented becomes more second nature to you. Your first reflex will be to do what brings more love in your life rather than shoot from the hip. And once you get to that point, you realize that all this hard work has really been worth it. Here's a letter from a man who would definitely agree. He managed to win back his wife, experienced a setback, and then discovered that love survives if you keep up these techniques.

Divorce Busting Works!!

My name is Don. My wife and I were separated for eight months, beginning in November. We lived apart and maintained a friendship, which I promoted and maintained per principles and guidelines I set forth from reading Michele's books and some books on personal development. My wife told me repeatedly that she held no hopes for our future together other than the maintenance of our friendship. My wife had a life of her own that included a short (four-month) relationship with someone else. Through the eight months that we were separated the friendship between my wife and me grew. A new trust in each other developed. I had made some serious changes in my life. I had made major shifts in my priorities.

My wife and I began dating again in June. We fell back in love with each other and she moved back in with me in August. I wish I could say that we lived happily ever after. I can't.

During the next few months my business began to falter due to a split with my business partner. The duty of support fell upon my wife for a few months. This is NOT the best thing for a new, second chance relationship. In January, just as my business was beginning to thrive again, my wife became disenchanted with our relationship. I can hardly blame her. It seemed that things were heading back to the way that they had become prior to our separating the first time.

I continued to work on the business and to employ the simple, unconditional friendship that has always been an ally in my relationship with my wife. Thanks to the continuing dedication to what

I had learned about Divorce Busting during my separation, my wife and I have come, once again, back to where we should be in our marriage.

This was, I believe, a final test of some sort, to show us that our marriage could go through a tough time without going through another separation and, probably, a divorce. Believe me, it does take two, ultimately, to keep the marriage together. But a single partner in the marriage can make the difference in whether the other partner wishes to remain in the marriage. My wife was able to see me in a different light during the tough time in our marriage the second time around. She saw me handle, in a solution-focused manner, what fate tossed at me. She was also able to observe me under pressure. After all was said and done, she had witnessed someone that had truly changed.

I am writing this so whoever reads it can know that this program works. It works not only to get your relationship back or back in order but it also works to *keep* your relationship in order. Keep at it and don't give up!!

Don

In the next chapter, I will tell you about several people who have improved their marriages by following the steps outlined in my seven-step program. Their stories will help to bring the ideas and methods in this marriage-enhancing program alive. Perhaps you will see some of yourself in their lives. If, on the other hand, you feel you have this material down already, you might want to turn to the next section in the book, "Common Dilemmas, Unique Solutions," to discover more about the application of solution-oriented methods to different life situations.

CHAPTER NINE

Pulling It All Together

Now that we've gone through the seven steps of my marriage-saving program, you may have some questions about how to pull all of this information together. It's like learning the individual steps of a dance but not yet seeing what it looks like for a couple to be doing the dance out on the dance floor. So now, we are going to go out on the dance floor with music: I am going to give you an in-depth look at how two couples turned their marriages around. Let me introduce you to Steve and Judy.

STEVE

Steve and Judy were married for fifteen years and had three children, aged ten, seven, and five. Steve had very fond memories of their early years of marriage but admitted that he and Judy had grown apart for quite some time. Nevertheless, he didn't see their distance as a crisis. He was a hard worker and provided well for his family. He didn't drink or stay out late with the guys and he was faithful. In other words, he thought he had been a pretty good husband and father. Judy was a stay-at-home mom who, to him, seemed content with her involvement with the children and their daily lives.

That's why Steve was shocked when Judy announced her grave unhappiness with their marriage. She was so unhappy that she was strongly considering divorce. Through her tears, she told Steve that she had felt isolated from him for years, that she didn't feel supported or loved, that she didn't even consider them to be good friends anymore. And when he asked her why if she had been so unhappy she hadn't told him, she grew furious, stating that she had tried for many years to get through to him but apparently he hadn't been listening. With that, she left the room.

Several weeks passed in between Judy's announcement and the time when Steve decided to begin the program for saving his marriage. During that time, things between Judy and Steve had deteriorated even farther. Judy seemed even more determined to end their marriage. Steve knew he had to act quickly. Here's how he used the program.

STEP NUMBER 1—START WITH A BEGINNER'S MIND

Steve had some *un*learning to do. When Judy told him of her discontent, he vacillated between intense anger and desperation. His anger stemmed from the fact that he believed that he had been a near-perfect husband and that Judy had temporarily lost her mind. He felt like a victim and was furious.

Steve had to learn that regardless of what he thought about their marriage, Judy had a different perspective and he had to do some soul searching to try to understand why she had been so unhappy. As long as Steve continued to play the blame game, he risked Judy's walking out the door. Even if he found her perspective hard to swallow, he needed to make every effort to be more empathetic—quickly. He also needed to accept that, whether he liked it or not, he was going to have to take responsibility for turning things around in their marriage. Because he vacillated between blaming Judy for her "craziness" and thinking that she had to agree to working on their marriage before any changes could occur, he had to familiarize himself with and internalize the notion that one person can change a marriage singlehandedly ("It Takes One to Tango"), and that one person had to be *him*. So he did.

STEP NUMBER 2—KNOW WHAT YOU WANT

Steve had some general ideas about what he wanted for his marriage, but his goals were too vague. He knew he wanted his wife to stay married to him and that he wanted them to be happy together. He also knew that he wanted the tension between them to disappear. But after learning about solution-oriented goal-setting, he realized that he had to fine-tune his goals. Here is how he did it:

ORIGINAL GOALS

GOAL 1—"I WANT MY WIFE TO STAY MARRIED TO ME."

GOAL 2—"I WANT THE TENSION BETWEEN US TO DISAPPEAR."

GOAL 3—"I WOULD LIKE US TO BE HAPPY TOGETHER."

REWORKED GOALS

GOAL 1—"I WANT MY WIFE TO STAY MARRIED TO ME."

Steve needed to break this goal down into something that was achievable within a week or two. It would probably take Judy a longer period of time to reconfirm her commitment to the marriage. Steve had to ask himself, "What will be the first sign that Judy is considering staying in the marriage?" His response to that question was the following:

"She will stop bringing up divorce in conversation."
"When she talks about the future, I will be included."
"She will start spending more time with me."
"We will start having family dinners again."
"We had a vacation planned. She will want to discuss plans for it with me."

GOAL 2—"I WANT THE TENSION BETWEEN US TO DISAPPEAR."

Steve needed to convert his goal into a positive action rather than the absence of something negative. He asked himself, "When the tension disappears, what will be happening instead?" His response:

"She will smile again."
"She will ask me how my day was."

"We will be able to be in the same room."

"She will initiate a pleasant conversation with me."

"She will answer my questions with more than one-word responses."

GOAL 3—"I WOULD LIKE US TO BE HAPPY TOGETHER."

This goal is obviously far too vague. Steve needed to ask himself, "When we start feeling happier, what will we be doing differently?" His response:

"We will get a baby-sitter once a week and spend time as a couple."

"We will talk more."

"We will make love more often."

"We will laugh together the way we used to when we were younger."

STEP NUMBER 3—ASK FOR WHAT YOU WANT

Although Steve's goals needed refinement, he felt confident that, given Judy's feelings about him and their marriage, asking her to change in any way was going to be counterproductive. So he decided to work on himself instead. He proceeded to Step Number 4.

STEP NUMBER 4—GOING DOWN CHEESELESS TUNNELS

Steve identified his "more of the same" actions very quickly. Initially, he approached Judy with anger. He couldn't believe she was refusing to give their marriage a second chance after so many years together. This infuriated him. However, he realized that it really didn't matter whether he felt justified in being angry because he was pushing her farther away with each angry word or action. He knew he had to work on himself to keep his frustration in check. He decided he would go for a walk, call a friend, or work on his car any time he felt his anger mounting.

Once Steve realized that his anger wasn't working, he became desperate—another "more of the same" strategy. He started begging Judy to reconsider her decision. He became despondent and cried often. He constantly reminded her of their marriage vows. He urged her to consider their three children. He bought her flowers and romantic cards. He tried to get her to reminisce about good times in the past. Nothing worked. In fact, Steve admitted to himself that these actions had inadvertently made things worse. So, hard as it might be, Steve understood that he had to stop pursuing Judy and pressuring her to stay in their marriage. He realized that he had no other choice if he wanted their marriage to last. "But what should I do instead?" he asked himself. He moved to Step Number 5.

STEP NUMBER 5—EXPERIMENT AND MONITOR RESULTS
Experiment

In addition to stopping his "more of the same" behavior, Steve decided to use the technique of "focusing on the problem-free times," asking himself, "What is different about the times in our marriage when we are getting along better?" When Steve reflected on this question, several scenarios came to mind. Steve was convinced that their marriage was significantly better before the birth of their children. Although Steve couldn't and wouldn't want to reverse their decision to have children, he started to think about how differently their life was structured back then. Here's what he discovered:

They spent most of their free time together.
They talked more.
They nurtured their common interests.
They complimented each other more.
Since Steve was happier back then, he participated more in general—doing housework, visiting in-laws, doing projects together.

Steve realized that over the years he had stopped noticing Judy. He stopped spending time with her or complimenting her. He also admitted to himself that he wasn't as helpful around home as he should be—he relied on Judy to provide the lion's share of child care and housework.

Steve decided that he could start being the "old Steve" again. He began complimenting Judy on the way she looked, he started doing small things for her like making coffee in the morning and bringing her a cup, he helped more around the house, he became more involved with their children. Additionally, since he realized that he used to be more lighthearted, he made an extreme effort, even though he didn't feel like it all the time, to be happier at home.

MONITOR RESULTS

Weeks one and two

Although Steve's making these changes sounds simple, it really wasn't simple at all because the rewards for doing so weren't immediate. In fact, at first Judy seemed either oblivious to his efforts or put off. She said little and kept her distance. The first time he brought her coffee, she asked, "Why in the world are you doing that?" Although Steve's feelings were hurt by this comment, he didn't let her know and he replied, "Just because I feel like it."

Despite the lack of obvious improvements Steve did notice that the fighting had ceased and that Judy was no longer bringing up the topic of divorce. Although Steve realized that this was one of his goals, he wasn't certain whether it was a fluke or not. He decided to reserve judgment. He did, nonetheless, feel somewhat uplifted by the relative peace around their home.

Week three

Steve continued his efforts to be more involved, more thoughtful, and more loving. He started to see a small, but noticeable change in Judy. She was no longer avoiding him. They were often in the same room together and although their conversation was generally superficial or child-related, he saw this as an improvement. Because he took to heart the idea that "Small Changes Matter," he felt encouraged by this development.

Week four

Because of the calmer atmosphere at home and their ability to spend time together, Steve felt tempted to ask Judy how she was feeling about their marriage. She told him that although she could tell he had been try-ing, she wasn't sure whether it would make a difference in the long run or not. As soon as he heard her response, he knew he had fallen back into his old ways of pursuing her and wanting reassurances, something she was not yet able to offer. Once he recognized that he had fallen off the "solution wagon," despite his feelings of discouragement, he picked himself up and brushed himself off and resumed his more solution-oriented actions. Steve promised himself he would not ask Judy for a relationship temperature check anymore unless he was positive he would like her answer.

Weeks five to eight

With a few minor exceptions, Steve was a model husband in the weeks that followed. He remained very involved and asked for little in return. There were occasions when he felt frustrated because Judy wasn't throwing her arms around him and professing her love and commitment to him, but he restrained himself from letting her know his true feelings. Several times he had to leave their home and go for a walk to recharge his solution-oriented batteries. By the end of the eighth week, his efforts were starting to pay off. Judy appeared to be softening. She called him at work, something she had not done in months, and asked if they could go out for dinner together because she had something she wanted to talk to him about. He immediately agreed and offered to call the baby-sitter.

When they hung up, Steve wasn't sure whether she had good news for him or whether he was going to get his walking papers. This made him quite nervous. His anxiety was making it difficult to envision staying on track—avoiding being desperate or pushy. In advance of their meeting, he reminded himself to "act as if." When Steve asked himself, "If I were to believe in my heart of hearts that the outcome was going to be positive, how would I handle this situation differently?" it became clear that, if he were more confident that Judy had something positive to report, he would exude more self-confidence in general. He would dress well for the occasion, appear to be relaxed and happy, be somewhat talkative and he would allow her to set the tone and pace of the important conversation. This plan differed sharply from what he would have done had he allowed his anxiety to take over. He felt prepared for their "date."

At dinner, Judy told Steve that she had really appreciated how much effort he was putting into their marriage and that she wanted him to know that it meant a lot to her. She really hadn't expected him to do the kind of soul-searching he had done on himself and she was pleased that he had. She loved seeing how his relationship with their children had improved. That meant a great deal to her.

However, despite her happiness with his changes, she was nervous about the improvements sticking. She worried that he would go back to his old ways if she were to let her guard down. She felt really torn because he had finally become the husband she had wanted for so long, but she worried that it wasn't going to last.

At first Steve felt defensive because he knew inside that he was a changed man, that he could never again go back to doing those things that created the distance between them. Just as he was about to express his dismay with her skepticism, he asked himself the basic solution-oriented question, "Is what I'm about to do going to bring me closer to her or push me farther away?" and the answer was obvious. Therefore, he told her that he understood her cautiousness and that he was going to have to work diligently to keep the positive changes going. He told her how much it meant to him that she was finally acknowledging his changes. He also suggested that it would really help him stay on track if she were to continue to be more forthcoming about her positive reactions to his efforts. She said that she would.

Despite the upbeat tone of their conversation, Judy wanted him to know that she could offer no guarantees or promises. She wanted to take one day at a time. This was a deal Steve could not refuse. Their dinner conversation shifted to more mundane topics and the evening ended on a positive note. Although Steve was on "cloud nine," he remembered not to overwhelm her with his enthusiasm. He just recorded his joy in his Solution Journal.

STEP NUMBER 6—TAKE STOCK

Week twelve

Steve decided it was time to take stock of their improvements. He asked himself these questions:

Q. On a one to ten scale, with one being "the pits," and ten being "great," where on the scale would you say you were prior to starting the program?
Two.

Q. Where on the scale would you say you are right now?
Eight.

Q. Are you satisfied?

Not yet.

Q. If not, where on the scale would you need to be in order to feel satisfied?

Nine.

Q. What might be one or two things you could do or that could happen that would bring you up a notch (from an eight to an eight and a half or nine) on that scale?

We would have to make love. Judy hasn't been interested in being touched yet. I understand, but how can we be close if we're not close physically?

Steve decided that, given all the progress in his marriage, he would just have to be patient. He understood how challenging this would be for him because he adored Judy and he longed to be close to her, to touch her affectionately and to kiss her. But he didn't want to take a chance of jeopardizing any of the progress they had made. So he promised himself he would just wait for signs that Judy was ready to be intimate, or at least more affectionate.

Happily, after several more solution-oriented weeks under their belts, Judy started to be more physical. She deliberately touched Steve on the shoulder several times in passing and kissed him good-bye on several occasions. She even hugged Steve after dinner one night. And then it happened—Judy expressed interest in making love. Steve was ecstatic—which is why he believed they finally were at a nine on the scale. Mission accomplished!

STEP NUMBER 7—KEEPING THE POSITIVE CHANGES GOING

Because Steve truly understood what he had almost lost, he never became complacent about having Judy back in his life. Every few months he reviewed his Solution Journal and reminded himself of what he had done to turn his marriage around. He promised himself that he would stay on track. This is not to say that they never argued or had rough times—they did. But he found that as long as they kept the lines of communication open and he stayed involved in her life and in the life of their family, things never deteriorated significantly. They also agreed that it was important to attend church on a regular basis, something they had stopped doing for many years. They found that their commitment to spirituality boosted their commitment to each other. Steve and Judy beat the divorce odds and have never been happier.

Here's another couple:

CAROL

Carol and Dean were married for twenty-five years and had two girls, ages twenty and eighteen. During the early years of their marriage, Carol and Dean were crazy about each other. They were inseparable; they truly believed that they were soul mates. They shared common interests and basic personality characteristics. They came from similar backgrounds— both grew up in a small Midwestern town and were of the same religion. Their families knew and liked each other. It seemed that everything pointed to a happy union.

But several years into their marriage, things changed. Carol worked part time as a dental hygienist and Dean had a key position in computer sales. Although Carol enjoyed her job, she considered herself a family person first. Dean, on the other hand, was spending increasing amounts of time focusing on his work. From a financial standpoint, his efforts were paying off. He received many promotions over the years and was earning a sizable salary. But his successes came with a price. Carol was feeling a great deal of resentment about his priorities. She wanted him to spend more time with her and the girls doing family-oriented activities. She couldn't understand why work was so important to him. She appreciated that he was the primary breadwinner for the family, but she thought he was going overboard with his involvement in work-related activities.

When Carol talked with Dean about her concerns, he became very defensive. Nothing changed. The more Carol resented Dean, the more she complained to him about his behavior. The more she complained about him, the angrier he became. The angrier he became, the more he kept to himself. Now, she was no longer just complaining about his work hours, she was complaining about everything he did. Never in their marriage had they been so distant. From time to time Dean approached Carol to make love in the evenings, but she just recoiled. She couldn't fathom how he could be interested in making love when they were so at odds. They went for months without being intimate.

Dean started spending even longer hours at work. Occasionally, he would call to say that he would be home late because he was going out with colleagues for a couple of drinks after work. When Carol complained to him about his going out socially, he just stopped telling her about his plans. Before she knew it, Dean was going out at least three times a week. Nothing that she said or did seemed to make a difference. She started to feel desperate and she confronted him, accusing him of having an affair. That conversation opened up a can of worms.

Dean denied having a physical affair but told her that there was a woman at work who really liked him, who appreciated his ambition and his talents. She frequently complimented him about his looks and his kindness toward others. He told Carol that this woman's positive attention confused him because all Carol ever did was criticize and belittle him; he never felt appreciated or sought after. Then, when Carol rejected his physical advances, he hit a low point. He started questioning his manhood. So, when this woman came along and started boosting his ego, he could hardly resist the temptation to respond. Although he stated that there had been no physical relationship so far, he was finding it increasingly difficult to resist the temptation.

Carol was devastated and absolutely furious. What started out as an angry conversation ended up as a shouting match, Carol blaming Dean for the problems in their marriage and Dean doing just the opposite. The pattern was familiar. That night they went to bed in separate bedrooms and said little to each other in the following days.

At first, Carol considered leaving Dean. She was so hurt and devastated, she almost convinced herself that leaving the marriage would be less painful than dealing with the problems they were currently experiencing. But Carol's parents had divorced when she was twenty years old and, despite the fact that she was an adult, she couldn't believe how much her parents' divorce had hurt her and their family. She swore she would never do that to her own children. Although still devastated and furious at Dean, she decided to try to sort through her feelings to see if there was any hope for their marriage. That's when she began the seven-step program.

STEP NUMBER 1—START WITH A BEGINNER'S MIND

Like Steve, Carol had some unlearning to do also. She had many preconceived notions about marriage and family that she had learned from her own childhood and she expected Dean to share those beliefs. Prior to children and careers, their values seemed to be more in line. Once they grew out of the "honeymoon period" in their marriage, their interests diverged and Carol started to be judgmental about Dean's choices. Carol believed that if Dean really loved her, he would feel and think the same way she did about life in general. She had to learn that no two people think and feel alike all the time, and therefore, successful couples have to learn how to communicate and navigate around their differences constructively.

Furthermore, Carol was always comparing how close they were during their honeymoon period with the level of closeness she felt at various times throughout their marriage. Nothing quite measured up. Instead of understanding that all relationships go through different stages (as I described in Chapter 2), Carol began to feel that there was something terribly wrong with her marriage. And this concern led her to become extremely critical about everything Dean did. Carol needed to be more realistic about her expectations of Dean.

On the other hand, wanting more family time was quite a reasonable request, but Carol's approach to Dean only seemed to backfire. Rather than blame Dean for his insensitivity, Carol needed to be willing to look inward to see if a more loving approach would have better results. Eventually she was willing to do that.

The more Carol thought about it, the more she realized that there were many telltale signs about Dean's unhappiness with their marriage—his long absences from home, his joining a health club to "make himself feel better," his weight loss (which Carol thought was due to stress), and his silences when he was home. Carol also noticed other uncharacteristic behavior from Dean; he bought himself a new wardrobe, colored his hair, and started carrying around a neon pager. Slowly, Carol came to the conclusion that Dean was in the throes of a midlife crisis. She wasn't sure what that meant to the future of their marriage, but she was sure that his thoughts about aging and what he wanted out of life were undoubtedly impacting on his feelings about their marriage and her. Now that she could see that Dean was "going through a stage," Carol became somewhat less defensive about Dean's actions.

STEP NUMBER 2—KNOW WHAT YOU WANT

When Carol thought about what she wanted to change about her marriage, this is what she said:

> First of all, Dean has to get that woman out of his life. He either needs to change jobs or he needs to tell her that it's over, and I need to know that he is finished with her. Second, Dean needs to realize the importance of our marriage. I need to feel as if I'm number one in his life again. Finally, we need to communicate better. We stopped talking so long ago, I can hardly remember what it's like to have a good conversation with him.

When Carol learned about the principles of solution-oriented goal-setting, she realized that her goals were far from clear and that she needed to further develop her ideas about what she wanted to change in her marriage This is what she came up with:

ORIGINAL GOALS

GOAL 1—"DEAN HAS TO GET THAT WOMAN OUT OF HIS LIFE. HE EITHER NEEDS TO CHANGE JOBS OR TELL HER THAT IT'S OVER."

GOAL 2—"DEAN NEEDS TO REALIZE THE IMPORTANCE OF OUR MARRIAGE. I NEED TO FEEL AS IF I'M NUMBER ONE IN HIS LIFE AGAIN."

GOAL 3—"WE NEED TO COMMUNICATE BETTER."

REWORKED GOALS

GOAL 1—"DEAN HAS TO GET THAT WOMAN OUT OF HIS LIFE. HE EITHER NEEDS TO CHANGE JOBS OR TELL HER THAT IT'S OVER."

Carol needed to break this goal down into a smaller step, something that was achievable within a week or two. It didn't seem likely that Dean would end his relationship with that woman immediately. Plus, even if Dean were to agree to changing jobs, there would be many small steps along the way. It would be helpful for Carol to identify the small steps leading to the ultimate decision of his changing jobs. Carol had to ask herself, "What will be the first sign that Dean is considering changing positions?" and "What will be the first sign that Dean is cutting himself off from his coworker?" Her responses to these questions were the following:

> "Dean and I will calmly discuss the situation about the other woman [OW]. He will acknowledge that her presence in his life is not good for our marriage and say that he is willing to have less contact with her."
> "We will discuss what he might do to make that happen."
> "We will talk about other job possibilities."

In essence, Carol realized that the first step in the process was to have an open discussion with Dean about her feelings and see if he was in agreement with her.

GOAL 2—"DEAN NEEDS TO REALIZE THE IMPORTANCE OF OUR MARRIAGE. I NEED TO FEEL AS IF I'M NUMBER ONE IN HIS LIFE AGAIN."

Carol needed to convert this goal into action-oriented terms. She asked herself, "When Dean recognizes the importance of our marriage again and I feel as if I'm more of a priority in his life, what exactly will he *be doing* differently?" Her response:

> "We will spend time together on weekends doing fun activities."
> "He will call me from work just to see how I'm doing."
> "He will initiate time together rather than my always having to be the one to say, 'Do you want to go out for dinner on Friday?'"

"He will show interest in my life by asking me about the things I'm doing."

"He will show interest in the girls' lives by calling them and talking on the phone."

"He will be more complimentary."

GOAL 3—"WE NEED TO COMMUNICATE BETTER."

This goal was far too vague. Carol needed to ask herself, "When we are communicating better, what will we *be doing* differently?" Her response:

"He will show me that he wants to talk to me by initiating more conversations."

"We will discuss topics that are more personal, such as our feelings for each other and our plans for the future."

"He will talk about his day at work."

"He will show interest in me by asking about my thoughts on various subjects."

"He will let me know that he is listening to me by acknowledging what I'm saying even if he doesn't agree."

"We will set aside a regular time to talk."

STEP NUMBER 3—ASK FOR WHAT YOU WANT

Once Carol identified her solution-oriented goals, she realized that most of the time when she talked to Dean she had been very vague and very negative. So she decided to ask him to sit down with her to discuss their situation. Here's what happened when she told him of her thoughts about what needed to change in their marriage.

They agreed to have a talk after dinner one night. Carol did everything right. She cleared her mind before the discussion and decided not to approach Dean angrily. As positively as she could, she told him about the changes that needed to occur in their marriage. She followed all the guidelines outlined in Step Number 3 including being very conscious of approaching Dean when the time was right. But despite her best efforts, things didn't go very well. In the time between their discussion and the argument that preceded it, Dean had done a great deal of thinking about their marriage and he wasn't so sure that he wanted to continue.

Dean told Carol that he had been unhappy for a very long time and that he refused to spend what remained of his life in a miserable situation. His father had died two years before and he had begun to realize that life is short. Because he and Carol were not close anymore, he questioned his commitment to spending the rest of his life with her. He also told her that their lack of sexual intimacy was a major problem for him. He couldn't fathom how insensitive she had been to his feelings. Furthermore, he couldn't understand why sex was so unimportant to her.

Carol became defensive and rehashed her unhappiness with their marriage. Once again, although she'd promised herself she wouldn't play the blame game, she reminded Dean about his role in the demise of their marriage. But Dean wholeheartedly disagreed and more strongly defended his position. He also informed Carol that he was not going to change jobs—his was going too well—and that he wasn't prepared to tell the OW that she was out of the picture. Carol was once again devastated.

In the days that followed, Carol reconsidered her commitment to their marriage. She was so surprised at Dean's reactions and the vehemence with which he stated them that she began to wonder whether Dean was still the same man she married years ago. She questioned why she would even want to stay in a marriage with a man who wasn't ready to drop the OW immediately. She wondered whether she had temporarily lost her mind. Carol cried incessantly that week, and felt desperate. She felt so much shame about her situation that she felt there was no one to whom she could turn. She was at a loss.

Once her tears stopped, she thought more about her marriage to Dean, reflected on their shared history, the happy times in their marriage, the thrill of birthing children together, and a sadness overwhelmed her. She also thought about the commitment she and Dean had made to each other and to God on the day of their wedding. "We said, 'Until death do us part,' and that's what marriage should be." So, for better or for worse, Carol decided that she was going to stop fighting with Dean and start fighting for her marriage. Realizing that Step Number 3—Ask for What You Want—didn't bring about positive results, she had to proceed with Step Number 4—Going Down Cheeseless Tunnels.

STEP NUMBER 4—GOING DOWN CHEESELESS TUNNELS

Carol realized that her marriage was truly on shaky ground. If she pushed Dean too much, she recognized that he would be right out the door. In fact, she believed that he would probably seek solace with his woman friend. This was the last thing that she wanted. It was enormously difficult for her to restrain herself from really letting him have it about his immoral and irresponsible behavior, but she knew that if she were to hound him about the OW or about anything else for that matter, their marriage probably wouldn't survive. She made a choice then and there to become solution-oriented rather than to allow her emotions to be her guide. That was a most productive thing to do. Hard, but productive. Carol recognized that if her marriage had a chance of surviving, she would have to look inward and change herself first. This was a truly humbling experience for her, especially because she felt so raw.

She also realized that, as unfair and unreasonable as it might be, it was Carol who had to woo her husband back. Because Dean had allowed his negative feelings about their marriage to fester for too long, he was less motivated to work on their marriage than she was. Carol decided to be realistic about this predicament. Although she believed that she had every reason in the world to think that Dean should be the one to court her, it was only going to happen in her dreams. The hard reality was that if their marriage was going to continue, Carol was going to have to take the lead.

Carol quickly realized that there was some merit in what Dean had been saying to her. In the early years of their marriage, she had been Dean's biggest fan. He could do no wrong. As time passed and their lives diverged, he could do nothing right. Although she still believed that his priorities had been askew, she also knew that criticizing was hardly the way to reach Dean. She could understand why Dean had reacted so negatively to her constant critical comments. She vowed to stop emphasizing his wrongdoings and find reasons to compliment him whenever possible.

She also figured out promptly that pressuring Dean to cut off all contact with the OW was premature. From what he said, it was clear that he wasn't ready to commit to their marriage, and because of that, was still deciding what he wanted to do about his relationship with the OW. Carol had learned enough about solution-oriented principles to know that if Dean felt cornered, he would probably opt to pursue the OW even if, in the long run, it wasn't in his or anyone's best interests. She knew that insisting upon an ultimatum was not going to work in her favor. So, as impossible as it seemed to her at the time, she promised herself that she would put the OW issue on the back burner for the time being.

At the same time, Carol had taken to heart what Dean had been saying about the lack of intimacy in their marriage. She wasn't quite sure what to do about the void in their relationship at this point, but she knew that something needed to change. She realized that her rejection of his advances over the months eventually took its toll and perhaps even played a role in his seeking affirmation outside of their marriage. Carol knew that her marriage would not be on firm ground until there were significant changes in their love life but given Dean's feelings, she thought she'd approach him about this matter at a later point.

In summary, Carol determined that these were the "more of the same" behaviors that she needed to stop immediately:

> Pressuring Dean on the issue of commitment to their marriage
> Pressuring Dean to end his relationship with the OW
> Being critical and negative
> Blaming Dean for their problems
> Expecting Dean to change first
> Rejecting Dean's advances

Then Carol asked herself "What should I do instead?" She was ready for Step Number 5.

STEP NUMBER 5—EXPERIMENT AND MONITOR RESULTS
Experiment

Carol decided to follow the advice outlined in Do a 180. You might recall that Do a 180 requires that you switch gears entirely and do the exact opposite of what you had been doing, even if it feels illogical and unnatural. For Carol, Doing a 180 meant that, even in her state of confusion, anger, and resentment, she try to be more loving, understanding, affectionate, and appreciative of Dean, no small feat indeed. Here's what she did.

She wrote him a letter explaining that she finally understood why he was feeling so distant from her. She also assumed some responsibility for behaviors that might have increased the distance between them, like being highly critical and giving their sex life a low priority. She refrained from explaining the reasons she had been critical or rejecting—she assumed he already knew that. She offered some genuine compliments, telling him that she was proud of his achievements at work and how much she appreciated the fact that they were financially comfortable as a family. She also mentioned that she noticed that he had been working out and losing weight and that he looked really good. She ended the letter by telling him how much she loved him and that she really wanted to work on their marriage and stay together. It took all the personal strength she could muster to finish writing her thoughts. She left the letter on his desk at home at a time when she knew he would be alone. She wanted him to have time to read the letter without responding or reacting immediately.

It was her hope that the letter would demonstrate to Dean her desire to maintain their marriage and her intention to treat him more lovingly. If everything worked as planned, she would continue to say kind things to him, refrain from criticizing, say nothing about the OW, and be more pleasant in general in the weeks that followed. She knew it was going to be incredibly challenging to stop herself from interrogating him about his so-called friend, but to do so would threaten her marriage. She also remembered the importance of observing Dean's reactions to her 180 behaviors to see whether or not her new plan was working.

MONITOR RESULTS

Weeks one and two

Carol really had her hopes up that the letter would be a turning point, but unfortunately, it didn't turn out that way. Dean didn't say anything about her letter for two days after he read it. Finally, Carol asked whether he had, in fact, read what she had written. He said that he had. She asked him what he thought about the letter and he told her that while he appreciated all the soul-searching she had obviously been doing, he was

starting to wonder whether it was too little, too late. He felt tormented by
the fact that he didn't know whether he was "in love" with her anymore.
He knew he cared about her and didn't want to break up their family, but
he felt so confused. He told her that he felt really guilty when she told him
in the letter that she loved him because he simply didn't feel that he could
say the same thing to her. This troubled him greatly. He said that he
needed some time to himself to sort things out.

Dean's response upset Carol tremendously. She had been feeling fairly
certain that Dean would be responsive to her heartfelt letter. That was not
the case. She started to imagine what her life would be like without him
and the thought terrified her. Despite their problems, in her heart, Carol
always knew that they would be together forever. Dean was pulling the
rug out from beneath her feet.

During the next few days, Carol slipped back into her old patterns. She
started to try to get Dean to see things her way again. She begged him to be
more reasonable. She reminded him that their problems were caused by
both of them. She cried and pleaded with him to give their marriage another chance. Dean visibly shut down during her monologue. He didn't
know how to respond. And then, when he continued being cold to Carol,
she told him that he was not himself anymore. She suggested that he was
going through a midlife crisis, that he was overreacting to their problems,
and that he would soon come out of his fog. She asked him to go to a therapist to sort out his personal issues.

Carol's theory could not have been met with more opposition. Dean
totally disagreed with her thoughts about a midlife crisis and felt that
Carol was minimizing what he was experiencing. But despite his negative
reaction, she felt compelled to try to convince him that his dissatisfaction
with life was just a stage many men his age go through. Dean would have
none of it. By the end of the second week, Dean decided to move into the
guest bedroom.

Weeks three and four

Carol realized immediately that she had to get a grip on herself and
stop pushing Dean in any way. Since she now knew how incredibly difficult this was going to be, she had to devise a plan to deal with her feelings
of insecurity. She decided to confide in a couple of friends about what was
happening in her marriage. They were extremely supportive and told her

that she could call them anytime she felt the need to talk. This comforted her tremendously. Carol also decided to speak to her pastor, who was supportive as well and offered to speak to Dean. Carol thought about his offer and decided to hold off for a while until she could get a clearer reading about the direction Dean was planning on taking.

Knowing herself pretty well, Carol figured out that she needed to keep herself busy in order not to obsess about the problems in her marriage. She made an effort to get to her health club at least three or four times a week. She joined a woman's book club that met once a month and she contacted some friends to get together a few times. She started a few spring cleaning projects at home too. She noticed that when she kept busy, it was a bit easier for her not to feel totally overwhelmed by what was going on in her life. She made a note in her Solution Journal: "Keep busy, Carol!"

Rather than work on their marital problems, Dean definitely kept his distance. They weren't fighting per se, but they weren't talking much either. Carol realized that if their marriage were going to get back on track, it was not going to be a speedy process. She tried to prepare herself for the long journey back to feeling close again. She decided that she would have to be patient, more patient than she had ever been before, and that she would have to let Dean know that she was going to be his friend while he worked through his confusion.

In addition, Carol admitted that Dean's reaction to her letter really caught her off guard. She assumed he would accept her with open arms after she admitted her shortcomings. When he didn't, she found herself being unproductive again—pushing Dean to see things her way. She knew that, no matter how hard it was for her to do, she needed to give him space to sort things out his way. Regardless of how convinced she was about the ways in which a midlife crisis might be affecting his thoughts and actions, Carol needed to stop trying to persuade Dean about it because it only pushed him farther away. Carol intended to get back on track and stick to her plan of backing off.

Weeks five to eight

During the next three weeks, Carol and Dean had several ups and downs. When she gave him space and said nothing about his lack of warmth or availability to her, things were calm at home. When she voiced any discontent or questioned him at all about his actions or intentions, things deteriorated. This was really traumatic for Carol because she felt so torn. On one hand, the calm felt better than the storm, but she also felt that she was sweeping things under the carpet. Each time she started to feel that they were avoiding the inevitable, she brought up the OW or the state of their marriage, always with poor results. That made her unhappy too. She felt caught between a rock and a hard place.

Finally, after one really bad day, she called her best friend and said, "I can't take this anymore. It's been two months and I'm going nuts." Her friend asked her what she was going to do. Together, they discussed all the options. They decided there were four possibilities—divorce, separate, stay together and continue to be miserable, or stay together and make a decision to stop focusing on the marriage and focus on herself instead. After considerable thought, she decided to take option four—stay together and focus on herself. She would no longer discuss the status of her marriage with Dean. She would be kind, respectful, and even thoughtful, but she wouldn't put the kind of energy she had been putting into their marriage. Instead, she would put it into herself.

Months three to six

Over the next three months, Carol saw some small signs of improvement. Although they weren't doing much together, Dean was spending more time at home. He even called her a few times from work. Although he always had an ostensible reason to call, in the past, he wouldn't have called for any reason. They also engaged in more conversation when he was home. On a few occasions, Dean asked Carol about her day and how she was feeling. They watched movies together on television a few times as well.

Although Carol was pleased about these small signs of change, she was cautious about not reading too much into them. She didn't want to be disappointed. She took what Dean had to offer, and then went about her own way. She was feeling much, much better about herself as a person and she realized how this "new Carol" was probably a whole lot more attractive than the whiny, insecure, negative one Dean used to know. This all seemed like great progress to her.

On the other hand, Carol was still in the dark about his feelings for the OW. Although she suspected that perhaps things had cooled down a bit, she really wasn't sure. She certainly wasn't going to get her hopes up until that woman was totally out of the picture. But all in all, Carol believed that things were at least somewhat better between her and Dean. Carol decided to figure out what she was doing that might have contributed to the improvements.

Carol had done some reading about men's midlife crises and felt more certain than ever that this was what Dean was dealing with. She learned that the only thing a woman can do when a man is questioning everything in his life, is to be supportive, not to be pushy, and most of all, to be patient. She discovered that it is very common for men to go through an intense period of questioning what they want out of life and a time where everything is up for grabs. Many of these men show signs of depression. Carol felt comforted to know that she wasn't the only one going through this nightmare and that for many, there was a happy ending. This allowed her to continue to back off and have faith that eventually Dean would come around.

Beyond backing off, Carol continued "acting as if," doing nice things for Dean, but not being pushy. She treated him as a friend might treat another friend. Although she had some friends and relatives wondering "how long she was going to put up with Dean's garbage," she felt good about her decision to do everything within her power to save her marriage. She still wasn't completely sure that her efforts were going to pay off in the end, but she felt that if their marriage ended in divorce, at least she could say to herself that she tried all that she could to make things work. This thought comforted her and allowed her to remain solution-focused.

Months six to eight

For the most part, Carol continued being positive and supportive, even when she didn't feel like it. Finally, her efforts were paying off. At the beginning of the seventh month, Dean asked if she would like to go out for dinner on the weekend. Needless to say, Carol almost had a heart attack. She was thrilled to death. But she knew how important it was to keep her cool so as not to overwhelm Dean and she calmly accepted his invitation.

Dinner went well and at the end of the meal, Dean told her that he appreciated how loving she had been over the last few months and that it was because of her that he now wanted to work on their marriage. He admitted that he had cut off the other relationship a month earlier and that he felt really good about his decision. He also said that he believed that they had a very long way to go before their marriage was as good as he hoped it would be. However, he now felt the desire to make that a priority. Carol was brought to tears. This is the conversation she had been hoping for for months. At last, Dean wanted to be her husband again! It was music to her ears.

She told him that she was thrilled with his decision and that she agreed about their marriage being a work in progress. In fact, she told him that she never wanted to go back to that old marriage again. Unless their marriage was more loving and caring, she wouldn't be happy either. He liked her suggestion. He grabbed her hand and squeezed it, the first sign of affection in at least half a year. Carol melted. They agreed to have an in-depth conversation about their relationship once a week, where they would discuss their needs, desires, goals, and what they needed to do to accomplish these things. They went home and for the first time in a very long time, slept in the same bedroom. Although Carol was disappointed that they didn't make love, she decided to feel good about what transpired that evening instead.

In the next month, things between Dean and Carol slowly improved. Dean was showing definite signs that he was interested in becoming closer to Carol. They were spending more time together, going out on "dates," were able to communicate calmly and enjoy each other's company. The only time things got tense is when Carol wanted Dean to be more affectionate than he was. They hadn't made love yet and this really bothered her. She didn't want to spend the rest of her life in a platonic relationship. She brought this up to Dean one time and he got very angry with her. He told her that he wasn't quite ready yet and that she would just have to back off. This hurt her feelings and they ended up not speaking for a day or two. But finally, Dean reassured Carol that everything would be okay in time. He asked her to be patient with him. She reminded herself how far they had come and how stupid it would be for her to blow the whole thing at this point.

The only other rocky time between them was when Carol became suspicious when Dean was late coming home from work. She worried that Dean might have become involved with the OW again. Her fears got the better of her and she discussed it with Dean. Although he could fully understand her mistrust, he told her adamantly that his relationship with that woman was over and that he preferred her not bringing up the past. Carol appreciated his feelings, but she felt he owed her some reassurance given their stormy history. He agreed reluctantly. Things ended on a positive note.

Months nine to twelve

In the next few months Carol and Dean's marriage improved to the point where it was better than it had been since they were newlyweds. They were intimate again and also the best of friends. They continued having regular open discussions about their marriage and about life in general. They understood the importance of spending time together and of being supportive of each other. They frequently complimented one another and expressed their appreciation for each other's contribution to their marriage. Carol and Dean decided that they needed to develop more common interests so they began playing bridge weekly and bike riding whenever their schedules and weather permitted.

At the end of the year, Carol and Dean felt as if they had been through the year from hell, but in many ways, it was a blessing. It brought them closer as a couple. They learned a lot about themselves and each other. Carol became an expert at remaining solution-focused even when the pressure was on. She thought that staying on track was the hardest thing she had ever done in her life because so much of the time she was feeling hurt and disillusioned. One of the most important lessons she learned was that she could feel one way and act another. This, she found, was greatly empowering.

This is not to say that Dean and Carol didn't have their share of ups and downs—they did. But every time things faltered, Carol asked herself, "What am I hoping will happen here?" "Is what I'm about to do going to bring me closer or move me farther away from my goal?" Then, she proceeded, if what she was planning to do had a good chance of achieving her goal, and she switched gears if what she was planning to do wasn't going to be productive. Eventually, since change is contagious, Dean caught on to Carol's solution-oriented ways and started incorporating this way of thinking and acting into his own life. When Carol was slow to fix things that were temporarily broken, Dean took the initiative. They were really on a roll.

STEP NUMBER 6—TAKE STOCK

Month twelve

Carol had made a conscious decision to wait until she sensed her marriage was on firm ground before she evaluated her progress more specifically. That's when she asked herself the following questions:

Q. On a one-to-ten scale, with one being "the pits," and ten being "great," where on the scale would you say you were prior to starting the program?

Two. She said this to herself as she smiled.

Q. Where on the scale would you say you are right now?

Nine.

Q. Are you satisfied?

Yes, but when we have more time under our belts, I will feel more secure about our changes.

Then Carol asked herself:

Q. How much time would have to pass without major setbacks in order for me to feel that these changes are permanent ones?

If we could maintain this level for three more months, I'd start to relax even more.

STEP NUMBER 7—KEEPING THE POSITIVE CHANGES GOING

Both Carol and Dean understood the importance of remaining solution-oriented if they wanted their marriage to stay on track. They had a fairly good grasp of what they needed to do to make that happen and they also had a handle on what they needed to avoid to prevent major backsliding. If they wanted things to stay on track, they needed to:

spend time together
talk regularly and openly
continue to nurture their physical relationship

Carol needed to:

> approach Dean in a constructive way if she were feeling down, disappointed, or insecure
> continue to compliment Dean and help him feel appreciated

Dean needed to:

> Be willing to discuss Carol's feelings about the past and comfort her, even if it was uncomfortable for him
> Not allow work to overshadow the importance of staying close and connected to Carol

The majority of the time, Carol and Dean were able to do what they needed to do to build on the positive changes that were occurring in their marriage. Like everyone else, they had their rough spots from time to time. But as the months passed, they truly began to feel that they had overcome a major hurdle in their lives and they were better people because of it. Sixteen months after the whole turmoil began, Dean asked Carol if she wanted to renew their vows and she very happily agreed.

Comment

Carol deserves a lot of credit. She did what many people in her situation could not have done. She kept her head at a time when it would have been easy to allow her emotions to drown her. She swallowed her pride and decided to save her marriage at a time when others might have thrown in the towel due to damaged egos. She continually reminded herself about what was truly important in life and focused all of her energy on loving Dean until he finally realized he felt the same way about her. In short, Carol's new and improved marriage is a credit to her blind determination to restore love in their lives. Dean deserves credit for not bolting when things got rocky; many people in his shoes do exactly that. He kept his heart open long enough to notice that Carol cherished him enough to stand by him through his ambivalence and confusion. At a time when millions of unsatisfied people leave their marriages thinking it is the more titillating thing to do, Dean should be commended for the strength he showed in giving his marriage a second chance.

Remember that Dean and Carol's marriage didn't heal quickly. In fact, it was six months before Dean showed any signs of coming around; if you ask Carol, those were probably the longest six months of her life. She had hoped that they would be able to repair their marriage the day after she gave him her letter, but Dean's emotions were not about to be controlled by Carol's timetable. If Dean was going to change his feelings and attitudes about their marriage, it was going to happen in his own time.

Dean and Carol's story should be encouraging if improvements are slower than you expected. Sometimes things take a lot longer than you want them to, especially when you are longing to feel closer to your spouse. But the problems in your marriage probably took years to develop and problem-solving can be a painstakingly slow process. In an age when we're spoiled by "instant everything"—fast food, microwaves, instant communication on the Internet, car phones, pagers that keep us in touch no matter where we wander—it's no surprise that we think marriage problems should shrink in a nanosecond. But sorry, it just doesn't work that way. Anything worth having is something worth waiting for. Don't forget that.

Perhaps as you've been reading the seven-step program, you've thought to yourself, "This is really helpful, but my situation is somewhat unique. I don't identify completely with the people Michele is describing." Although I've tried to give you a cross section of examples of folks doing effective divorce busting, I know that there are situations that are special. If you are in one of those marriages, you know what I'm talking about. Although it's impossible to address every situation couples encounter, in the next section, I will address the questions most commonly asked of me over the years. I hope, if you haven't already, you will find yourself and your marriage in the pages that follow. If not, write me, I'll include information about your situation in a future book!

Part 3

Common Dilemmas, Unique Solutions

Over the years that I've been teaching people to become solution-oriented I've noticed that there are certain circumstances that make applying these methods and achieving positive results a bit more difficult. That's why I want to devote a section in this book to addressing these complex situations. Suffice it to say that if I were to write about all the areas of relationships that present major challenges, I could spend the rest of my life writing . . . and, for that matter, I just may! But for the purposes of this book, I have chosen four topics to tackle in-depth. They are:

- Infidelity, including Internet affairs
- Depression
- Sexual problems
- Midlife crises

CHAPTER TEN

Infidelity

I t's been estimated that 20 percent of married women and 37 percent of married men have been unfaithful to their spouses. There is little that is more devastating than the discovery that your partner has strayed. Affairs corrode trust, the basic building block of marriage. If your spouse has been unfaithful, I'm sure you have difficulty imagining moving beyond your pain, rage, sadness, and disillusionment. You are probably desperate for answers about how the affair could have happened and how your spouse—the person you thought you could trust—could have betrayed you. You might even be questioning your commitment to your marriage.

But you should know that most marriages do survive infidelity. That's the good news. But *how* they survive is another matter. Some couples stay together but never truly rebound from the hurt, while others are able to mend their marriages completely. In fact, many say their love becomes even stronger than before the affair. How well couples mend depends upon what they do or don't do to facilitate the healing process. This chapter will offer you information about the steps you need to take to turn the crisis of infidelity into an opportunity to make your marriage better than ever.

LET THE HEALING BEGIN

Over the years I've been practicing marital therapy, I've helped many, many couples get their marriages back on track after infidelity. And although it is no easy task, I have observed definite patterns in the marriages that have been successful in overcoming infidelity. I want to share my observations with you.

Before I outline the steps both the unfaithful partner and the hurt partner must take to heal their marriage, I want to tell you one important thing about recovering from infidelity; the healing process always takes longer than you think it will or should. Since infidelity is such a major breach of trust, it takes time to recover and rebuild, even if your commitment is strong. Sometimes it takes months, sometimes it takes years. If you were the unfaithful partner, you will have to be extremely patient with your spouse. You might not fully understand how devastating it is for him/her to have learned about your affair, but whether you understand or not, you should brace yourself for a rather long road to recovery.

If you are the hurt partner, you will also have to be patient. Just when you think you're feeling better and you're beginning to see light at the end of the infidelity tunnel, something reminds you of the affair and you go downhill rapidly. The road to full recovery is a jagged rather than a straight line. You will feel as if you're on a roller coaster and, for all intents and purposes, you are. When you hit a low, you will feel tempted to tell yourself that working on your marriage isn't worth it, that it's just too painful. But take it from me, the alternative—separation or divorce—is no less painful. There's no running away from the nightmare. The only way to get to the other side is to go through the pain.

The following guidelines are written for couples where both spouses want to make the marriage work. Your situation might be different; perhaps your spouse isn't certain s/he wants to continue in the marriage. If so, keep reading because I will address your situation in the section that follows.

THE BETRAYED PARTNER

Although both partners may feel hurt and betrayed in the marriage, the phrase, "the betrayed partner" refers to the spouse who is faithful rather than the one who has had an affair.

KNOW THAT IT'S NORMAL TO FEEL A WHOLE RANGE OF EMOTIONAL RESPONSES

Once your suspicions have been confirmed or you have been told about the infidelity, you probably will feel shock, disbelief, rage, anger, hurt, devastation, disillusionment, and intense sadness. No, you are not going crazy. These are normal emotions, given the situation. Also, expect your feelings to vacillate. You may feel one way at one moment and a completely different way five minutes later. You may cry a lot and find it difficult to sleep or eat. You may feel completely obsessed with thoughts about the affair and have a hard time concentrating or doing anything else. Know that for the time being, your emotions are in the driver's seat. As difficult as that might be, it's completely normal. And although you probably have convinced yourself that you are going to be miserable for the rest of your life, you won't. You will move beyond this eventually and you will be able to reclaim your life. I know it's hard to believe this when you're in the midst of feeling this way, but it's true. Allow yourself to feel your feelings.

EXPRESS YOUR FEELINGS AND ASK QUESTIONS ABOUT THE AFFAIR IF YOU SO DESIRE

Rather than lick your wounds and pull away from your partner, it's helpful to discuss your feelings with your spouse and allow him or her to help you through this process. If you feel angry, say so. If you feel hurt, tell him or her that too. Even though it's painful to discuss your vulnerability, when you do, it will give your partner the opportunity to reassure and comfort you. This is an important part of the process.

In addition to talking about your feelings, it is very likely that you will have lots of questions about your spouse's relationship with the other person. I suggest that if you are full of questions, ask them. However, be aware that there are advantages and disadvantages to asking detailed questions. The primary advantage is that you will be apprised of the facts rather than allowed to let your imagination run wild. The truth might pale in comparison to what you've been dreaming up. Knowing the whole truth and nothing but the truth takes the guesswork out of the healing process. So ask if you must.

On the other hand, if you ask lots of questions, you might not like the answers. In fact, you might be devastated by the actual details of the affair. So, you need to weigh the pros and cons. Are you the sort of person who won't let things rest until you've gotten to the bottom of things? If so, ask away, but be prepared to steel yourself for some unpleasant information. Conversely, if you feel you'd be better off just putting the whole thing to rest without digging up the details, so be it. Some people do better that way. The choice is yours.

If you decide that you're the sort of person who needs to ask questions, know that your questions will come in waves. Just when you think you've asked everything you need to know and more, a day or two will pass and you'll think of something else. This is normal too. Remember, this is a process, not a quick fix.

In all likelihood, your spouse will probably not be as eager as you to talk about the affair. After all, s/he probably feels shame and remorse and doesn't appreciate having his/her "face rubbed into it." It's likely that your spouse is hoping you will want to just put this whole thing behind you and close the door on the past. And although this is what will eventually need to happen if the two of you are going to make it as a couple, now may be too soon. You simply can't rush things. If your spouse has been giving you a hard time about talking and thinking about the affair incessantly, make it clear that this is a necessary—and temporary—part of the process you need to go through. Your spouse should read the section later in this chapter that describes what s/he must do to help you feel better.

If you ask your partner questions, listen to him/her without attacking. People tend to defend themselves when attacked, and the last thing you want your spouse to do is to defend his/her deceitful behavior. Just listen to your spouse's responses and consider letting him/her know that, though you are outraged by what happened, you appreciate the fact that s/he is sharing openly now. While you may not like what you're hearing, the fact that your spouse is willing to talk, even though it might not be his/her favorite thing to do, is a good thing. It shows that s/he cares tremendously about your feelings. That's good, right?

SPEND HEALING TIME TOGETHER

In addition to discussing the affair, you need to have healing time with your spouse, time when you are *not* discussing the affair at all. It doesn't matter what you do, just spend time together. Take a walk. Get a baby-sitter and go to a movie. Go out for dinner. Take a drive. Rent a video. Just hang out together. Lots of people in your shoes have told me that they feel their best when they are with their spouses.

Ask your partner to make himself/herself available to you. Spend more time together than you normally would. If thoughts about the affair pop into your mind randomly, force yourself to dismiss them at this time. Remind yourself that there will be another time for you to broach the subject again. Make conversation about the affair off-limits during the time you've set aside to be together peacefully.

ASK FOR REASSURANCES

As you move along in this process, there will be days when you feel confident and strong about yourself and about your partner's love for you. There will be other days when you feel insecure about everything. You may become doubtful that your spouse really loves you. This is also very natural. Many people tell me that when they're with their spouses, they feel confident, but when they're apart, insecurity sets in. They worry that their spouses might become deceitful again. A five-minute delay in returning home can set a whirlwind of worries into motion.

Regardless of when or why you feel uncertain and shaky, you are entitled to have your spouse reassure you. After all, you've been through a lot. On those low days, ask for reassurances. There's nothing wrong with asking your partner for help in feeling better. That's what marriage is all about, teamwork.

However, it is often the case that when people feel mistrusting or insecure, rather than ask for reassurances, they accuse and attack their partners. If you end up accusing your spouse, I can guarantee you that your spouse will become defensive and unloving. Now, you're probably saying to yourself, "Of course, I'm accusatory, s/he violated my trust!" Although this is true, you should remember the message in this book—be solution-oriented. If you want to accuse your partner and let him/her have it, all you will get is defensiveness. I think you want more than that. You want to be reassured that your spouse is being loyal, that s/he loves you very much, that the delay in getting home had to do with traffic rather than a stop at the other person's apartment. You want to be told that everything is okay.

As you go through this healing process where you and your spouse are trying to rebuild the trust, you deserve to know your partner's whereabouts. You have a right to ask and your spouse has an obligation to keep you informed. However, I want to stress once again that how your spouse reacts to your questions may have a great deal to do with how you ask them. Don't assume, don't condemn, just ask. In fact, it helps to remind your spouse that you are feeling scared and uncertain and that's why you're asking. If you attack, expect to be attacked back. Instead, try: "I know it was probably nothing, but when you came home late from work, it really scared me. I started to wonder whether you stopped by to see her. I hate feeling this way, so help me with it, please. Tell me why you were late," instead of storming around, being angry, and then blurting out, "Where were you, were you with her?" Get the picture?

IDENTIFY WHAT MIGHT HELP AND ASK FOR IT

If your partner has been unfaithful, it's likely that you have been hurting so much that you just want your partner to do something to fix it and make the pain go away. One of the problems with this wish is that your partner, even if s/he is willing to do whatever it takes, might not know where to begin. Sometimes it's hard to know what to do to help a loved one through a difficult emotional period, especially if you have been the cause of some of the pain.

Although your spouse needs to take responsibility to ease your discomfort, it is essential that you guide the way. No two people are alike. No two roads to recovery are identical. What might help your spouse recover from the infidelity might be entirely different from what you need right now. So you have to "teach" your spouse what you need from him/her to get over this.

When I say that, I bet you might be thinking, "I'm so upset, I don't even know what might help." That, too, is perfectly normal. I'm going to help you sort through this. I want you to think back to the times that you were feeling better and ask yourself that old familiar solution-oriented question, *"What do the two of you do differently when you feel more optimistic and hopeful about your life and your marriage?"* Really analyze what you and your spouse do when things are a bit better. For example, some people tell me that they are more likely to feel positive when there has been a lot of physical contact; hugging, kissing, and holding hands. Other people have said they feel better when their spouses keep saying, "I love you," or "I'm sorry." Identify what works in your situation, even if it only works a little.

Once you have figured out what you find helpful, tell your spouse about it. Remember to be specific. Say, "It really helps me when you hold me at night or when we snuggle in bed," or "I find it enormously helpful if you call me several times a day from work."

IDENTIFY WHY THE AFFAIR HAPPENED

If you have just learned about the infidelity, you might be too hurt or too defensive to take to heart what I am about to say. If so, read this section anyway, because you'll need to come back to it eventually.

If your spouse has had an affair, it's tempting to believe that it was due to his/her flawed and immoral character. And this may be true in part, but if your analysis stops there, you won't learn anything from this ordeal and that would be sinful too. In order to divorce-proof your marriage, you need to have a more thorough understanding about the factors that lead to the infidelity.

There are lots of reasons people choose to have affairs. Some people who have affairs are aware of their motivations, while others are not. But whether or not a person can readily offer an explanation for having an affair, it helps to try to have a deeper understanding of the issues involved.

LOOKING FOR LOVE IN ALL THE WRONG PLACES

Many people who are unhappy in their marriages seek emotional and/or physical connection elsewhere. Sometimes the relationship with the other person (OP) begins as a friendship and becomes physical gradually. At first, they talk about neutral subjects—work, people they know in common, world events. But soon after, the conversations become more personal. If they're married, they confide about the problems that they're experiencing with their respective spouses. They start fantasizing about each other and talking about their mutual attraction. People in these relationships often try to convince themselves that they didn't see the affair coming, it just happened. They purport that the feelings of passion took them by surprise and the temptation eventually became too great. But why were these people seeking this sort of intimate friendship outside their marriages in the first place?

"I feel taken for granted"

People become vulnerable to having an affair when marriages go flat, when romance goes out of their lives. This happens when couples aren't spending enough time together and they don't make their relationship a priority. They become like two ships in the night. If leading parallel lives is an acceptable way of life for both partners, there isn't a problem. But more often than not, one spouse feels neglected, taken for granted, and ignored. If these feelings are allowed to fester, in time, they often lead to feelings of anger and resentment. When this happens, any attention from outside sources begins to feel very welcomed.

The excitement that comes from a new relationship makes the hurt person feel alive again. For the first time in a long time s/he hears compliments rather than criticisms. S/he sees intense interest rather than apathy or disdain. S/he feels appreciated, attractive and wanted again—sexy, smart, good-looking, interesting, and desirable. They do fun things together. There is a euphoria and intense feeling of passion that's hard to be without. Those in the midst of this passion frenzy often lose sight of the fact that these "Hollywood feelings" are only transient. What matters to them is that, instead of feeling unimportant or pushed aside, they now feel special again.

If you have taken your partner for granted, it's essential that you start paying him/her more attention. No matter how busy you are, you must schedule dates together. It doesn't matter what you do, you can't lose touch with each other. Talk. Ask each other questions. Do fun things together. Unless you do this regularly, you will keep putting your marriage at risk. There is no mystery to this. You need to value your marriage and nurture it so that your spouse won't feel the need to seek attention elsewhere.

"I can't stand the criticism"

When couples are having problems, they are hurting so much inside that they end up hurting each other. They criticize, put down, and condemn each other. They endlessly focus on their partners' faults. Eventually, the blaming takes its toll. Sometimes, when people become saturated with the constant barrage of complaints, they find themselves seeking the company of those who are more appreciative.

Since the focus tends to be on people's good qualities in new relationships, compliments rather than criticisms are more forthcoming. Relationship expert Ellen Kreidman says, "People have affairs not because of how they feel about the other man or woman, but because of how the other man or woman makes them feel about themselves." Feeling appreciated can be highly seductive.

Are most of your interactions with your spouse about things s/he is doing wrong? Be honest. I know that you are feeling angry and resentful, but if you are often critical, you may be pushing your spouse into the arms of another, more supportive person. Although you didn't *make* your spouse have the affair—that was his/her choice—you might have made spending time with you a less desirable choice. No one likes to feel nagged or unappreciated. No one likes to be constantly criticized. If you don't appreciate your spouse, someone else will. You have to find another way to get through to your partner. Even if you have every reason in the world to be unhappy, you need to review the techniques in Chapter 6 and find strategies that are more positive and, without a doubt, more effective. If your marriage is going to thrive after this crisis period is over, you will need to take a kinder and more supportive approach to your differences.

"Our sex life is sorely lacking"

Other people stray, not because their emotional needs are unmet, but because they are unhappy sexually. In Chapter 13, I will address the area of sexuality more thoroughly, but for now, let's look at some of the reasons people grow dissatisfied with their sexual relationships with their spouses.

Sometimes, when there is a sizable discrepancy between the spouses' sex drive, the more highly sexed spouses complain that their partners simply aren't interested in sex. Other times, people say that they're bored—sex with their spouses isn't passionate or creative enough. Some people lose their physical attraction to their partners. Others complain that their spouses are simply poor lovers and aren't able to excite them. They turn to new sexual partners to fulfill these needs. Unfortunately, less highly sexed people have a hard time truly understanding the void their partners feel about their sexual relationship and therefore are not proactive in doing something about it.

Has your sex life been at the bottom of your priority list? Sexual intimacy is a very important part of a good relationship. If your sexual relationship has been less than satisfying to you or your partner, whatever the reason, this deserves your attention. If your spouse has been complaining about sex, it's important that you not brush his or her comments aside. When one person is sorely unhappy sexually, it makes going outside the marriage for sexual satisfaction too great a temptation. Read Chapter 13 about sexuality and get some ideas about what you can do differently to make your sex life a more important part of your life together as a couple. Even if the reason you haven't been interested in sex is that you've been unhappy in your marriage, you need to address this issue. Don't take your sex life for granted.

The ego boost

If a person isn't self-confident, s/he might seek the approval of others to restore a sense of self-esteem. That's why, when some people feel insecure or question their attractiveness, they may try to test the waters and become flirtatious. Occasionally, these flirtations lead to affairs.

This is especially true for people who are going through some version of a "midlife crisis," a subject that will be explored in depth in Chapter 12. They often feel depressed about the fact that they are getting older and their bodies are showing signs of age and wear. They wonder if the opposite sex still finds them attractive, and they become bound and determined to find out.

No matter how old people get or how long they are together as a couple, they still need to feel attractive. Do you compliment your spouse?

When you think s/he looks good in a particular outfit or that you've noticed s/he has lost a few pounds, do you say so? Do you say flattering things on a fairly regular basis or is that rather unusual for you? Compliment your spouse. Let him/her know that you are attracted to him or her. Regardless of how long you've been together, you need to let your spouse know that s/he is special. If you won't, someone else will.

A cry for help

Sometimes people have affairs because, in their minds, they've tried everything to get their partners to understand that there is a problem in the marriage, but nothing ever changes. Eventually, they decide to get involved with another person and leave telltale signs about their actions in various places. Some people write in diaries and leave them in plain view. Others take personal phone calls within earshot. Phone bills and restaurant receipts are left lying in obvious places. Although few people acknowledge or are even aware of their intent to disclose the facts about their affairs, they nonetheless are so "careless," one can't help but wonder about unconscious motives. For many of these couples, the disclosure of the affair, although incredibly painful, serves as a wake-up call and they begin to address as a team the underlying issues in their marriage.

Have you ignored your spouse's attempts to let you know about his/her unhappiness? Hindsight is always twenty-twenty, but can you recall times when your spouse told you that s/he was unhappy in your marriage? This is different from those conversations when spouses complain about day-to-day things. These are the kinds of "sit-down,-I-need-to-talk-to-you," conversations. If so, did you respond with defensiveness? Did you minimize your partner's feelings? Were you tuned out when your spouse shared openly about what s/he wanted to change or improve about the marriage?

As tough as it is, we need to try to hear what our spouses are saying when they are telling us about their needs. In order for a marriage to remain vibrant, it needs to continue to change. The more you can be open to hearing your spouse's heartfelt words, no matter how painful, the better you will be able to adjust those aspects of your marriage that need to be fine-tuned. If you shut down when your spouse shares, your marriage will move well beyond the fine-tuning stage. Don't let this happen to you.

Keep in mind that even if you flagrantly ignored your spouse's requests for change, it doesn't mitigate the fact that s/he made a very poor decision. That's a separate issue and one that I will deal with in the next section. However, if you want your marriage to improve, which I know you do, in the future, you will need to be more sensitive when your spouse appeals to you to improve your marriage.

The one-night stand

Sometimes, even in perfectly happy marriages, people can make really bad choices. A late night at the office with a seductive coworker, or an out-of-town trip and an evening with a few drinks too many, can be the backdrop to a slip into temporary insanity. This does not in any way excuse such behavior, but it happens. In this case, the actions say less about the quality of a marriage and more about a person's impulse-control skills. One-night stands don't make dealing with the issues of infidelity any easier. A breach of trust is a breach of trust.

Sexual addiction

Sometimes, no matter how much sex a couple is having, or how varied or passionate it might be, it isn't satisfying to a person who is sexually addicted. People with sexual addictions have an insatiable need to engage in certain sexual behaviors, even if it means hurting those closest to them. Unless the addicted person sees his/her behavior as a problem and takes responsibility to change, there is little the other partner can do to put an end to the excessive behavior. Ultimately, the addicted person needs to acknowledge the problem and be willing to learn impulse-control skills with professional help.

ASK YOUR PARTNER IF S/HE WANTS TO CHANGE THINGS ABOUT THE MARRIAGE

It is my hope that the last section got you thinking about the reasons your partner might have decided to be unfaithful. I realize that if you are feeling hurt, you might not feel all that interested in knowing about your spouse's needs, but that sort of attitude will create problems in the long run. Unless you understand and are willing to do something about your partner's unhappiness (if, in fact, s/he is unhappy), you may find yourself in this same position a few months or years down the road. Your marriage can't be a happy one if either spouse is unhappy. If you are uncomfortable talking about deeply personal issues, get professional help. But go to a solution-oriented therapist, someone who believes in marriage and is experienced in helping couples beyond infidelity. As painful as it may be, this is a great opportunity for both of you to talk openly about your hopes, dreams, and aspirations for your marriage.

LEARN HOW TO THOUGHT-STOP

When you discover an affair, it is common to think about it constantly. As time goes on, these thoughts tend to diminish, but this is not to say that you forget about your partner's affair. This won't happen, so don't sit around hoping it will. Sorry. Even when things are great between you, you will probably have times when you start feeling bad again because those negative thoughts just pop into your head. Although this is normal, you might decide that these thoughts are getting in the way of your being happy and you might want to do something to get more control of them. You can learn how to zap those thoughts.

First, I want you to know that it's useless to do this too early on in the process. Painful though it might be, you have to allow yourself to go through the full range of emotions first. This takes different amounts of time for different people.

Second, *you* have to be the one to decide to practice the thought-stopping method. You need to feel committed to freeing yourself of negativity. It can't be because your spouse is tired of hearing you remind him/her about the affair. So, are you ready to learn a method for changing your mental channel when the show you're watching is destructive? Then get your remotes ready.

THOUGHT-STOPPING

Say you are in the midst of a pleasant time in your life and you start to feel bad because you recalled a detail about the affair. The moment the negative thought occurs to you, envision a big, red stop sign. Then force yourself (and I do mean *force*) to immediately think of something else, something more pleasant. Try to imagine all the details in your mind's eye of a more soothing scene or situation.

At first this will feel awkward and artificial. That's okay. In fact, because your mind is a powerful force, you may find it really difficult to shift gears. You need to be persistent. Even if you are successful at thinking about something more positive, it is likely that you will start to think about the affair once again. That's okay too. Just gently remind yourself to get back on track and envision that big old red stop sign. Then *stop,* and do not proceed with negative thoughts.

With a bit of practice, you'll find that you have more control over what you think about and when you do, you'll have more control over how you feel. If you think about negative things, you will feel crappy. When you think about more positive things, you feel better. The point is, you can choose what you think about and influence your emotions by so doing. In fact, once you get skilled at thought-stopping, you'll find yourself using this technique in other kinds of challenging situations you encounter. It really works!

FORGIVE

One of the hardest steps in the recovery process after infidelity is forgiveness. Yet, without it, marriages can't thrive. People who stay together but don't forgive live in shallow, meaningless relationships. They just go through the motions but feel no joy or closeness. Don't make that choice. Choose love. Forgive.

The lack of forgiveness imprisons you. It takes its toll on your physical and emotional health. It keeps you stuck in the deepest of relationship ruts. No matter how justified you feel about your point of view regarding your partner's insensitive behavior, you still are miserable. When you wake up each morning, a gray tint shadows your life. You can't feel joy because you're too busy being angry or feeling disappointed.

In the face of these fairly obvious disadvantages, you hang on to your belief that since you feel let down, you must not "give in." To you, giving in means forgiving, letting go, making peace. To do so would be tantamount to giving up your soul; so you keep your distance. You interact in perfunctory ways, never allowing your partner to step over the emotional barrier you've erected. And though the distance often feels intolerable, forgiveness is not on your short list of solutions to your dilemma.

I have worked with so many couples who say they want to heal their relationships after affairs and yet when they're offered the tools to do so, they can't seem to move forward. These are the couples who, instead of finding effective ways to get beyond blame, continue to repeat their mantra, "Our problems are your fault and you must pay." As long as they maintain this mind-set, they are doomed to failure. How very sad. Even sadder are their children, who, on a day-by-day basis, observe their parents being "right" but "miserable." What lessons are they learning about love?

If any of this strikes a chord with you (and you wouldn't be reading this if it didn't), you need to internalize that forgiveness is a gift you give *yourself*. Letting go of resentment can set you free and it can bring more love and happiness into your life. It opens the door to intimacy and connection. It makes you feel whole. Forgiving others takes strength, particularly when you feel wronged, but the fortitude required to forgive pales in comparison to the energy it takes to hold a grudge. The person most hurt by holding out or blaming is *you*.

"All this sounds good," you tell yourself, "but how can I ever forget what my partner did to me?" Good question. You don't! Forgiveness is not the same as forgetting. You will always remember the affair. But when you forgive, the intense emotions associated with the affair will begin to fade. You will feel happier, lighter, more loving.

Just keep in mind that forgiveness isn't a feeling. It is a decision. You decide that you are going to start tomorrow with a clean slate and that you are going to do what you must to begin creating a more positive future.

So promise yourself that, no matter what, you will not go another day blaming your partner and feeling lonely. Make peace. Make up. Make love. I promise you that the benefits of deciding to forgive go far beyond anything you can picture in your mind's eye at the moment. Your decision to forgive will create a ripple effect of exponential changes in your life.

THE UNFAITHFUL PERSON

If you are the partner who had an affair and your spouse still wants your marriage to work, it's time to push up your sleeves and get to work.

Rebuilding trust and repairing your marriage is hard work, but it can be done. I've seen it happen many, many times. First of all, I want you to know that most people who have had affairs didn't mean to hurt their spouses. They often feel very bad about the fact that the affair has caused so much pain and wish they could turn back the hands of time. Although you can't change the past, you can change the future. I'm going to show you the steps you need to take to get your marriage back on track.

END THE AFFAIR

If you are dedicated to saving your marriage, if you haven't already, you need to stop the affair—cold turkey. Affairs and marriages generally don't go together very well. If you want to rebuild trust, you need to start being trustworthy, and that means that you need to stop having intimate relations of any kind with the OP. If you have become emotionally attached, I know this will require a great deal of personal strength. But the sooner you cut the ties, the better off your marriage will be.

Don't fool yourself into thinking you can just be friends or that the phone calls can continue because you're not having any face-to-face contact. No contact means *no contact.* You need to tell the OP that you've decided to renew your commitment to your marriage. If this relationship has been satisfying unmet needs in your marriage, it will be even more challenging to cut the cord, but you need to find healthy ways to get your needs met within the context of your marriage. I'm going to help you do that. I don't think you should stay married and be miserable. I think you should make your marriage great. Now's a good time.

EXAMINE THE REASONS THE AFFAIR OCCURRED

If you haven't already, review the information in the preceding section about the reasons people choose to have affairs. Hopefully, you will see yourself in one of those explanations. You are not an evil person because you decided to be unfaithful. You made a mistake—a *big* mistake—but a mistake nonetheless. You and your spouse can learn from this experience and do what it takes to make your marriage stronger.

If you had the affair because of personal reasons such as a sexual addiction or a thoughtless one-night stand, you need to take full responsibility for your actions. You need to change your behavior. If you are sexually addicted, you should definitely get some professional help. Many therapists are trained in the area of sexuality and can offer you methods for having a healthier, safer, and more satisfying sex life.

If you decided to have an affair because of unhappiness in your marriage, you've probably figured out that an affair doesn't solve problems, it only creates them. Even if your unhappiness was due to an unsatisfying sex life, although an affair might have satisfied your immediate sexual needs, it only made your marriage more troubled.

Rather than run from your marital difficulties, you need to identify specifically what you'd like to change about your relationship. Refer back to Chapter 3 and review your goals for your marriage.

If this is soon after the discovery of the affair, your spouse probably won't be very open to hearing about your needs or what might have led you to having an affair. All s/he cares about right now is his/her own feelings. That's because s/he feels incredibly betrayed and hurt and it's hard to get beyond that at the moment. Be patient and that will change and there will be a time when a discussion of your feelings will be more well received. If your marriage is going to improve, you need to be clear about what you want to be different in your marriage so that when the time is right, the two of you can work on this together. Do your homework. Identify what you need in your marriage, and be prepared to discuss it as soon as your partner seems ready to do so.

SHOW REMORSE

Your partner needs to know that you are truly, sincerely, sorry about what happened. You probably can't apologize often enough. You can say it, write it, send flowers. Be creative. Love means *always* having to say you're sorry. In addition to saying you're sorry, you need to demonstrate that you are trying to understand the pain your partner is feeling. Tell your partner that you feel bad about hurting him/her. Show your remorse in your actions, on your face, in your eyes. Although a simple "I'm sorry," doesn't take away the pain, it sets the recovery process in motion.

You should also keep in mind that your spouse may not respond exactly the way you want him/her to when you show remorse. S/he might be sarcastic or withdrawn or even unkind. This doesn't mean that s/he isn't listening to what you're saying or truly considering your apology. That unproductive behavior is just a defense. Ignore it. Keep showing your remorse. Eventually, it will be appreciated.

PROMISE CHANGE

I've worked with couples who don't survive infidelity. There are many reasons they don't, but one of the consistent themes running through these marriages is that the person who had the affair did not commit to being monogamous in the future. S/he never said, "I won't do this again, I promise." Some people fail to say these words because they think it is self-evident. Others don't promise this change because they are too proud. Whatever the reason, failing to promise monogamy makes your partner wonder whether the two of you are on the same page about the future of your marriage. So, don't hold back. If you can honestly say that you are committed to being monogamous, let your partner know in no uncertain terms that that is your plan.

SHARE DETAILS

If your spouse is the sort of person who requires lots of information in order to feel better about the affair, you should be honest. I know this is very difficult and you may be tempted to withhold information, thinking that you are protecting your spouse. But many in your spouse's shoes have said that the worst part of the infidelity were the lies and deception that followed the disclosure. It's time for you to come clean and clear the air. As tough as that might be, it's a lot easier than lying, covering up, and being discovered again. That corrodes trust tremendously. So share, even if it hurts.

Sometimes you will question whether sharing information is a good idea because your spouse reacts so badly to the things you've said. But if your spouse determines that the road to recovery is paved with brutal honesty, that's the path you need to take no matter how uncomfortable it makes you feel. There will be times when the two of you will feel close as a result of this new honesty and you will begin to feel that your truthfulness has really paid off. Then, just when you thought you were out of the woods and the questions would cease, a whole new slew of questions get thrown your way. You feel as if you're getting the third degree.

Remember, healing is a process, not a quick fix. Just because your spouse was fine on Monday doesn't mean s/he will be fine on Thursday. It also doesn't mean that sharing information isn't working. Some people think, "I told him/her what happened. If that was so useful, why is s/he still having a problem and needing to talk about it constantly?" That's just the way improvement happens . . . in waves. You need to continue to be forthcoming, from now until forever.

OFFER REASSURANCES

If you read the section meant for your spouse, you know that your spouse will be mistrustful of you and s/he will probably want you to account for any time spent apart from him/her. Although you may have decided to turn over a new leaf, your spouse is still reacting to what happened. This is completely normal, and for now, you owe it to your partner and to yourself to bend over backward to prove your trustworthiness. You might be thinking to yourself, "I decided to stop the affair and be trustworthy, I don't know why s/he just doesn't trust me now." Your spouse is feeling very insecure right now and needs all the help you can give him/her to get back on stable ground. You need to extend yourself—even if you don't think you should have to—to help your spouse feel more secure. Along these lines, do what your spouse asks. Here are some things s/he might ask of you:

- Call from work often.
- Limit out-of-town travel temporarily.
- Offer complete travel itineraries and phone numbers.
- Carry a pager.
- Talk about your day in detail.
- Spend more time together.
- Be willing to answer any and all questions about the OP and about your whereabouts.

Remember, once your spouse feels more trust in you and in your marriage, many of these requests will stop.

EXPECT UPS AND DOWNS

I really want to emphasize this point. The road to recovery is a zigzag, not a straight line. At first, the bad days will definitely outnumber the good ones. In fact, there may not be any good days to speak of. But slowly, as you begin to talk and make sense of what happened, you will have your positive moments. Moments will turn into days. Then, you will actually have a stretch of a few good days at a time. Just when you start to get optimistic, something will happen that will remind your spouse about the affair and bring back those unpleasant feelings. This rockiness and instability will occur for a very long time. You need to expect that. It doesn't mean that this problem is insurmountable, it just means that this problem is on its way to being resolved. It happens slowly, much too slowly for you. And what should you do in the meantime?

BE PATIENT

Even though you might feel a great deal of remorse about what happened, there will be times when you have a hard time understanding why your spouse seems intent on hanging on to the affair. From your standpoint, the whole thing is over and you want to just move on. However, if you convey this emotion to your spouse, s/he will feel that you are not empathetic, that you have no idea what s/he has been going through, and that will set both of you back considerably.

I realize that your need to move on has little to do with your insensitivity. In fact, one of the primary reasons you want to put the past in the past is because you don't want to see the hurt on your partner's face any longer. But be that as it may, you have to move at your spouse's pace. You won't be able to speed things along with your anger.

Continue to answer questions and be reassuring. If your spouse still wants to know where you've been and what you've been doing, continue offering information. It won't last forever, even though it seems that way right now. This is a transitional period. There has been a major breach of trust and it takes time to heal. Be patient, be loving, be responsive, and you will get through this.

TALK ABOUT THE CHANGES YOU'D LIKE TO SEE IN YOUR MARRIAGE

With some time under your belt, you may notice that your spouse seems more receptive to having a conversation about your needs. If this is the time, then go for it. There are a few things to remember as you enter into this discussion. You should review the goals you wrote down earlier and make sure they are positively stated, action-oriented, and broken down into small steps. Then, when you share your goals for your marriage with your spouse, you need to make sure that you say them in such a way that your spouse doesn't feel blamed. One way that you can do this is to use what's referred to as "I-statements." Let me give you an example of what I mean.

When people take responsibility for their own feelings, it's easier for others to listen in a nondefensive manner. Here are some illustrations of "I-statements"

Say: _____	Instead of: _____
I would like to make love at least twice a week.	You never want to make love.
I feel hurt when you spend so much time on the computer.	You are a computer fanatic.
I would like it if you would agree to having a budget.	You don't care about finances.
When you go out with your friends, I feel left out.	All you care about is Tom.

Second, don't overwhelm your spouse. It's important that s/he knows everything you're feeling about what you want to change in your marriage, but not necessarily all at one time. Plan on tackling one or two points at first and see how things go. Some people in your partner's position are eager to know how their spouses are feeling and what they can do to improve things. Others aren't quite so open-minded. In either case, go slowly. You have a lot of time to get to know each other again. You don't have to tackle every concern in a one-hour discussion. Take your time. Proceed lovingly.

NOW WHAT?

If both of you follow the advice outlined and ignore friends and relatives who ask, "Why do you put up with that?" or "I can't believe s/he hasn't gotten over this yet," you will start to feel that your marriage is moving in the right direction. If this isn't true in your case, you should consider seeking outside help. As I suggested before, choose your therapist carefully. Find someone who is solution-oriented, pro-marriage, and experienced in dealing with the issue of infidelity who will help make your marriage strong again.

Once your marriage is back on track and you are feeling good about each other again, you might consider doing what so many other couples do: renewing your marriage vows. You can do this privately—just the two of you—or you can invite close friends and relatives to the occasion. The renewing of vows helps people feel that they are making a new commitment and getting a fresh start. Celebrate your success in turning your marriage around and rising above adversity.

Once you and your spouse have gotten things back on track, you must never take your marriage for granted. It took a lot of hard work to get yourselves to the point where you are now and in order to sustain the changes, you need to make your marriage your number-one priority. Reread Chapter 8 on keeping positive changes going. Keep your love alive.

WHEN S/HE WON'T END THE AFFAIR

Perhaps your spouse is in the midst of a passionate affair and refuses to end it. This is not the optimum situation as you can well imagine but it's not time to give up hope just yet. For one thing, you should know that most affairs end within six months. Second, affairs usually don't result in marriage, and when they do, most end in divorce. So, if you're desperate to save your marriage, and you have enough patience to wait this thing out, you may just be able to turn things around.

If you are considering trying to save your marriage when your partner is unwilling to end the affair, you can count on receiving lots of advice from people who know about the situation. They will undoubtedly tell you to stop being a doormat and go on with your life. You need to be the one who calls the shots on this one. This is, after all, your life. You need to decide how you want to handle it. Trust your instincts. Don't let anyone else tell you what to do. If you're not ready to give up on your marriage, keep fighting.

If you decide to fight for your marriage, prepare yourself for a tough battle because your pride and emotions are going to constantly get in the way. It's hard enough to recover from betrayal when your spouse ends the affair and is trying his/her best to be supportive and loving. It's another matter completely when your spouse refuses to do what is in the best interests of the marriage. Fighting for your marriage under those circumstances takes courage, stamina, and blind determination. There will even be days when you question your sanity. And perhaps days when you should! But here you are. You want to make sure you've done everything humanly possible to make your marriage work and I'm going to see if I can help you.

REREAD THE LAST-RESORT TECHNIQUE

In Chapter 6, I wrote about the last-resort technique. Reread that section (page 124), because everything I wrote there applies here as well. When you feel your spouse slipping away because s/he is emotionally and/or physically involved with someone else, you will probably do everything you can to try to get your spouse to stop seeing that person. You will rant, rave, scream, cry, beg, and plead. Although these reactions are perfectly normal, by now you should know that they will not bring about the results you are hoping for. If you determine that you want to try to save your marriage, the very first thing you need to do is to promise yourself that you will stop chasing, pushing, pleading, and pursuing. If you don't, I promise you that your spouse will find the OP a more attractive option.

In addition, unlike the suggestion I made in the previous section where I told the faithful spouse to feel free to ask questions and talk about hurt feelings, you need to gather all your strength to *stop* talking about the affair. In fact, it behooves you to stop asking questions about their relationship completely. The more you ask, the more your spouse will feel pressured. The more your spouse feels pressured, the more s/he will want to flee. Control yourself.

I know that stopping the pursuit and interrogation is incredibly hard to do. In fact, if you decide to do it, it will be the hardest thing you've ever done in your life. But if there's a chance your marriage might work after your spouse comes to his/her senses, this is the course you must follow.

You also have some investigative work to do. No, I don't mean snooping around to find out what is *really* going on. Since you can't approach your spouse with any information you discover, you are only hurting yourself by snooping. You need to figure out what is so darn appealing about this OP. Do they have a great sex life whereas yours has been paltry? Does s/he flatter your spouse a great deal, building his/her ego? Is s/he spontaneous, willing to do things at the spur of the moment, when you like to have things planned months in advance? Is s/he a good listener, always interested in what your spouse has to say?

You need to find out what need your spouse is fulfilling by spending time with this person so that you can do a better job fulfilling that need yourself. You need to make some changes. Don't tell your spouse that you are going to change or that things will be different, just start acting differently.

Since you are probably an emotional wreck right now, you probably aren't too upbeat or even pleasant when your spouse is in your presence. Although this is perfectly understandable, it's not a good thing. That's because the OP is probably *quite* happy when your spouse comes around and that's what you're competing against. You need to do your best to be in good spirits and perky when your spouse is there. Yes, I know that I'm suggesting you do the impossible, but that's my job. I'm telling you to do what has worked for other people.

You should know that this could take a while, possibly months. You will be more successful in staying the course if you are taking care of yourself. How can you keep your sanity while you are doing this? Visit my Web site, www.divorcebusting.com. You will get lots of good ideas and support there. Keep yourself busy. Do things you enjoy. Spend time with friends. Develop a new hobby. Go back to a neglected old hobby. When tempted to discuss the affair, go for a walk. Call a friend who supports what you're trying to do. Write in a diary. Record your triumphs over temptation in your Solution Journal. Give yourself permission to stay in bed one day with the covers over your head. Join a health club and exercise at least three times a week. You get the picture?

By virtue of the fact that you care so much about your relationship, it means you have great values and you are a great person. Treat yourself like the great person that you are. Surround yourself with people who appreciate this loving quality in you. You deserve it.

I need to warn you that there will be days when you completely blow it; when you ask questions, and even rant and rave. So, expect these days. When they occur, don't be too hard on yourself, just pick yourself up and get back on track. You might even apologize to your spouse for losing it. You won't get the "Oh, that's okay, I know this is hard on you too," that you're hoping for, but at least s/he will recognize that you understand how counterproductive ranting and raving really are.

If all goes according to plan, if you keep a low profile with regard to your reactions about the affair, and if you keep being the person your spouse wants you to be, eventually your spouse might realize that the grass isn't any greener on the other side. That's when s/he will start showing interest in your marriage again. I truly hope and pray for you that that will happen. If it does, there will still be a lot of work to do to get your marriage out of the woods.

BACK IN MY HEART AGAIN

If you've spent months swallowing your pride and zipping your lips in the hope your spouse would eventually come to his/her senses, you will be overjoyed when that day happens. However, that won't be the only emotion you will experience. Now that you've got your spouse back, it's very likely that you will feel resentment creeping up on you. In fact, it might begin to overwhelm you. This is normal too.

Up until now, you were in a crisis mode, doing what you had to do to get your marriage on track. That meant sweeping your negative feelings under the carpet. Now that you are shifting into another gear, you have the "opportunity" to feel emotions that you put aside for so long. The most important thing to remember here is that you shouldn't overreact to these emotions. Don't tell yourself, "Maybe I made the wrong decision," or "If my marriage was meant to be, I wouldn't be feeling this way." That's rubbish. You've been through an enormous amount of turmoil and you're bound to have all sorts of feelings once the period of intense danger has passed.

As time passes, you and your spouse will be able to talk more honestly about what you've been through during this difficult time. If, when you discuss your ambivalent feelings, your spouse recoils or becomes defensive, it's time to hold off for a while. This is not to say that you will never be able to share openly. You must be able to do that if your marriage is going to be a good one. But timing is everything.

You might also be looking for strong signs that your spouse is truly in love with you. It's natural for you to want this kind of reassurance after what you've been through. However, don't go setting up little tests that your spouse can fail. Don't say to yourself, "Unless s/he says 'I love you' next week, it means that this reconciliation is a farce," or "If we don't make love within the next two weeks, it means s/he is still in love with the OP." Again, you need to be patient. Several months ago, you would have been thrilled to have your spouse commit to working on your marriage. Even if the pace of the reconciliation is slower than you would like, remember how far you've come. Don't screw things up now. Take a deep breath and remind yourself that you are definitely moving in the right direction.

In time, your spouse will be ready to address the issues in your marriage. Use the information you've learned in the seven-step program to help improve your marriage. If you feel you need outside help, find yourself a good therapist or take a marriage education course in your area. Just don't lose sight of how far you've come and that you're the primary reason you're still together. Be proud of yourself.

IF IT'S STILL NOT WORKING, TRY THE "AFTER THE LAST-RESORT TECHNIQUE"

Sometimes, even after you've done all the right things, your spouse still refuses to stop seeing the OP. At some point, you may start to feel that you can no longer go on this way. Everyone will feel that from time to time, but what I'm referring to here is the point that some people arrive at when they decide enough is enough. Rather than throw in the towel completely, there's one more thing you can do to make sure you've left no stone unturned. I call it the "After the Last-Resort Technique." If you've come to the end of your rope, before you hang yourself or someone else, give this technique a shot.

However, you shouldn't do it unless you are prepared to end your marriage because that's just what it might do. However, it might serve as a wake-up call to your spouse. It's hard to predict what will happen.

Tell your spouse that you love him/her enough that you are prepared to let go, then back off completely. Don't spend time together. Don't speak on the phone unless it's about your children. Have as little face-to-face contact as possible. Don't do nice things anymore. Don't call. Don't e-mail. Don't initiate contact of any sort. Don't allow your spouse to feel that there is a relationship between you any longer. Continue this emotional cutoff until your spouse gets the point that there will be no relationship of any sort until and unless the OP is *completely out of the picture*. If your spouse starts to show some interest in making this happen, the burden of proof now becomes his/hers. You need to insist that you are shown proof that the relationship with the OP is a thing of the past. Don't listen to promises, just look at behavior. If your spouse proves to you that the relationship is over, make it clear that your spouse has only one chance to win back your trust. If you choose to put energy into your marriage again and there are *any* signs of betrayal, it's over forever.

This last, last-resort technique is one that will force you to take a strong stand. It's not for the faint of heart. Once you make the statement that you're done, you have to be willing to follow through. If you waffle, you will lose all of your credibility. So don't use this method unless you're prepared to see it through all the way to the end. Hopefully, when you get to the end, you will find that sticking to your guns was well worth it.

INTERNET INFIDELITY

The Internet has opened up an exciting new reality. It connects millions of people from all over the world to create a global community. People from all walks of life are meeting on-line, communicating, supporting each other, and sharing important information. But there is a dark side to on-line relationships—Internet infidelity. I receive many letters each month from people whose partners have turned to the Internet to fulfill sexual needs. Here are a couple of examples.

I have experienced the Internet destruction of a family. I don't know if inappropriate sex talk was used at first but I do know my husband was looking for "a friend" to confide his sexual desires to. I do know that there were wild fantasies. It seemed that once one step was taken, another step followed. After digging for information, I discovered that my husband had opened a private post office box and a private charge card. He purchased a laptop computer and got an Internet provider. He started surfing the net for porno sites and several times he paid to get into the more graphic ones. A while later, he told me he wanted to record our lovemaking, so he purchased an inexpensive surveillance camera. He never used it in my presence.

Unfortunately, it was my thirteen-year-old son who informed me about the Internet stuff. He wanted me to know it was not him visiting the sexual sites such as "Bound and gagged." He found the addresses to these sites in the history file. I was so sad.

Help! My husband of twenty years has been into cybersex for at least two years. I didn't realize how bad the situation had gotten until he came back from overseas and I found some letters he had written to another woman. I let things go until I discovered that he was in actual contact with a woman. When I confronted him, he lied and then sort of confessed and said he would stop. Well, he hasn't and now he is not only talking to her, but to others as well—this includes guys and other couples. He is also e-mailing pictures of himself (private areas as well) to whomever he talks to on the Net and soliciting relations. I feel like I don't know him anymore. I feel angry, betrayed, and my self-esteem is at an all-time low. The worst of it is that his teenage children know what he is doing as well. What should I do?

Millions of people visit sexually-oriented Web sites every day. Some engage in erotic dialogue with willing partners in chat rooms devoted to various sexual interests—group sex, bondage, fetishes. Whatever your particular bent, you can find a like-minded community of people eager to "talk dirty." Others pay to view pornography. Some purchase inexpensive video cameras to send images of themselves engaged in sexual acts. Real-life affairs are often the result of people meeting online at sex sites or in other kinds of chat rooms or message boards.

One of the reasons cybersex is so rampant is because of its accessibility. You just have to go into the next room and turn on your computer to find a "singles' bar" with thousands of eager and willing partners. You don't have to make small talk. You don't even have to dress up or brush your hair. There is complete anonymity. You can pretend to be anyone you want to be, or anyone you think your cyber-partner might want you to be, and no one will ever know the difference.

How can you tell if your spouse is engaged in cybersexual activity? Here are some questions you should ask yourself. Is your spouse

1. Spending increasing amounts of time on the computer and less time with you?
2. Becoming increasingly private and secretive about his/her online "business"; switching screens abruptly if you walk into the room?
3. Becoming angry and defensive when asked about his/her computing activities?
4. Lying or being deceptive?
5. Considerably less interested in being intimate or sexual with you?

If you answered "Yes" to several of these indicators, it's possible that your spouse may be involved in some sort of cybersex or real-life affair. If so, and you are troubled by it, what do you do?

An honest, straightforward approach is your first line of defense. Don't bother gathering an enormous amount of evidence before confronting your spouse about his/her behavior. If you are concerned, it warrants your taking action.

As usual, when asking for what you want, you must state it positively (use I-statements) rather than in a blaming fashion, and in an action-oriented rather than vague manner. Tell your spouse that you've been concerned about his/her behavior. Specify exactly what behavior is troubling you. Explain why this is disturbing to *you*. Own your discomfort. For example, instead of saying, "You are really upsetting me. I know you've been doing things online that are sexual and you've been lying about it. I won't put up with it," say, "I've been upset by the fact that you've been spending lots of time on the computer recently and you appear to be very secretive about it. Every time I walk into the room, you switch screens or log off. I feel scared that you might be involved in inappropriate online relationships."

There are several ways your spouse might respond to your accusations. S/he might admit you are right and express remorse, deny the accusation completely, or acknowledge it's happening but tell you that you are reading too much into it, that it's no big deal. Let's look at each of these responses separately.

1. "You're right, I'm sorry." Of course, this is the ideal response, and one that doesn't happen nearly as often as it should. If you are fortunate enough to have your spouse react this way, you should seize the opportunity to have an in-depth, heart-to-heart conversation about the reasons your spouse has been surfing the net for sexual/emotional satisfaction and the impact this has been having on you. If your spouse has been surfing simply out of curiosity, once s/he understands the impact this behavior has been having on you, if s/he is truly remorseful, the behavior should stop. If your spouse's actions are due to the fact that something has been missing in your relationship, you and your spouse need to commit to working on those issues. Look at this as a chance to improve your relationship and follow the guidelines offered in this chapter about real-life affairs; the same advice applies.

2. "Yes, you're right, but it's no big deal." Your spouse may tell you that s/he has been involved in erotic conversations over the Internet but that s/he doesn't see it as a betrayal of your marriage. In fact, s/he might say that this sort of interaction prevents him/her from having an actual affair, that the cybersex is no real threat to your marriage, and that you should stop being so controlling.

If you feel reassured by the fact that your spouse is not involved in a real-life affair, you might decide not to make an issue of his/her involvement over the Internet. Chances are, however, if you are reading this section, you feel quite strongly that your partner's behavior—whether having intimate conversations about life with another person or acting out sexual fantasies with a group of strangers—is a betrayal of your marital vows. Intimate online chatting and cybersex have all the characteristics of real-life affairs—secrecy, intimacy, and sexual fulfillment. That's why, no matter what your spouse tells you, his/her behavior feels like a betrayal. You're not crazy if you feel that way.

If your spouse takes the "You're overreacting" stance, rather than debating the issue, you should point out that *to you,* it is infidelity. Talk about your hurt feelings and your feelings of betrayal. Tell your spouse that you understand that s/he may see it differently, but since you are in a relationship, s/he needs to take *your* point of view into account and take care of *your* feelings. Don't debate who's right and who's wrong because that won't get you very far. It's important to remain solution-oriented regardless of the kind of problem you're tackling.

If you think your spouse might be open to it, you might consider collecting some articles about Internet affairs and giving him/her the chance to read what experts in the field are writing about this new subject. This may educate your spouse and allow him/her to see that you are not alone in your feelings. However, if your spouse appears to be defensive, it's unlikely that these articles will make a difference. If so, don't push it.

Once you make it clear that you are offended by the behavior, you need to also be clear as to what you expect your spouse to change. Follow the guidelines outlined in Chapter 4. You must be specific and action-oriented and your requests must be reasonable. For example, you can't ask a person whose job entails being on the computer much of the day to avoid the computer entirely. In that case, you have to figure out what your spouse could change so that you will feel more reassured that his/her online behavior is strictly work-related.

It may be the case that your spouse is completely unwilling to consider your requests. If so, your first line of defense—a straightforward request—must be deemed unsuccessful, in which case, you need to continue reading the sections below, which address your situation.

3. "You're imagining things"—the complete denial. This is the toughest and, unfortunately, the most typical response to allegations of Internet infidelity. If your spouse has reacted defensively and told you that you are flat-out wrong when your instincts have told you otherwise, you will be very tempted to spend the next few days/months snooping, spying, hiring private detectives, setting surfing traps just to prove your point. My advice? Don't bother. It's an enormous waste of time, effort, and money. Trust yourself. If you feel confident that there's something to be concerned about, unless you're truly a paranoid person, there's probably something to be concerned about. Don't start playing the hide-and-seek game. It's addictive and highly destructive.

Rather than try to prove that your spouse has been engaged in sexual activity online, sit down and focus instead on how the excessive time spent online has been interfering with your marriage. Talk about what's been missing in your relationship and what you'd like to change. Be direct about your expectations and wishes. If your spouse says that s/he is willing to invest more energy in your marriage, it will, by definition, change what s/he is doing online. You can only be in one place at a time. If you doubt your spouse's sincerity when s/he commits to making changes in your relationship, keep it to yourself. Take the offer at face value. Only time will tell if your spouse is being honest about his/her intentions.

If things change for the better, so be it. If not—if the excessive online behavior continues—you have some choices to make. No matter what book or article you read, seminar you attend, or therapist you consult with on this issue, there are no single solutions that work for everyone. Like everything else in life, you have to be your own expert and decide which solution works best for you. I will offer you a number of different ideas. As you read them, notice which one(s) feel right to you. Then give it a shot and see if it is helpful. Remember, you should only continue doing something if it starts to work. This list begins with the simplest, most direct strategies and broadens out from there.

TRY TO CONFRONT YOUR SPOUSE ONE MORE TIME

Before you can be absolutely sure that it's time to bring out the bigger guns, you might try confronting your spouse one more time to see his/her reaction. Follow the suggestions above about the way that you approach your spouse. Don't be accusatory or angry, just calmly tell him/her that what's happening is really hurting you and why. If your spouse has that, "I can't believe we're talking about this again" look on his/her face, stop what you're doing and wait a few days to see if your feedback had any impact. If so, great. If not, try something different.

DO SOMETHING DIFFERENT

Review the section on the technique of doing something different in Chapter 6. You need to change your approach if you want your spouse to pay attention to you and your requests/needs. Change anything. Here are a few examples to jump-start your imagination.

1. Crazy as it sounds, you might consider showing your spouse a genuine interest in his/her online activities. Promise that you will not be judgmental or get angry. Tell your spouse that you want to find out what has been turning him/her on. If s/he is willing to include you, although it may make you uncomfortable, consider joining in. For one thing, it's entirely possible that your fears about your spouse's activities may be considerably worse than what's happening in reality. You will have more information about what is actually going on and you can make a rational decision about what you need to do next. Second, since the illicitness and secrecy of online activity are often a turn-on, once your spouse shares openly about it, the thrill might be diffused.

2. If in response to your spouse's spending inordinate amounts of time on the computer at night you have been sitting around waiting for him/her to quit, why not get creative? Be less predictable and make yourself less available to your spouse when s/he is offline. Your spouse knows that no matter what s/he does, you will be there waiting. Stop waiting and see what happens. If your spouse has been pulling away by being online, stop pushing.

Why not go out with friends? Give your spouse a chance to notice that if s/he doesn't invest more energy in you, you won't be there anymore. If you have children, I know this will take some planning, so plan.

3. Since your spouse gets a charge out of online dialogues, try e-mailing your spouse a flirtatious message. Get your spouse turned on *to you* via the very tool that you fear is taking him/her away from you.

4. If you are convinced that nothing in your marriage will change unless and until your spouse is confronted with hard evidence about his/her behavior, then you might consider purchasing a software product that takes "snapshots" of online activity for review later. If you decide to go this route, you must be prepared for two things.

One—You might find what you've suspected to be true. You might discover the evidence you've been searching for and unless you are totally prepared to see or read the information, you may become very upset. Ask yourself, "Do I really want to do this?" "Am I prepared for what might be bad news?" If, after considering all the possible outcomes of your search, you still believe it's the only hope for change, go ahead. Gather your information.

Two—Even though your spouse might be involved in behavior that is unacceptable to you, your surveillance might not be appreciated, to say the least. S/he might feel that you have invaded their privacy and become angered and defensive. In fact, although you will want to be discussing the evidence you've found, your spouse might want to do nothing of the sort. S/he might be so incensed that you have been "spying," that s/he will refuse to take any responsibility for his/her own actions and, instead, blame you. Then you will be back to square one, minus the amount you paid for the software.

If, after trying many innovative strategies, the only change you see is a change for the worse, it's time to consider the following:

For some people, engaging in sexually-oriented activities over the Internet becomes a full-time preoccupation. They're either doing it or thinking about doing it constantly. Their desire to be online supersedes their desire to interact in their own real-life relationships. If your spouse has been unwilling to change his/her behavior despite your protests, it may mean that s/he is one of those people. You may even feel that your spouse has become addicted to online sexual experiences. If so, you can try to educate your spouse about the subject of addiction. Offer him/her articles to read about various forms of Internet addiction.

Chances are, your spouse will not want to read the articles or admit that s/he has a problem, but by broaching the subject, you have laid the groundwork for future conversations that may be more productive. Even if these articles don't convince your spouse that s/he has a problem, it will help *you* feel better in that you will realize that this issue is bigger than your marriage. There are many excellent Web sites devoted to Internet addictions and, of late, several new books; take advantage of the information. It helps to know what you're dealing with.

If your spouse is obsessed with being online or engaging in sexually oriented activities via the Internet and nothing you do seems to make a difference, ultimately you are faced with three choices:

1. Keep doing what you're doing and be miserable. Yes, believe it or not, this is a choice. You may not feel as if being miserable is a choice, but it is. If what you've been doing hasn't been working and you continue to do it, you are, in essence, *choosing* to be miserable. Sometimes we have to do this for a while before we really tire of it. You need to ask yourself, "Am I sufficiently convinced that I haven't been able to change this situation?" "Am I ready to do something else, or am I still holding out hope that if I keep trying to get him/her to stop, somehow it will work eventually?" If you are not entirely fed up with trying to change your spouse, you'll need to choose to be miserable for a while. Keep doing what you're doing until you hit rock bottom. Then you'll be ready for a change.

2. Detach. I worked with a woman named Jessica whose husband, Ken, visited sexually-oriented Web sites. Jessica wasn't entirely sure what Ken was doing online, but she wasn't happy about the things she discovered when Ken was out of town one day. He had visited chat rooms and X-rated Web sites.

Jessica was also a devout Christian. She tried to get Ken to admit he had a problem and get some help. But Ken would have none of it. He enjoyed his time online and felt that Jessica was interfering. They argued a great deal about this.

Although her religious beliefs ruled out divorce as a viable option, she was finding it extremely difficult to be married to a man who enjoyed visiting pornographic Web sites and chatting with other women. Jessica felt torn most of the time and was extremely unhappy. After months of soul-searching, she made a decision. She decided that when she vowed to God that she would stay married, "For better or for worse," she meant it. She recommitted herself to her husband and set out to find a way to live with him without being miserable.

I met with Jessica a number of times and found her to be an amazingly resourceful woman. She had many ideas about what she needed to do to revamp her life to make it more satisfying. For starters, she decided that his sexual behavior was an addiction rather than a malicious act aimed at angering her. This helped her to be less reactive when he chose to surf the Net. Jessica decided to try to focus on the aspects of their marriage that she enjoyed, and there were many. Jessica also promised herself that she would stop nagging him about the time he spent on his computer. She let *his* problem be *his* problem.

Jessica was fortunate in that she loved her work and had an extremely close network of Christian women friends who supported her. When she was feeling down or frustrated, rather than try to change her husband, she turned to her friends to vent and for support. She worked extremely hard at separating herself from her husband's problems. On most days, she had an excellent handle on things.

Over time, Jessica discovered that her marriage was improving. Although she still felt very strongly that Ken's sexual behavior was morally wrong, she went about her business and made her own life fulfilling. She noticed that she was beginning to feel less anger at Ken, which had its payoffs. He was becoming kinder and more considerate. The time they spent together was more enjoyable. There was less tension between them.

She also noticed that, although Ken continued to surf the Net occasionally, that he was spending significantly less time doing so. By emphasizing what she loved about Ken and detaching from the rest, Jessica managed to minimize the impact his cyber activities had on their marriage. This wasn't an easy task, but neither was divorcing the man she loved and to whom she had made a lifelong commitment. On most days, they are very happy together.

Like Jessica, you can decide to detach from your spouse's online obsession. You can focus on the good times, rare though they might be, and ignore the rest. You can put more energy into making yourself happy as an individual. You can decide to let go of the fantasy that you are going to change your spouse at this point. Sometimes, people feel an enormous sense of relief in letting go of unrealistic expectations. You may feel liberated once you make the decision to let the online obsession/addiction be your spouse's problem.

However, I completely understand that the idea of detaching might not be appealing to you. You may be asking yourself, "How can I detach from this sort of unacceptable behavior? I can't!" If that's how you feel, don't do it. Remember, there is no single correct way to respond here. This is *your* life—not mine, not your therapist's, or your friends'. You have to decide what is in your and your family's best interest. If you can't live with the idea that your spouse is involved in an unhealthy way online, don't.

On the other hand, if the idea of detaching has piqued your interest but you think it might be overwhelmingly difficult to do, you can consider finding a support group (like Alanon). You can also network through your religious organization. Just be certain that the group is supportive of your goal to stay in your marriage and that they are nonjudgmental about your decision to detach.

3. Prepare to separate or divorce. One of the choices you can make is that you are not going to live your life with someone who is obsessed with cybersexual activities. If you feel that this behavior has interfered with your marriage to the point that you no longer want to stay together, you should consider giving your spouse a firm ultimatum before you move out or begin the divorce process. Sometimes a dramatic but genuine threat acts like a wake-up call.

THE ULTIMATUM

If your spouse has been unwilling to change, and you have come to the end of your rope, one of your clear choices is to give your partner an ultimatum. But a word of warning: *Do not give an ultimatum unless you are willing to follow through. Do not make an empty threat.* If you are at the point where you see no other option, you can set a boundary by saying, "I don't mean for this to sound like a threat, but I can't live like this anymore. It's too upsetting to me. Either you come with me to counseling [or quit spending time on the computer], or I need to end this marriage. It's not what I want to do, but I feel this is an unhealthy situation for me. I am willing to schedule an appointment for us to see a therapist, but I need to know right now if this is something you are willing to do."

You can deliver a message such as this face-to-face, in a letter or e-mail, or over the phone. How you do it really doesn't matter. *That* you do it does. Your spouse will either take you up on your offer or decline. However, s/he might react defensively at first and then soften a bit. Wait a few days to see what happens and then, if s/he hasn't responded, ask for an answer. Then act. Either schedule a therapy appointment with a solution-oriented therapist, or go see a good attorney.

Just because you are seeking legal advice doesn't mean your marriage is over. Once your spouse sees that you are really serious about following through with your threat, s/he might decide to get some help. Since laws vary from state to state, ask your attorney if there is some way to issue a formal but nonaccusatory announcement of your intention to begin divorce proceedings. If so, you might consider going that route first.

For example, in Illinois, the state in which I live, it is possible for an attorney to issue a praecipe summons rather than file a petition of dissolution of marriage. In a petition, you must allege grounds for the dissolution of your marriage (marital misconduct such as mental cruelty, adultery, etc.) and ask for the relief you're seeking. Your spouse will be served with a copy of the petition and the summons, and s/he will be expected to respond in writing within thirty days or be "defaulted." If your spouse is defaulted, it is assumed that s/he admits to the charges and that the divorce will not be contested. Naturally, these accusations, even if true, are likely to make your spouse defensive and ruin chances of reconciliation.

Under the praecipe-summons procedure, a request is simply filed asking the court to issue a summons. No grounds for the dissolution of marriage are necessary. Enlightened attorneys who use this procedure find that it sometimes serves as a wake-up call to the spouse who has been unmotivated to change. (Gitlin)

Although your state may not offer such an option, there may be something comparable that your lawyer can do to shake up your spouse. Perhaps a letter from the attorney acknowledging your visit to his/her office and your intention to dissolve your marriage will suffice. Discuss these options with your attorney.

But in the end, it is your spouse who will have to decide to change. Once a person is obsessed or addicted to a particular behavior, s/he won't make the decision to change unless they have suffered some losses. They need to realize that their behavior is causing serious problems for them. Only then will they be willing to look inward. By filing for divorce, you are doing what you can to pull the rug out from beneath your partner's feet. This might help shake things up. But again, it might not. That's why you should be fully prepared to move on with your life if you take this path.

CHAPTER ELEVEN

Dealing with the Depressed Spouse

Dear Michele,

My husband suffers from depression. He's been like this for about two years. He's also very much into a "victim mentality." He believes that everything that ever goes wrong in his life is my fault. My career is pretty successful and he can't stand it. He knows that he's depressed; however, he refuses to do anything about it. I try to go on and just live my life, but it's so hard. I am not happy like this and I am so tired of crying and being unhappy myself. Can I really do anything that will make a difference in our marriage? Also, what do you think of medication?

Dear Michele,

I am convinced that my work-obsessed, grumpy husband has been changed from the smiley, fun-loving guy I married by some chemical imbalance. If I didn't have the confirming evidence of witnessing what happened in the few weeks after he started taking an antidepressant, I might doubt myself too. The medication really helped but then he stopped taking it and he got depressed again. Now he knows what the problem is, but he still chooses not to get treatment for it. What solution-oriented method should I use to approach him?

Depression affects approximately twenty to thirty million Americans, making it the most common psychological problem in America. When depression hits, it affects everyone in the family. Sometimes depressed people turn inward and tune out the world, other times they can be quite unpleasant, even to well-meaning family and friends. Although depression makes people feel incredibly isolated and lonely, it's no picnic being married to someone who is depressed either. At first, most people are nurturing and sympathetic to their unhappy partners. However, when "cheering up" efforts fail and the depression lingers, even the most patient spouses begin to feel resentment, frustration, and rage.

If you are married to someone who you believe is depressed, you've probably been experiencing a multitude of feelings yourself. You simply may be worried about your partner. You are probably also feeling frustrated that your spouse is seeing everything—his/her life, marriage, career—through the distorted, hazy lenses of depression. If your spouse is the sort of person who has withdrawn from you, the silence and emotional void in your marriage must be very, very painful. If your spouse has blamed you for all of his/her unhappiness, resentment, anger, and hurt are to be expected. If your spouse vacillates between being distant and accusatory, you undoubtedly feel as if your life is in a state of flux, never quite knowing what to expect.

You ask yourself, "Why can't s/he see that s/he has a problem?" "Why won't s/he do something about it?" "Why can't s/he just snap out of it?" "Why won't s/he recognize how hard I'm trying to be understanding and helpful?" You feel exasperated.

Despite your strong conviction that depression is wrecking both your lives, you can't seem to get your spouse to agree with your diagnosis or to do something to help himself/herself. And in the meantime, you feel helpless to do anything but painfully watch your relationship worsen with each passing day. What's a loving, committed spouse to do?

To help you develop a plan for overcoming the hurdle depression puts in the way of a satisfying marriage, I want you to have a better understanding about why people get depressed and what happens to them when they do. However, it is beyond the scope of this book to offer you a comprehensive explanation about depression and its impact on family members. There are many good books you can and should read on the subject. I highly recommend *Breaking the Patterns of Depression* by Dr. Michael Yapko (Doubleday). It offers a thorough explanation about depression and what a person can do to free himself/herself from its toxic grip.

HOW CAN I TELL IF MY SPOUSE IS DEPRESSED?

First of all, you should know that everyone goes through periods in their lives when they feel down or melancholy. It's part of being alive, and is not something to be concerned about. That is not considered depression. If, however, a person feels extremely down day after day for several weeks or more, depression is a strong possibility. Depression often prevents people from carrying on their normal lives. Although stressful life events, like a death in the family, financial problems, a debilitating illness, or relationship problems can trigger depression, sometimes depression appears to come out of the blue.

There are many symptoms of depression. Some people experience practically all of them, while others only a few. The major thing you should be concerned about is a significant change in how your spouse feels and/or interacts with you and your family. Here are some typical symptoms:

Changes in sleeping habits	(excessive sleep or insomnia)
Changes in eating habits	(compulsive eating or no appetite)
Lethargy	Lack of motivation
Loss of pleasure	Irritability
Loss of concentration/poor memory	Excessive crying
Apathy	Withdrawal
Thoughts of death or suicide	Loss of interest in sex

WHY IS MY SPOUSE DEPRESSED?

Although you might be frustrated with your spouse for being so down in the dumps and find it impossible to fathom why s/he doesn't just pick himself/herself up by the bootstraps and get on with life, it isn't quite that simple. Depression is a serious mood disorder that makes it difficult for people to function. Unless they actively fight the depression, they can't just snap out of it.

But what causes depression? Depression is a complex disorder. There are no single causes, nor are there single solutions. There is evidence that depression is not a purely biochemical or genetic disorder, nor is it purely a psychological disorder. It's both. Although brain chemistry undoubtedly affects how we think, feel, and behave, it's also true that how we think, feel, and behave affect brain chemistry.

BIOLOGICAL CAUSES

It is certain that genetics and biochemistry are correlated with depression. Having a family history of depression increases your risk for developing the disorder. However, it is unclear whether this increased risk is due to a genetic vulnerability or the fact that the depressive thinking patterns that accompany depression can be learned and passed down from generation to generation.

Depression can also be caused by imbalances in brain chemicals called neurotransmitters—serotonin, norepinephrine, and dopamine. Among other functions, these brain chemicals appear to play an important role in the regulating of the secretion of hormones, such as estrogen, progesterone, cortisol, melatonin, and endorphins, which are also believed to affect emotion.

OTHER BIOLOGICAL CAUSES OF DEPRESSION

In addition to fluctuating hormones or brain chemicals, there are other biological components to depression. Certain chronic illnesses like heart disease, hypothyroidism, stroke, diabetes, cancer, and Alzheimer's disease have been linked to depression, as well as some medications such as certain diuretics and heart medications, blood pressure drugs, and some drugs used to treat arthritis and Parkinson's disease. Occasionally, steroid medications and cancer treatment drugs also cause depression. Depression may also be a warning sign or symptom of a serious underlying disease such as a brain tumor, multiple sclerosis, or cancer of the pancreas.

Use of alcohol and nicotine has also been associated with depression. Although it was originally believed that depressed people abused these drugs, it is now thought that the drugs themselves can actually cause depression. Vitamin deficiencies such as B_{12} and folate have also been linked to depression.

TRIGGERING EVENTS

When life throws hardship our way, it's not unusual for people to become depressed. However, after dealing with their grief and sadness, most people get their lives back on track within a reasonable period of time. For some, though, the road to recovery from these stressful life experiences is considerably more rocky. Getting back on track is a more elusive goal. The stressful event sparks a bout of depression that is hard to shake. Some events that have been known to trigger a more lasting depression are the following:

Death of a loved one	Job loss
Financial loss	Any major life change
Childbirth	Divorce
Midlife crisis	Menopause
Breakup of a relationship	Children leaving home
Loss of health or independence	

PSYCHOLOGICAL CAUSES

It is believed that depression is triggered by pervasive negative thoughts about ourselves and the world around us. In other words, if we spend the majority of our time thinking pessimistically, we are bound to get depressed. Then when depression sets in, it's harder to break free from the persistent negative thinking. When thinking is distorted in this way, people start to convince themselves that the negative thoughts are true, and that things will never improve. Depressed people search for clues about their unhappiness in their past and focus on every negative experience, deepening the depression. Their glasses are half empty. Hopelessness sets in. In short, from a psychological perspective, twisted thinking is at the root of a problem with depression.

From this perspective, the depressed person needs to learn how to change the way s/he looks at his/her life. S/he needs to recognize that his/her thinking has been distorted and learn how to think about things more objectively. People can learn skills that are designed to change their thinking patterns.

But what kinds of negative thoughts get people stuck? Depressed people ruminate about many things including poor self-esteem, anxiety, anger/ sadness over childhood experiences or other past experiences, guilt, hopelessness about the future, confusion about life goals and so on. Sometimes negative thoughts have less to do with the depressed individual and instead revolve around *interpersonal* issues such as feelings of resentment, hurt, and anger toward other people in their lives. Although research shows that healthy relationships tend to guard against depression, unhappy relationships trigger feelings of despair. This is especially true if the depressed person feels s/he has tried to improve the relationship for a long time to no avail.

WHAT ARE THE TREATMENTS FOR DEPRESSION?

There are many actions a depressed person can take to help himself/ herself. Here are some ways to get started:

GET A COMPLETE MEDICAL PHYSICAL TO RULE OUT BIOLOGICAL CAUSES

It is just common sense to eliminate any physiological causes by getting a thorough medical checkup. A physician can determine whether illness, medications, hormone fluctuations, or some other underlying condition is prompting feelings of depression and make a recommendation to address the problematic physiological aspects. Make sure you are not taking any over-the-counter or prescribed drugs that can contribute to depression. That includes antihistamines, tranquilizers, sleeping pills, and narcotics.

BEGIN THERAPY WITH A GOAL-ORIENTED THERAPIST

Make sure the therapist adheres to a goal-oriented, skill-building therapy model such as solution-oriented, cognitive, behavioral therapy rather than one that is focused on analyzing the cause of the depression. These therapy models offer clients specific tools for breaking the patterns of depression.

MEET WITH A PSYCHIATRIST OR FAMILY DOCTOR TO ASSESS THE NEED FOR ANTIDEPRESSANT MEDICATION

There are many different medications available that are effective in dealing with depression. No two people react the same way to specific antidepressants. Some people experience little or no side effects, whereas others are much more troubled by them. For this reason, it's important to consult with a physician who is knowledgeable about the broad range of medications available. Frequently, a trial and error process is necessary to discover the medication of choice for a particular individual. Medications should be monitored by a physician.

Also, it is important to keep in mind that unlike aspirin or other pain-relieving medications, antidepressants do not work immediately. It may take several weeks before relief is felt.

Although many people feel that medication is a lifesaver during a serious depression, it is important to combine this approach with psychotherapy. In addition to altering body chemistry, the depressed person needs to make significant changes in his/her lifestyle in order to make future relapses less likely. Psychotherapy can help people explore what they need to change and offer tools for accomplishing these goals.

EXERCISE AEROBICALLY AT LEAST FIVE TIMES A WEEK

Research has shown that regular exercise guards against and alleviates depression. Among countless other health benefits, strenuous aerobic exercise stimulates the release of endorphins, the body's natural opiate.

CHANGES IN DIET—EATING AND DRINKING MORE HEALTHFULLY

A well-balanced diet ensures a healthy body, which is nature's best defense against the stressful symptoms of depression. But in addition to simply eating healthfully, there are other things you should know about the role of diet and depression. For example, when blood sugar is low, mood swings are likely. Slow-acting or low-glycemic carbohydrates, along with high-quality fats and proteins, are believed to stabilize blood sugar levels and, therefore, are considered valuable resources for combating depression. Additionally, it is believed that omega-3 fatty acids, especially DHA from fish or fortified eggs, and supplements of DL-phenylalanine and vitamins B_6 and C are important depression busters. Consider consulting with a nutritionist or naturopath to help design a depression-fighting eating plan.

ALTERNATIVE HEALTH APPROACHES

Finally, there are many alternative methods for dealing with milder forms of depression such as herbal therapy including St. John's wort, the most thoroughly researched natural herb, acupuncture, and meditation. Unlike Prozac and other antidepressants that require a prescription from a physician, St. John's wort and other herbal remedies are available over-the-counter. Acupuncture, a form of Chinese medicine that has gained popularity and acceptance in medical circles in the United States, is based on the idea that a life force called Chi flows through our bodies, but can sometimes become blocked. When this happens, health problems can occur. Acupuncturists place thin needles in certain spots on the body to unblock the flow of Chi, thus restoring the balance. There are many American schools and colleges of acupuncture and Chinese medicine. In states where acupuncture is licensed and regulated, you can get the names of practitioners by calling the state department of health or the department of licensing. Just make sure that the acupuncturist is board-certified.

How should I approach my spouse?

Perhaps you have been reading the treatment options and thinking to yourself, I would love it if my spouse would just try *anything!* But I don't even know how to approach him/her. Or perhaps what you've done so far hasn't worked. Keep in mind that, like every other problem I've addressed in this book, there are no single paths to a solution. You pick a starting place and keep trying alternatives until you hit on something that works. But before you do anything else with regard to this problem, you need to be clear about your goal.

As I see it, your goal should be to convince your spouse *to do something* about being down in the dumps. You want your spouse to take an action. It's not important that s/he admits, "You're right, I'm depressed," or that s/he chooses the particular treatment option you have been hoping for. What matters is that there is movement of any sort. As long as your spouse is willing to do *something,* you are headed in the right direction.

I'M CONCERNED ABOUT YOU

As with any other problem, it's best to start with the simplest, most straightforward approach. When you have your spouse's full attention, say that you are really concerned about him/her. Point out that your partner's behavior has changed toward you and/or other loved ones. Be specific. Give examples about these changes. For instance, say, "You hardly say a word at home to anyone. That's not like you." Or, "Last night when you snapped at me at dinner, I was really concerned because you seem so angry lately. It seems as if you are feeling really down." It's important to be concrete. Instead of saying, "You've seemed listless lately," say, "You haven't left the house for five days in a row, this isn't like you." Tell your spouse that you believe s/he is depressed and that it has been coloring the way s/he thinks and feels about things. Suggest that there are many different things s/he can do to feel better, and that if s/he is open to it, you will help him/her get the help s/he needs.

At this point you should stop, look, and listen. See how your spouse is reacting. If it is positive, you can begin to explore some of the alternatives I've discussed in this chapter and see if anything sounds appealing. If so, try to get your spouse to commit to taking an action. Remember, it doesn't matter what s/he does, it just matters that s/he is willing to do something. If s/he is willing to create a plan of action, you will need to keep your eyes open to see if s/he follows through. If so, be supportive and congratulatory. This will encourage him/her to continue to do what it takes to feel better. If not, perhaps a gentle reminder might do. Sometimes a person is more open to taking suggestions to heart after s/he has had some time to let the ideas percolate a bit. A second reminder might do the trick. However, if more time passes and nothing changes, you can safely assume your spouse is resisting your suggestion. Time to try something else.

If, when you approach your spouse, s/he reacts defensively—either disagreeing with your diagnosis about depression or refusing to do anything about it—you have to stop trying to get him/her to see things your way. You might try varying your language. Rather than use the phrase "depression," talk about his/her being down in the dumps, moody, or in a rut. Sometimes people feel less threatened by terms that are slightly less clinical or pathological. Using the phrases "down in the dumps" or "in a rut" make the depression seem more "regular." And in the end, whether someone is in a rut or depressed, they have to do many of the same things in order to feel better. So, don't get hung up on labels, just see if you can find something to call your partner's state of mind that will motivate him/her to seek help. If your partner still disagrees about being down, rather than argue, ask him/her if s/he would be willing to talk to a therapist anyway—just to sort things out. If the answer is "no," you need to stop discussing your concern for a few days and try a back-door approach.

Coming in through the back door simply means that you have stopped trying to convince your spouse that s/he is depressed and that s/he should go to a therapist, but you continue to suggest activities that are proven to be effective in alleviating depression. For example, since being active often helps, you might ask your spouse to join a health club with you or go for a walk together. Just don't say, "It will help you feel better." Act as if you are asking him/her to keep you company. Don't allude to the fact that you are acting out of concern for his/her mental health.

However, since you are reading this chapter, it is more than likely that your spouse has vehemently resisted your help. You've probably wondered time and time again how a person could feel bad and not do anything about it. There are many reasons people put off getting help. Sometimes their thinking is so clouded that they fail to recognize how out of sorts they really are. Other times, they are embarrassed to admit they have a problem. Seeking professional help makes them feel like failures. Particularly when someone prides himself/herself in being independent, ego often stands in the way of asking for help. Some people refuse to seek therapy because they just don't believe in it. Perhaps they've heard stories from friends or acquaintances about go-nowhere therapy experiences. Some people do nothing about depression because they assume it will eventually go away on its own. Others do nothing because they feel hopeless about the possibility for change.

However, there is another reason your spouse may be resisting your suggestion to seek help. If s/he has told you that *you* are the cause of his/her unhappiness, your spouse probably feels that you (of all people) are not exactly the best person to be shelling out advice. If instead of acknowledging your partner's negative feelings about your marriage (which is counterintuitive), you insisted that depression is the culprit, your partner is probably digging in his/her heels because agreeing to seek help would feel like admitting s/he's wrong and you're right. Although this kind of thinking is absurd, it is probably part of the reason your spouse is stuck in neutral.

If your spouse has blamed you for his/her unhappiness and refuses to see the role that distorted thinking has played in the problem, I have some very strong advice for you. *You need to stop defending yourself and telling your partner that s/he's depressed.* This is only making your spouse more determined to prove you wrong. S/he will recall and rehash each and every unhappy moment in your marriage to provide evidence that you have destroyed his/her life. Research shows that when you ask depressed people about their lives, what they tend to remember are depressing events. Happy people, asked the same question, tend to remember happy events. So, a person's current mood state has everything to do with how s/he evaluates his/her life. If you have thought that your spouse's thinking is off-base and that his/her perceptions about your life together is biased, you are absolutely right. But whatever you do, you need to stop trying to get your spouse to see the light. You know you're right, I know you're right, and for now, that will have to be enough. The most loving thing you can do right now is to stop trying to prove to someone who isn't thinking clearly that s/he isn't thinking clearly. Understand?

This may make complete sense to you, yet you may be asking yourself, "If I don't try to uncloud my spouse's thinking, what should I be doing in the meantime?" That's what the rest of this chapter is about—solution-oriented strategies for dealing with your depressed spouse.

One more thing: before you read the specific techniques, remember:

- Be patient.
  If your spouse is fairly depressed, it may take a while for him/her to either get help or to start to do the things that will provide relief from the depression. Don't expect change to happen overnight. Don't become impatient and revert to your old ways of trying to convince your spouse that s/he is depressed. Just stay solution-oriented and have faith that things will improve because eventually s/he will want life to be different. Change can be a slow process.

- Try not to take things personally.

  Yes, I know it feels next to impossible to remain calm when your spouse is telling you that you are the source of misery in the world or when s/he is nasty and unloving. You need to remember that your spouse's mind is temporarily out of order and you should try as hard as you can not to take things s/he says personally. Unhappy people say things they don't mean or that they shouldn't. They're miserable. They're lonely. They're desperate. They just aren't thinking clearly. Their accusations aren't a reflection of you. They are a reflection of the hurt and pain your spouse is experiencing right now. When your spouse condemns you, rather than defending yourself (if that's what you've been doing), say something like, "I'm sorry you're feeling so bad about us. I certainly wouldn't have intentionally done anything to hurt you."

The suggestions above will require a great deal of self-esteem and self-control. You have to feel centered and good enough about yourself to not allow negative comments about you define you. You will be more likely to be able to accomplish this sort of detachment if you take the time to feed your soul. Do things that make you feel good. Don't let your depressed spouse be the center of your world. Surround yourself with people who love you and who understand your situation. Don't hang out with people who say, "Why in the world would you want to put up with that?" They don't understand. They've been victims of the divorce trap. If these "protective" folks are good friends of yours, tell them, "I appreciate your caring, but I want to make my marriage work." Then, stop complaining about your spouse to them; they don't appreciate what it takes to stay married. Find other friends to support you. Weathering this depression storm will probably be the hardest thing you've ever done. But if you hang in there and your spouse begins to see the light of day, you'll understand why the wait was well worth it.

WHAT TO DO WHEN YOUR SPOUSE IS DEPRESSED

The techniques in this section will sound familiar to you because they are the same ones I've written about throughout the rest of the book. Here you will learn to apply these methods to your situation. If you need a re-fresher course, reread Chapter 6.

THE MEDIUM IS THE MESSAGE

Some people have told me that since their spouses see them as the cause of their depression, it detracts from their credibility as advice-dispensers. On the other hand, their spouses have been more receptive when the concern comes from other respected and loved friends and rela-tives. You might consider asking someone your spouse loves to have a heart-to-heart with him/her and confront the issue of depression.

Before you take this step, I must tell you that it is somewhat risky. For one thing, if your spouse believes that you put a friend or relative up to the task of confronting him/her, it is highly likely that your spouse will be an-gry at you. The only way this works is if it appears to happen naturally. Even then, if your spouse thinks the conversation originated with you, there might be some negative repercussions. Having said that, this method does work sometimes.

Another strategy that has some merit is that of letter writing. Count-less people have told me that although their discussions about their spouses' depression had failed miserably, letters seemed to have worked. If you haven't already written your spouse a letter expressing your concern and love, you might consider this option. It is important that you not try to prove the fact that s/he is depressed, but rather that you emphasize your love, caring, and concern that s/he is feeling bad and unhappy. Ask your spouse what s/he would like you to do to make things better.

Leave the letter where your spouse will find it, but say nothing. Wait and see if s/he responds. Don't get frustrated if your spouse says nothing. Observe his/her behavior in the days that follow to see if there is any change at all. Resist the temptation to ask what your spouse thought about the letter. Let your spouse take the lead here. If nothing is said and nothing changes, scratch letter writing off your list of effective strategies to try in the future.

FOCUS ON THE EXCEPTIONS

Life isn't *always* bleak, even for depressed people. There are moments, hours, even days when the depression seems to slip into the background.

The problem is, your partner fails to notice these exceptions and fixates on the times when s/he feels down. This "half-empty glass" perspective compounds the problem in that it makes your spouse's bad feelings seem even worse. You can help your spouse build a more objective view of things by catching him/her in the act of being happier, more involved, more upbeat, and subtly bringing it to his/her attention. Let me give you an example.

Angie's husband, Bart, had been depressed for several months. He was withdrawn, accusatory, and showed little interest in their three children. Angie had tried everything she could think of to get Bart to go for therapy, or at least admit he had a problem. Nothing worked, and Angie was starting to question her commitment to their marriage. She couldn't envision spending the rest of her life with a man who showed little caring or interest in her or their family.

Before deciding to divorce, she consulted with me. I told her to catch Bart in the act of feeling a little better, acting more like his former self, and then reinforce his behavior by complimenting him and acknowledging his efforts to be part of her life.

Over the next few days, Angie noticed that Bart had taken some steps to be involved with their children. He read them bedtime stories, bathed them, and seemed to talk more than he had in previous weeks. Although she didn't consider children being read to or bathed to be remarkable acts—fathers are supposed to do that sort of thing—she realized that because of his depression, it probably required an extra push on his part to motivate himself. She decided that rather than take these actions for granted, she would let him know how much she appreciated them. "The kids really seemed happy that you read them to sleep last night. It means a lot to them. I know that you're not always in the mood to do that, but I'm glad you pushed yourself because they love having you be part of their lives." Then she said nothing more.

Then Angie came home from work one day and heard Bart playing his guitar. Although this is something he used to do on a regular basis, he hadn't played guitar in weeks. Although prior to our meeting, Angie wouldn't have attributed much significance to his making music, she now recognized that guitar playing was part of the "good old Bart," and something she wanted to encourage. She simply commented, "It's good to hear music in the house again." He said, "Thanks." Three days later, he began playing guitar again on a daily basis.

Angie decided that instead of urging him to do something about his depression, she would help make him more aware of the fact that he wasn't depressed all the time. When Angie paid more attention to Bart's better times, not only did this help Bart, it also helped Angie. Like Bart, she learned that his depression wasn't all-pervasive. This helped her to see her husband as a person who had his occasional bouts with depression as opposed to his being a depressed person and encouraged her to be more upbeat and less cautious in his presence. It's entirely possible that Bart's improved mood was, in part, a reaction to Angie's more optimistic stance.

So, if you haven't already, put focusing on exceptions to work for you. Don't talk about depression at all. Just let your spouse know how much you like what is happening when s/he is less unhappy, more cooperative, more involved, or more himself/herself. Then watch what happens next.

ACT AS IF

It's clear that Bart's depression had taken its toll on Angie. She became resentful, hurt, and most of all, tentative. She felt as if she were walking on eggshells around her husband and worried that the littlest thing she might do wrong could set Bart off; she had been operating in a defensive mode for weeks. Angie hated coming home because she dreaded the feeling of doom and gloom that had permeated their home.

You don't have to have a degree in psychology to begin to imagine how Bart might have been reacting, not only to his negative thinking and feelings in general but to Angie's defensive behavior. Her sulkiness and cautiousness might have triggered him to react negatively. Of course, Angie believed that Bart's unhappy behavior was not caused by her in any way, and yet, when she began searching for and expecting good things to happen, he started acting less unhappy. Interesting, isn't it?

Although you might not be aware of it, you may inadvertently be signaling to your spouse by your own behavior that you are expecting him/her to be grouchy or sad. Ask yourself, "If I thought that my spouse was fine and in a really good mood, how would I approach him/her differently? What would I do that I haven't done in a long time because I've been nervous about his/her mental state?" Then, whatever it is you would do or used to do in the past when things were less shaky, start acting as if. Do the things you would do if you felt more confident that your spouse was okay or that there would be light at the end of this depression tunnel. Just start acting more confident about that and watch what happens.

Andrew was very upset about Jessie's state of mind. She seemed depressed and very disengaged from him. Because there was a history of depression and failed marriages in her family, Andrew was fearful that depression might destroy their marriage as it had done to those of two of her sisters. He vowed not to pressure her at all. Although prior to Jessie's withdrawal, they communicated their feelings about themselves and their lives very often, he didn't want to force her to open up. Andrew decided to give her space to sort out her own feelings and pretty much left her alone.

But time didn't heal Jessie's wounds; she got more and more depressed. Although Andrew wasn't sure how to handle things anymore, he got inspired by the act-as-if technique. He realized that, when he felt more confident about their marriage, talking to Jessie about her life used to be a very important part of what they did together. He realized that he had given her space because that's what he thought she needed and he feared doing anything wrong. However, when he asked himself how he would handle things differently if he felt more confident that her depression was just a passing phase and that their marriage was not in jeopardy, the answer was that he would do what he had always done when Jessie was upset. Andrew decided he would talk to Jessie and show his concern. If she initially resisted his pursuing her in this way, he would persist. That's what had always worked for him in the past and that's what he was going to do now. And it worked! Jessie started sharing her feelings more openly and seemed relieved that he expressed his concern for her and their relationship. Eventually, Jessie agreed to go for counseling and within a short time, she was feeling much better and their marriage improved.

Do a 180

Life is funny. Someone you love gets depressed. You try to cheer that person up. You say, "Things aren't so bad," or "You'll feel better tomorrow," or "Why don't you take some medication?" or "Please get some help." You assume your suggestions are viewed as acts of love and that they will help your loved one feel better. Unfortunately, it doesn't always work that way. Sometimes the very things you do to try to help your spouse feel better make him/her feel that you don't understand the depth of his/her despair, and that makes your mate feel more depressed.

I know that your suggestions and pep talks are well-meaning. But as I've stressed before, well-meaning, even logical approaches don't guarantee effectiveness. Sometimes you have to do the exact opposite of what you've been doing to achieve positive results. Here's an illustration.

Mike was a retired trucker who could no longer work due to a back injury. He sat at home doing very little and feeling sorry for himself. He complained about being unhappy but never followed through with any of my suggestions to consider less physically demanding employment or other activities that might help him feel better. His mood did not improve.

I asked him about his wife and what she thought about his current situation. He told me that his wife was a nurse and that she was very concerned about him. She tried to get him to socialize with neighbors and relatives but he just didn't feel like it. She tried to get him to consider finding a "lightweight" job, but that wasn't too appealing to him. He knew she loved him and that she was frustrated with his lack of progress. I asked him if he would mind if she came in for a session without him and he agreed.

Adrian was an intelligent, loving woman who had a wonderful sense of humor and a bright outlook on life. She was very upset about her husband and was at her wit's end. She felt that she had tried everything to cheer him up and get him involved in life again. She said that even the neighbors had noticed that he would go days without leaving home or chatting with them as he had done in the past.

I began by acknowledging her efforts to help her distressed husband and letting her know that she was working very hard to motivate him to do something for himself. I talked to her about my seesaw analogy—the more one person does of something, the less the other person will do. I told her that she was the hopeful/positive one in her marriage, which allowed him to be the pessimistic one. She was always suggesting a new plan of action, while he did nothing. I asked her if she was ready to throw the ball back into his ballpark and without hesitation, she said, "Absolutely."

I told her that my suggestion was going to sound weird, but that I thought she should try it as an experiment. She needed to become outwardly less optimistic to give him a chance to rise to the occasion and defend himself. I suggested that she go home and tell him that she'd been expecting too much from him. She wanted him to go back to the times when he was happy, fun-loving, and interactive, but now she realized that because of his back injury, he might never be the same. I told her to tell him that she recognized that what she needed to do was to establish a life without him and find enjoyment without his presence. She should apologize for having missed this point and placed too much pressure on him. I suggested she tell him not to worry, she wouldn't be pushing him anymore because she was committed to becoming more realistic about his condition. And then she should end the conversation.

Adrian laughed out loud; she understood completely. She told me that she loved it and asked if I could think of any other creative ways to get the message across that she had "given up on him."

I suggested that Adrian go to nursing homes in their area, pick up four or five different brochures, and without saying a single word, leave them scattered throughout the house in plain view. If her husband asked about them, she was to be vague, saying that she was just checking them out as possible referrals for clients, nothing more.

Then I told her to start making lots of social plans for herself without consulting with him or asking him to join her as she had done in the past. Mostly, I urged her to keep her eyes open to see how he was responding. Two weeks later, she returned with an update.

When she apologized to Mike about her pushing him, he was speechless. In fact, he started to tell her that it was natural for her to want him to feel better. She acknowledged what he was saying, but went on to say that her approach wasn't in his best interest so she was going to stop completely. He appeared confused, even somewhat miffed.

A day or two later, she noticed that he had picked up one of the brochures she had left on their nightstand. After that, his behavior took a turn for the better. He started looking for a job immediately and had several interviews lined up by the time she had returned for her second session! She noticed that he was talking to the neighbors and even invited them for dinner, which totally flabbergasted her. He began talking more at home and his attitude seemed vastly improved. She was amazed.

Although Adrian was tempted to compliment him on his changes, I warned her that if she were to become the positive one again too quickly, Mike would revert to being the negative one. I suggested that she say nothing and if he asked whether she noticed the changes in him, she was to say, "Yes, I guess so, but I was wondering if the changes were going to last." In other words, I urged her to allow *him* to prove to her that he was on the mend, rather than *her* proving to him that he could do it. She understood and agreed. I saw her one more time and she reported things were much improved.

Whether it is logical or not, sometimes doing a 180 is the only way to break free from patterns that aren't working. The trouble is, when your spouse is depressed, thinking about doing a 180 feels risky. You fear that your spouse will think you've really given up on him/her and worry that it will make your spouse feel even more depressed. When you abandon your "more of the same" strategy, it's common to worry that your new approach will backfire. But you need to remember that the only way you can really screw up is by doing what doesn't work.

So it's time for you to consider doing a 180. If you've been patient and understanding, it may be time to take a strong stand and set limits for how you'll be treated. If you've been calling your spouse on his/her behavior, you should probably let things slide and show more understanding and patience. If you've been bending over backward to please your spouse, you might try pleasing yourself instead. If you've been trying to get him/her to talk about what's wrong, you probably should stop acting so concerned. If you've been saying in many different ways, "Things will get better," you need to stop being a cheerleader. The long and the short of it is that no matter what you've been doing in regard to this depression, if it hasn't been working, you need to start doing a 180 right now.

GET A LIFE

Sometimes no matter what you do to help your spouse or get him/her to see the light, *any* effort you make to improve the situation becomes more of the same. You've been focusing your entire life on trying to make your spouse happy or getting him/her to understand how depression is wreaking havoc in your lives and your spouse is not responding. It's time for you to do something entirely different—get a life. Stop trying to fix things. Focus on yourself for a while. Make yourself happy for a change.

Look, if nothing you have done has worked, it may mean that your spouse needs to hit rock bottom before s/he will do anything about changing his/her behavior or getting help. You can't do it for him/her. It's true that some people don't change until things get really, really bad. That's when they feel motivated to do something about their situation. You can't help someone hit rock bottom. The only thing you do is to prolong the agony by helping them feel good enough so that they can put off being proactive.

Ask yourself, "What haven't I been doing lately because I've been so concerned about my spouse's mental health or the state of my marriage?" Make a list of all the activities you've put aside and start penciling them into your calendar. You need to start enjoying your life again, with or without your spouse. This is especially true if you have children. It's bad enough to have a depressed parent, but it's tragic if you have two. You need to make sure there is laughter and happiness in your home and in the lives of your children. You can be a role model for your children, letting them know that life is wonderful and that you enjoy being alive. It's entirely possible that by your making yourself happy for a change, you will also be a role model for your spouse.

If you are a natural caregiver, you may feel guilty at the thought of "abandoning" your spouse to seek personal satisfaction. This will prevent you from doing what you need to in order to increase the chances your marriage will be saved. There is no reason to feel guilty. You are showing your love and caring to your spouse by being willing to dare to try something different when all of your efforts to boost your spouse's spirits have failed. Focusing on yourself and your children is a great thing for you to be doing. So just go and get started and watch what happens.

ONE LAST THOUGHT

Although I said that one of the most loving things you can do is to stop paying attention to your spouse and start focusing on yourself for a change, I want you to know that there are some circumstances when you should not turn your back on your spouse. If your spouse has been talking about death or committing suicide, hurting himself/herself or threatening others, you need to contact your local mental health center or a suicide prevention crisis center. Talk of suicide should always be taken seriously. The professional to whom you speak will be able to direct you to the best course of action given your unique circumstances.

CHAPTER TWELVE

Surviving His Midlife Crisis

Although this chapter is geared toward women, don't skip over it too quickly if you are a man whose wife has suddenly questioned everything about her life. You will find much in this chapter to which you can relate, especially if you are married to a Walkaway Wife. The same advice applies to you if you are a woman married to a man who doesn't quite fit the "midlife" criteria. Men are "maturing" early these days. Some men in their late twenties and early thirties have been known to go through an emotional crisis that sounds, smells, and looks a whole lot like things their older friends experience. So keep reading.

I started calling my husband the Grumpmaster General. He's unhappy (sometimes he'll even call it miserable) and as he sees it, it's mostly because of me. Every time I "fix" something that bothered him (like lose weight, keep house better, initiate sex more), those things turn out NOT to have been that important after all, and then he names something ELSE I've done all wrong.

Since moving out, he has had LASIK eye surgery so he could stop wearing glasses, and has even talked about liposuction and plastic surgery. And now he wants to start his own business. It looks to me like he's dissatisfied with just about everything, and is desperately trying to change things and control things in an effort to make himself happy. If only he'd change himself INSIDE and stop looking to change me or look younger or become the boss of a company— he's looking for happiness in all the wrong places.

After a nineteen-year marriage of fun, faithfulness, and overcoming many obstacles, my husband started finding himself not happy with work, home, me, kids, life in general. Then he started focusing on my flaws and has made them bigger than life and "the target for all his bad feelings" and seems to think if he can just get rid of me, then all his problems will be over. He has rewritten our history to where "nothing was ever good" and does not respond to my changes—my making myself happy, financial concerns that seem to be improving, nor all the wonderful things our family (two adopted kids) have built together. His own father and grandfather had hormonal drops/MLC/ midlife depression, also. He seems to be desperately looking for an instant, easy way out. I fear for our kids so I've suggested we at least hold out until they're grown, which still isn't ideal (that would be four more years) but that seems to just make him panic. He wants to sell our beautiful home, have me leave, and seems to think everything, including our happy, well-adjusted kids, will be great after that.

Does any of this sound familiar? If so, welcome to Midlife Crisis Land. It often strikes men between the ages of thirty-five and fifty-something. You think your marriage is decent. Oh yes, you realize that there are ups and downs, but you also know that no marriage is perfect so you don't get too bent out of shape about it. Then strange things start to happen. You and your spouse are arguing all the time. He starts telling you that he's unhappy in the marriage. In fact, he's always been unhappy being with you. What about all of your fond memories? It was a sham, he tells you. He confesses that he loves you, but he's no longer *in love* with you. You're too fat, too thin, too demanding, too laid back, not sexual enough, too boring, too critical, too unloving. He wants a divorce.

You're crushed. Here's the man you love, the man you vowed to spend the rest of your life with, and he can find nothing good or right about you and your life together. You feel hurt and spend days trying to sort out where things went wrong. Because you love your husband and you want to keep your marriage together, you keep a running list of his complaints and, after you get over your initial shock and defensiveness, you start trying to fix things like a crazy woman. You lose weight. You get a new hairstyle. You buy new clothes. You start being nicer and more affectionate. You stop doing things that annoy him. You bend over backward trying to please him, but his needs seem to be a moving target. Nothing you do makes a difference.

Then his behavior becomes even stranger. He spends long hours with his buddies, works out at a gym trying to win an Arnold Schwarzenegger look-alike contest, buys a new wardrobe, uses new cologne, dyes his gray hair, trades in his cheap reading glasses for colored contact lenses, and if he's financially able, buys himself new expensive toys with motors. If all this weren't enough, he finds a lover who can convince him that he is immortal, sexy, smart, and successful, and that life would be wonderful if he just rode off into the sunset with her. What's going on here? Hold on to your hat. You've entered Midlife Crisis Land and you are in for quite a ride. Why do men act as if their minds have been abducted by extraterrestrial beings? And more important, why didn't these beings take men's bodies too so that it wouldn't be quite so confusing?

Many men wake up one morning and realize for the first time in their lives that they aren't going to live forever. They notice their bodies aging. Their waists are growing, their hair is graying or gone. Their reading glasses have become an annoying necessity. Their sex drive isn't what it used to be. There are wrinkles on their faces along with sagging skin. And then there are those little aches and pains in their joints and other body parts that weren't there the last time they looked. It all adds up to a very depressing epiphany . . . "I'm a middle-aged man." The old gray man, he ain't what he used to be.

Suddenly, he's scared. Life is passing him by, and the only thing slowing him down, he thinks, is you. You and all that you have come to symbolize are his emotional shackle. He's tired of feeling responsible for putting food on the table, buying name-brand clothes for the kids, sending them to college, and having to show up at work every day. Because men often define themselves through their work, if he's been less than successful or less than satisfied with his career, he feels as if he's a failure. He becomes depressed. His only salvation, he convinces himself, is to be free of you.

First, you need to know that you are not the cause of all his unhappiness. There may be things about your marriage that need to be improved and you, like everyone else, aren't perfect, but the emotions he's pinning on you have much, much more to do with him and the way he's handling things right now. He feels so bad about himself that he is striking out, and you just happen to be within striking distance. If you've been feeling dumped on, this is why.

Here's the tricky part. Part of you desperately wants to save your marriage and do what it takes to make him happy. Another part of you keeps asking yourself whether you should be putting up with this insanity. You wonder whether you've lost your mind. "Why in the world," you ask yourself, "would someone subject herself to this kind of abuse?" Your friends worry about your husband but they're even more worried about you. They think you've lost your marbles for considering spending one more day in a thankless marriage.

There are days you agree with them and just when you feel like throwing in the towel (or better yet, throwing it at him) you remember your vows. You remember your children. You remember your history together and what your marriage was like before he pulled the rug out from beneath your feet. You loved him dearly. In fact, you still love him dearly. Despite all that he has said and done recently, you find yourself longing for him. You want him to just snap out of this temporary insanity long enough to put his arms around you and tell you that everything is going to be okay. You can't seem to shake the feeling that love is a decision and you made the decision long ago to stay together "till death do us part."

So you feel desperate to get him to realize that he is going through a phase that will pass. You try to convince him that he's misjudging, misreading, and overreacting. You tell him that things aren't as bad as they seem. You promise things will change soon and that he will feel better about his life. But you notice that he's not buying it. In fact, the more you try to convince him that he's overreacting or undervaluing the good things in your marriage, the more he pulls away from you, blaming you loudly as he goes. You feel abandoned, betrayed, and emotionally empty. Throw an affair into this mix and you start to feel yourself falling apart.

You're at a loss, you don't know what to do. You want to make your marriage work, but it's hard to imagine how even the best divorce-busting techniques could be effective in dealing with a person who is in La-La Land. Despite your frustrations, the bottom line is you want your marriage. So what's a woman to do?

Before you decide to take on the project of saving your marriage, you need to realize a few things:

THERE ARE NO GUARANTEES

Although most men do come to their senses eventually, not all do. You could do all the hard work, and in the end, still get divorced. At the very least, you'll be able to honestly say to yourself that you tried everything. And if you have children, you are teaching them a very, very important lesson: that you must do whatever you can to make your marriage work. Your children will benefit from watching you, no matter what happens in the end.

THIS IS GOING TO BE A LONG HAUL

Midlife crises don't end quickly; they may last months or years, and you need to brace yourself for the journey. Many of the problems addressed in this marriage-saving guide are somewhat less intractable and easier to resolve. Wading through a midlife crisis is a process that simply takes time. You can't rush it. You can't bull your way through it. You just have to remind yourself constantly that there are no quick fixes. And, however long it really takes, it seems a whole lot longer.

EXPECT A ROLLER-COASTER RIDE

The midlife crisis is going to be a full-fledged roller-coaster ride. You will go up and you will go down. Just when you think your husband is showing signs of improvement, he lets you know that, as far as he's concerned, nothing has changed. It's all par for the course. The unpredictability of his moods and his reactions will drive you nuts. But then there will be those times that keep you going, times when, for just a brief moment, things seem normal again. If you ask people who have successfully survived a midlife crisis, they will tell you that the roller-coaster ride was the only route to getting there. So like it or not, fasten your seat belt and invest in a large supply of Dramamine.

WELCOME TO LIMBO LAND

One of the worst parts about how long it takes for your spouse to work his way through his existential dilemma—and how rocky the road will be—is that you will feel that your life has been put on hold. You will feel angry and hurt that you have to wait for him to realize something that he should just have known at the start—that your marriage is worth saving. You will resent the fact that it will feel as if he is calling all the shots. You have to wait for him to change his mind about you and your relationship. You have to wait for him to want to be with you. You have to wait for him to feel better about himself and his choices. You just have to wait. He's setting the pace right now. Not knowing about the outcome of all this will be maddening at times but, for now, you will just have to accept this state of uncertainty .

TO SAY YOU WILL NEED PATIENCE IS A
BIG, BIG UNDERSTATEMENT

If you are a take-charge person, you are about to learn one of the hardest lessons in your life. You are not going to be able to control or exert influence on your partner to speed up this process. You are going to hear and see things that you think are unfair and unjust and you are going to learn very quickly that you are not going to be able to educate your spouse about his wrongdoings. You are just going to have to let things happen, go with the flow. The answers to this puzzling midlife crisis must come from him. You won't be able to guide him or facilitate the process. This will require an enormous amount of patience and self-control. Think about the most challenging thing you've ever done in your life in regard to being patient. Now multiply that by a million. You're beginning to see what I mean.

One of the things that you *can* do to boost your chances of remaining patient is for you to read all that you can about your spouse's midlife crisis. Do research on the Internet and go to bookstores. Talk to people who have overcome this stage in their lives. Just immerse yourself in as much information as you can. Once you become educated about what your spouse is feeling and thinking, it will be easier for you not to take things quite so personally. That will help you remain on track. Don't count on your spouse to help you understand his feelings because he might not understand them himself. Even if he does, he might not want to talk to you about them.

DON'T DEFEND YOURSELF

The best thing you can do when your spouse shares negative feelings about your marriage, his life, or even you is to be a good listener. Acknowledge what he is saying. Tell him that you feel bad that he is so upset about things. Tell him that you wish things had been different. Apologize for things that warrant it. Let him know that you are hearing and taking to heart the things he is unhappy about. This will be challenging because you will be listening with one ear and thinking about what you'd love to say in response at the same time. Resist the temptation to say it. Even if you are "right," pushing the issue will push him away. Don't do it.

DON'T ASK QUESTIONS OR MAKE DEMANDS

It's very important that you give your husband space. He needs time to think, feel, and experiment, even if part of his experimentation involves another woman. If you start making demands right away, you will probably lose him. There may not be much that you can do right now to make things better, but there are a ton of things you can do to make things worse, like interrogation and issuing demands. You will have to develop many strategies to stop yourself from blowing your stack or nailing him to the wall; this will be unbelievably challenging. But that's precisely what you need to do. Discover what helps to keep you on track, whether it's taking a walk, going for a run, calling a friend, logging on to your computer, reading a book, or standing on your head.

FOCUS ON YOURSELF

Although you have read this advice many times in this book, it is here that it is most applicable. It is absolutely essential that you find ways to make yourself happy during this most difficult time. "Easy for you to say, Michele," is what you're thinking. I know, I know. It's hard to imagine how you could be happy while your life is falling apart, but if you are going to come out the other side of this midlife crisis, you are going to have to do it. Whether you were an incredibly independent person to begin with, or someone who preferred doing everything with your man, you are going to have to develop and discover ways to find inner peace *without* him right now. You need to do this for you, for your husband and for your children, if you have them.

Although your husband can choose to put his decision about your marriage on hold, you cannot and should not put your own life on hold. Once you get over the shock of what's happening and grieve, you need to get out a piece of paper and a pen and write down the concrete steps you are going to take to make your life as fulfilling as possible. You need to re-store your sense of self. You are a wonderful person and you should remind yourself of this whenever possible, because you won't be getting lots of compliments from your spouse. You will have to find your goodies somewhere else. Here are some things women have done to help them feel good about themselves and their lives during their transitional periods. This list is by no means comprehensive. I include it simply to jump-start your imagination.

Spend more time with their children

Keep a journal

Re-invest themselves in spiritual activities

Further their education

Join a support group

Devote themselves to their careers

Spend more time with friends

Begin a new hobby

Join a health club

Read self-help books

One more thing to consider. Even if your husband won't go—and whatever you do, you shouldn't press the issue—you might consider going for therapy. If you find someone you like, s/he can help you sort things out and feel better about yourself. Find a professional who is trained in solution-oriented methods and who is pro-marriage. If you go to a therapist who doesn't understand what you are working toward and the methods you are using to get there, s/he will probably try to discourage you from continuing on your marriage-saving path. Be very clear from the start that you are determined to save your marriage. Also, make sure your therapist doesn't subscribe to the "You should tell him how you feel" methodology. It won't work, I promise you. If the therapist suggests that you need to disclose your feelings or that therapy won't work unless your husband joins you in treatment, it should be an immediate red flag for you to find someone else.

I DID IT MY WAY

The one thing you will have to keep in mind throughout this journey is that your husband will have to find his own answers. No matter how much you want to help him, he will not find comfort in the articles you cut out for him, the therapy appointments you want to make for him, the heart-to-hearts you want to have with him, or anything else you wish to do. In the same way that you can't force a baby to walk before he crawls, talk before he babbles, getting through a midlife crisis is a process.

If you have children, you know that there have been times when you've needed to stand back and let them fall so they improve their balance and learn how to get up again. Similarly, you will need to stand back and allow your spouse to find his way. I realize that I have told you this before, but I'm saying it again because I know you will need to take this to heart. You might find yourself reading and rereading this section. Letting go is amazingly difficult, but unless you do, your marriage probably won't work out. You have to learn how to detach from your husband's confusion and let him struggle through it until he sees a clearing.

COMING HOME

I know you are going to have a hard time believing what I'm about to tell you now, but if your husband does eventually decide to recommit to your marriage, life will not be a bed of roses right away. For starters, you have just spent a very long time putting aside *your* emotions and needs. You've had to be incredibly strong. Perhaps your spouse has had an affair and while you've been fighting for your marriage, you've had to put your feelings of rage and despair on the back burner. So, if your husband decides to work on your marriage, although you'll be very relieved, you should expect to be flooded with many other intense emotions. This is normal. It doesn't mean you've made a mistake. It just means you're human.

The way to move beyond these intense feelings is to make your marriage better than it ever was to begin with. This means that you and your husband have lots of issues to work out. You need to identify which parts of your marriage need to be improved. You will need to change, but your husband will need to change too. He will need to show you that he wants to invest his heart into your relationship. He needs to show empathy for what you've been through all these months. But don't expect these changes to happen immediately; it will take time. You will need to continue to remain patient.

Furthermore, if your spouse had an affair that he's decided to end, as much as you'd like him to be thrilled about the fact that the other woman is no longer in his life, it's unlikely that this will happen. Even if his intentions to work on your marriage are good, he will probably be feeling a sense of withdrawal just as someone would if they were giving up a drug. He might feel sad. He might be depressed or irritable. Don't assume he's second-guessing himself. Don't assume he thinks he wants to go back to her. Let him be. He will come out of his funk much more quickly if you, in a sense, give him "permission" to feel that way for a while. This shows him that you know that feeling sad when you end something is normal. It is. Don't make anything more out of it than it is.

But don't lose sight of the fact that you have come such a very, very long way. Think about how things were when he first hit his midlife crisis. Remember how devastated you were and how impossible he was. Things really have changed, haven't they? You should be very proud of yourself. And you should give yourself permission to feel the whole range of feelings you are experiencing right now. Just don't blow all the hard work by slipping back into old ways. You will feel better soon. You and your spouse need to work as a team to get your marriage back on track. You've gotten this far, you can reach your end goal . . . a loving marriage. Just hang in there.

In all honesty, I've never had to do what I am suggesting that you do and I can only imagine the strength it would take to stick to your plan. But I see people do it all the time. Here is a letter from a woman who successfully worked on herself until her husband came back from the brink of a midlife crisis. Use this as an inspiration!

Dear Michele,

Last year at this time (Valentine's Day) I was an emotional wreck! However, here I am a year later and my husband is "in love" with me again and can't stop telling me or showing me! Last Valentine's Day, my husband informed me, again, how miserable he was and how he needed to leave us (married seventeen years and three children). He told me he did not love me and never had loved me. That "I" was his problem and he wanted to find happiness and passion without me. I suspected an emotional affair with another woman.

Well, I am here to tell you that your methods work and you CAN save your marriage BY YOURSELF, if you really want to put forth the time, effort, and PATIENCE that it will take.

MY suggestions:
Don't *push* your husband into therapy with you!
Don't insist on talks about your relationship.
Don't pry and become obsessed with other women he might be seeing.
Work on yourself!
Actions speak louder than words. Change *your* behavior and attitudes *now!* The only person you have *any* control over in this world is *you!!!!*
Men *hate* relationship talks and if they resist therapy, go by yourself!
Don't pursue your husband . . . lovingly *distance!*

I am so happy with my husband's "recovery" and our wonderful NEW marriage. I feel like I am on my honeymoon again after seventeen years. I have no anger or unresolved feelings, now that my husband is surrounding me with such love. I have grown so much over the past year and have much success in many areas to show for it. You see, I was unhappy too, just in denial over the dismal shape of my marriage. I don't appreciate the way that my husband rocked my world, but I am better for it in many ways.

I see no need to live in the past, as the present is wonderful. I have "moved on." All the "talk" in the world cannot create the profound changes that Michele's approach does so effectively.

Louise

CHAPTER THIRTEEN

Overcoming Passion Meltdown

No book on divorce prevention would be complete without a chapter devoted to having a loving and satisfying intimate relationship. Without physical closeness, it's difficult for spouses to feel connected emotionally and spiritually. A nonexistent or unsatisfying sexual relationship triggers low-grade ill will that permeates your life and colors most of your interactions. At first, you fool yourself into thinking that sex isn't that important and that as long as the rest of your marriage is working, everything will be okay. But slowly, almost imperceptibly, things start falling apart.

You find yourselves arguing more often. Every small annoyance becomes magnified. You feel like opponents rather than teammates. You feel hurt and misunderstood. You practice self-protection rather than cooperation and compromise. You stop caring about each other's feelings and needs. You stop being kind.

And yet, as crucial as sex is to having a loving marriage, too many people take their love lives for granted. They know that sex isn't what it used to be, that the passion went out of their marriages years ago, but they do little to revive it. They hear their partner's complaints about not enough frequency, fire, variety, spontaneity, intensity, or emotional connection, but they figure, "He'll get over it," "If she weren't so critical, I'd be more interested," "He just has a one-track mind," or "She's never happy." And nothing changes.

But lingering unhappiness with one's sex life is a formula for marital disaster. It leads to emotional divorces, infidelity, and, inevitably, real divorces. Unless both partners agree to a sexless marriage and are content with that, a marriage void of sex, passion, and intimacy is a marriage doomed.

If you are reading this book, I recognize that it's possible that your spouse doesn't want anything to do with you, has left home, or is emotionally distant. Having sex with you might be the last thing on his/her mind right now. You'd love to put into practice some of the techniques you will read about in this chapter, but you have an unwilling partner. I want to encourage you to read this chapter in its entirety, even if you feel hopeless, because I will clear up many misunderstandings and myths about having a healthy sex life. This information can only be helpful to you in the future.

Second, I also realize that you might be someone whose marriage isn't quite that shaky, and you already understand how important your love life is—you just haven't had a whole lot of success thus far convincing your spouse of it. You'll be reading this chapter, saying to yourself, "Yes, I wholeheartedly agree, but *what do I do* to get my spouse to understand my point of view?" Good question. I will offer you specific tips to help you get your spouse to place more priority on your sexual relationship.

Finally, maybe you're someone whose spouse isn't about to pack up and leave, but s/he has been complaining of being unhappy sexually. If so, arriving at this chapter is nothing short of providential. It will help you understand why your spouse has been so miserable and it will outline the small steps you need to take to rejuvenate your love and make your marriage more satisfying all around. It may help you rediscover feelings of passion you long since thought were dead. And if you aren't completely convinced about the damage a less-than-desirable sexual relationship can have on a marriage, read on. The following is but a small sample of the hundreds of letters I've gotten from people who are feeling a void in their intimate relationship.

I have been married for twenty-seven years, three kids, five grandkids, but I'M YOUNG . . . forty-nine, and my husband is forty-nine. We have not had intercourse more than six times in the last three years. My husband can achieve and maintain an erection long enough for oral sex for him PERIOD. I have tried to beg, plead, talk calmly, ignore the problem, threaten, show him literature, etc.

Well, in the last three months we have had sex zero times. He now says he cannot maintain an erection long enough and feels no desire. He takes medicine for high blood pressure, Prozac for depression, and medicine for sleep. I am convinced that these are the culprits and made an appt. for him with his internist to discuss it but he refused to go. In a loving, calm way I tried to tell him that I understood how hard it would be for him to talk about but that he needs to. To this he responded that "we are too old to be having sex all the time" and that I am obsessed with sex and need to get over it. I told him that I am unwilling to live in a marriage this way but he doesn't seem interested in doing anything about it. We are at an impasse . . . he thinks I expect too much and I say this is way too little.

The sexual aspect of my relationship is what keeps me up at night. My wife and I have had a rather up and down sexual relationship over the ten years we have been together. It was very intense and satisfying in the first year or so and then things began to dwindle off. We have had many discussions (always initiated by me) about our sex life, and she has indicated that she did not feel good about herself because she had gained a lot of weight and until she did feel more attractive she could not respond well.

Recently, she has lost a lot of weight as the result of a job change that required her to be much more active. For a while, this seemed to spark her sex drive, but recently she has backed off in this area. She has also backed off on our relationship, which may account for the lack of interest in sex.

I don't know at this point what the hell to do!! Now she is more desirable than ever, but she has backed off in her interest for me. She says that she just is not interested. I, of course, have not helped matters by being angry and frustrated because I want her more than ever and am being shut down or limited to quickies once in a while. This is driving me crazy.

This lack of sex is more than just a lack of physical attention. It goes deep into a woman's heart. I think in a normal marriage a couple can fight about anything but then they can make love and soothe the bad feelings . . . sort of like a rebirth and start again—a forgiving ritual. But when you are deprived of even that, only bitterness and resentment and desperation accumulate. I have a husband who is a good guy . . . great father . . . good provider, but I have no lover. I'm angry about the wasted years; the years I could have been loving, but spent agonizing about why I was being deprived. It's so much more than sex. It's feeling wanted, and sexy, and desired by the man that you are committed to for life. LIFE! It messes you up in the head.

If having a healthy sex life is so important, what gets in the way? Although there are many different kinds of sexual problems that can create barriers to having an enjoyable sex life, it is beyond the scope of this chapter to cover them all. Instead, I am going to tell you about one of the most common sexual problems driving couples apart . . . that of low sexual desire.

How low is low?

First of all, be assured that almost everyone goes through phases when lovemaking may not be tops on his/her list of things to do. Only when there is a *persistent* lack or dramatic loss of interest or ability to feel aroused should people take steps to investigate alternatives.

Second, unlike vitamins, there are no recommended minimum daily requirements to ensure a healthy sex life. Sex once or twice a week might be great for one couple, yet grounds for divorce for another. Low sexual desire is a problem only if a person experiencing it is troubled by it, or, because of a sizable discrepancy between one person's level of desire and that of his/her partner's, it is creating friction in the marriage. In either case, it's time to take action. The sooner, the better.

Desire discrepancy—when one person is satisfied with very little sex, while the other wants lots—can become a breeding ground for marital problems. The person wanting or needing more sex always feels shortchanged and rejected. The person who is satisfied with less often feels pressured, criticized, or condemned for not living up to the more highly sexed partner's expectations. Rather than try to understand each other's needs, spouses often blame each other for their differences. And it is often the case that the person wanting more sex decides to seek satisfaction outside the marriage or leave.

Who's got the headache?

If the sentence "Not tonight, dear, I've got a headache" conjures up an image of a woman telling her husband she's not in the mood for sex, it is not without reason. It is estimated that approximately forty million women have little desire for sex. As a couples' therapist for over two decades, I've lost count of the number of times I've heard women say, "Sex is the last thing on my mind." They tell me that they prefer doing just about anything—clipping their pets' toenails, balancing checkbooks, or cleaning out ovens—rather than having sex with their partners.

> I am a thirty-nine-year-old mother of a two-year-old. My problem is I have lost my sex drive—I just don't ever feel like it. When my husband and I do have sex, it's always great and I think, why don't we do this more often? But when I think about it later, I would much rather take a hot bath and go to bed early.

However, before you jump to the conclusion that women have a monopoly on headaches, hold on to your hat. You may be in for a surprise. Apparently, despite the enormous number of women who aren't interested in sex, they do not have a corner on the deflated libido market. In fact, many women have been telling me what men dare not . . . it is their *husbands* who are the ones who are just saying no. Read one of countless letters I received after writing an article about low sexual desire in women.

> I just read your article and I'm furious. There are many, many of us women who would LOVE to have a spouse interested in sex. Do you realize how humiliating it is to have a husband who simply isn't interested in sex, touching, kissing, or anything of a physical nature, and then to read articles that perpetuate the myth that men are always more interested in sex than women? This is a bunch of hooey! I've spoken to many women who have this same problem . . . their husbands simply aren't interested. I cannot believe my circle of friends is so different from the average. None of these men are "get-

ting it on the side" . . . they simply are not interested. In my case, my husband of twenty-six years has never been as interested as I in sex, and the last five years it has been nonexistent. Give us a break, lady!

Why don't we hear more about low sexual desire in men? What explains male and female latent libidos? And more important, what can be done to pique sexual desire and bring back those loving feelings?

Why men aren't talking

There are lots of reasons we don't hear more about low sexual desire in men. For starters, talking about sexual problems is very personal. Most people don't do it. And because men pride themselves on their achievements and their independent problem-solving abilities, they are less likely than women to discuss their failures or shortcomings publicly. They prefer working out personal problems themselves.

But perhaps the most significant reason we don't hear much about low sexual desire in men is this. When a woman lacks sexual desire, as confusing or disconcerting as it might be, there are subtle societal expectations that women aren't supposed to be sexual beings; jokes about women's headaches are as American as apple pie. Not so for men. "Because masculinity is *defined* by men's virility and their sexual potency, thinking about, let alone *admitting* to a lack of interest in sex *out loud* strikes terror in men," says Dr. Dennis Dailey, certified sex therapist and University of Kansas professor. So no wonder they don't like to talk about it, think about it, let alone seek help. Men feel an enormous amount of shame to which women often can't relate.

Why we aren't in the mood

Since low sexual desire is common in both men and women, what causes it? Experts agree that a complex mix of physiological, psychological, and relationship factors fuels sexual desire.

Physiological factors

When a person is not "in the mood," it may have something to do with hormones. For example, fluctuating levels of testosterone—one of the primary hormones responsible for sexual desire in both men and women—can account for low sexual desire. In men, testosterone levels often decrease with age, causing a "male menopause," a condition analogous to its female counterpart. When this occurs, it can and often does dampen sexual desire.

Women's sexual desire can also be a result of fluctuating testosterone levels. Judith Reichman, M.D., author of the book *I'm Not in the Mood,* offers new evidence about the crucial role testosterone plays in women's sexuality and how small doses of this hormone can ignite sexual desire.

There are other physiological factors people should consider when examining possible causes for low sexual desire. Illnesses such as circulatory problems, diabetes, or heart, liver, and pituitary disease, can cause sexual dysfunction, which, in turn, can be at the root of libido problems. Medications such as antidepressants, tranquilizers, blood pressure medications, birth control pills, chemotherapy, alcohol, and other illicit drugs can also impact negatively on desire.

Psychological factors

Women's psychological issues

Women often tell me that the sky could be falling, but that doesn't stop their husbands from wanting sex. Conversely, unless a woman is in a positive frame of mind, she's probably not too interested. A myriad of issues can leave her feeling down in the dumps. For example, low self-esteem, stress, poor body image, grief over the loss of a loved one, fatigue, and depression are likely to put a damper on her sexual appetite. Additionally, women who were sexually, physically, or emotionally abused as children might carry unresolved feelings about these experiences into their relationships with their partners. As a result, true intimacy might feel threatening and, therefore, unappealing.

Beyond having negative personal feelings, women seem to have a much more difficult time putting their "to-do list" out of their minds to relax long enough to be turned on. To them, sex becomes more appealing when the dishes are completely done, the laundry is folded, the phone calls are made, job responsibilities are completed, the children are asleep or away, the dog is outside, the counters have been dusted, and so on. Then, and only then, can women concentrate on being intimate with their partners. Men often resent feeling as if they are the very last item on their wives' priority lists.

Men's psychological issues

Since men generally don't talk about their feelings as much as women, women often incorrectly assume they don't have any. But men are prone to having the same feelings that women do, feelings that can get in the way of their desiring an active sex life. These feelings include depression, which can be triggered by a job loss, death of a loved one, low self-esteem, stress, fatigue, a midlife crisis, and so on. As with women, traumatic childhood experiences and misinformation about sex can provoke negative feelings about sexuality.

One thing that is different for men, though, is that even if a woman is not entirely in the mood, she can do a good job at faking it. She can decide to have intercourse and no one will ever suspect that her mind is on her shopping list. Not so for men. Without desire, there is no erection, and without an erection, there is no intercourse. When men experience sexual problems such as impotence, performance anxiety, or difficulty pleasing their partners, it is easy to see how they might anticipate unsatisfying and humiliating sexual encounters and, therefore, avoid them entirely.

Relationship issues

Beyond physiological and psychological causes, there are relationship issues that can be at the root of a decreased libido.

• Passion meltdown—New relationships affect our brain chemistry such that our sexual arousal is at a peak. Over time these chemicals simmer down, as does our sexual passion. People who have low testosterone might be highly stimulated during this courtship period but not so shortly thereafter. Even in healthy, long-term marriages, people need to become creative to avoid sexual boredom.

• Lack of attraction—Changes in appearance, such as weight gain or poor health habits might make a person feel "turned off." Whether it's flat-out wrong or even unfair, many people lose interest in being sexual when their spouses have let their physical appearance slide.

• Arguments about sexual frequency—Oddly enough, the more a couple argues about differences in sexual appetite, the more it can become a problem.

• Poor communication skills—Communication is an important part of any healthy relationship. If a couple is unable to discuss their sexual issues openly and honestly, sexual problems are difficult to resolve, making sex less desirable.

• No sexpertise—Low sexual desire can be the result of sexual encounters that continually leave a person feeling empty. There are many reasons this happens. A primary cause is that one spouse simply doesn't know how to turn the other one on. This is often due to a lack of honest and open communication about sex and what each partner finds stimulating and sensual. Some people shy away from frank discussions about sex because they feel embarrassed, worried about hurting their partners' feelings, or they have the misconception their partners should *just know* what to do without being told. This is unfortunate because most people are lousy mind readers.

In my practice, I am continually amazed at how often couples avoid talking about sex. They will do anything to steer clear of conversations that relate to their intimate relations. Even when I ask them if they feel more comfortable discussing these issues at home, when I'm not around, they tell me that they never talk about sex. I find this hard to fathom. How are you supposed to know what your partner likes, dislikes, dreams about, hopes for, and so on, if you don't talk?

However, even when communication is good, some people don't know their own bodies well enough to offer guidance. They haven't "practiced" enough on themselves. And if you don't know what lights your fire, how in the world is your partner supposed to know?

• Nagging—Men's number-one complaint about their wives is that they nag too much. Criticism and nagging—justified or not—are often major libido busters. But women say that they nag because, when they are forthcoming about their feelings, their partners discount them and are totally unresponsive. This kind of insensitivity is another major libido buster.

• Anger and resentment—Frustration over unpleasant, day-to-day interactions or unresolved, long-standing relationship issues can get in the way of a person feeling amorous. Nothing squelches sexual desire quite as effectively as unexpressed feelings of resentment or anger. Harboring negative feelings is a good way to build a wall around you. This wall prevents people from opening their hearts . . . and their arms to their partners.

• Gender differences—There are differences in the way men and women think and feel that make a satisfying sex life challenging sometimes. As I explain the differences, you may be thinking that they do not apply to you or your marriage. As with any stereotype, there are exceptions. However, the issues I am about to address are so commonplace, I'm certain they will resonate with you in some way. If not, skip this section and read ahead.

Most women need to feel emotionally connected or close to their spouses in order to desire sex. This means that they need to spend time together, talk about personal issues, and do fun things as a couple. In short, they need to share their lives. Once women feel this emotional bond, they are much more receptive to their husband's advances and to initiating sexual encounters themselves. For most women, without this connection, sex is just not appealing. If men go for long periods of time without paying attention to their wives, women shut down emotionally and simply aren't interested in being physically close. In fact, it's the last thing on their minds.

Men, on the other hand, work the other way around. Talking about personal issues and investing themselves emotionally in their relationships are things that don't come quite as naturally to them as to their wives. They have to work at it. They usually don't derive the same thrill from an intimate discussion that their wives do. It takes an effort to share themselves emotionally in this way. However, most men are quite willing to do that *if* they first feel connected on a physical level to their wives. If their sexual relationship has been made a priority and men feel a sexual bond to their wives, then they are willing to extend themselves, opening up in the way their wives desire.

If women feel that their spouses haven't been involved in their lives, they wait for their men to be more loving, attentive, and talkative. They're not particularly interested in being sexual until this happens. On the other hand, if men are unhappy, they stop paying attention to their wives until their women touch them, are sensual, flirtatious, and sexual. He's waiting for her to change, she's waiting for him to change. I've seen many, many marriages go down the drain while both spouses wait passively for the other one to make the first move.

Misunderstanding fuels the distance and waiting game. Many women think a man's need to have sex is just like scratching an itch. They believe that men have biological needs that have nothing to do with emotions or feelings. They think that for men, sex is just a physical release. Because of all the years I've been working with couples, I know this simply isn't an accurate description of how most men feel.

Although no man would disagree that there are times when sex is simply a physical release, this is not the primary motivator or reason men desire sex with their wives. Most men tell me that having a good sexual relationship with their wives makes them feel loved, attractive, connected emotionally, good about themselves as sexual beings, caretakers, and lovers. Many men pride themselves on their ability to please their wives sexually. Since a man's self-concept is often so strongly linked to how he thinks of himself sexually, an unsatisfying sex life often makes him feel less than a man.

But what is most striking about men's reactions to unsatisfying sexual relationships is how important sexuality is in terms of their feeling emotionally bonded to their wives. It really makes them feel close. It brings out loving emotions men often don't feel in other situations. Many women don't understand this part of the male psyche.

Conversely, men completely misunderstand women when they aren't interested in being sexual, a misunderstanding that also fuels the cold war. Since men's need to be close to their wives physically is so important to how they feel about themselves and their marriages, they can't understand why women are so uncaring and cold. They become angry and hurt at the thought that their wives simply don't care about their feelings. And when their wives tell them, "You spend no time with me and then you expect me to want to have sex!" men think that women are using sex as a weapon— "Since you aren't the person I want you to be, I am going to punish you." Although it may feel this way sometimes, it simply isn't true.

Women shut down sexually for several reasons. They are hurt because they don't feel loved and appreciated and they can't put thoughts of resentment and anger out of their heads. If they do have sex, he's fantasizing about an incredibly sensual sexual encounter, while she's thinking, "I can't believe that he came home late without even calling. He hasn't had a meaningful discussion with me in two weeks. I feel like a single parent." Not exactly an aphrodisiac.

• Hormonal differences—There is a physiological gender difference that can also create misunderstanding between couples. Although this isn't always the case, testosterone (one of the main hormones responsible for sex drive) is twenty to forty times more prevalent in men than women. This means that, although men definitely experience problems with low sexual desire, it is less common for men than women. The fact that men generally have much more testosterone than women means that they think about and desire sex more often; they can't understand what it's like *not* to feel the sexual feelings that they do. So many men say, "I know my wife likes sex, but she doesn't show interest in pursuing me. What gives here?" People with high levels of testosterone often can't understand why everyone doesn't spend as much time fantasizing about sex as they do.

Conversely, women with low levels of testosterone don't understand what it's like to live in the body of a person who has a lot of testosterone running through it. I know a woman who, because of her concern about low sexual desire, had a complete physical and was diagnosed as having very low levels of testosterone. Her physician prescribed a testosterone supplement. As soon as it took effect, she found herself looking at other men in ways she hadn't for a very long time. She noticed intermittent sexual thoughts throughout the day. She thought about masturbating, something she hadn't done for a while. In other words, with a higher level of testosterone in her body, her mind and emotions were working differently, very differently. She began to appreciate what her spouse might think and feel over the course of a day, every day. In addition to boosting her sexual desire, this experience with testosterone helped her to be more understanding and empathetic about his sexual needs.

Now that you know some of the reasons people may not be feeling sexual desire, you might be asking yourself, "What do I [we] do about this?"

Tips for the spouse with a lower sexual drive

If sex is the last thing on your mind, here are things to consider:

1. Make having a satisfying sexual relationship a bigger priority in your life. There are at least two very important reasons that you should take your sex life off the back burner and pay attention to it. The first is your relationship with your spouse. Your marriage depends on it. Your spouse's feelings about himself/herself depend on it. Your future together depends on it. You have to stop thinking you can have a great relationship without satisfying sex unless your partner wholeheartedly agrees. Don't resign yourself to passionless lovemaking or a relationship void of true intimacy. Even elderly and chronically ill people can enjoy a robust sex life.

The second reason is that unless you are truly enjoying your intimate relationship, you are really cheating yourself! If you aren't all that interested in sex at the moment, you are probably thinking, "I don't feel cheated at all," but I'd like for you to take a moment and think back to a time when sex was more fulfilling. Really think about it. Wasn't it wonderful? Didn't it feel great? Recall what it felt like to be a more passionate, sensual person. Didn't you feel better about yourself? Wasn't it more fun?

When you think back to times when things were better between you sexually, you may ask yourself what happened to your passion and what caused this change in you. You may also wonder if you will ever feel the same way about being sexual as you once did. Perhaps it's the seesaw phenomenon at work; the more one person does of something, the less the other person does. Well, this holds true for sexual issues as well. Since your spouse has been the one to focus on sex in your marriage and you have felt pressured about it, you have backed away. In fact, it's entirely possible that the cat and mouse dynamic in your relationship has dampened your desire, even fooled you into thinking you don't like sex anymore. But this isn't necessarily so. Your negative feelings or apathy may have more to do with the chase than sex itself.

In order to change this, one of two things must happen. Your spouse can stop chasing (and you better believe that this will be one of my suggestions), or you can become more proactive for making things better between you. Since you are the one reading this, I am going to strongly suggest that it is *you* who has to take charge of changing things. You need to start to figure out the steps you ought to take to feel more passion and desire. Make feeling sexier your pet project. If you don't, you are missing out on one of life's greatest joys, feeling truly intimate with the person you love. Don't shortchange *yourself*. Forget about doing this strictly for your partner or the marriage, do it for *you!!!*

How? Promise yourself that you are going to commit to doing what it takes to improve your sex life. Don't stop until you see signs that things are improving.

Start by telling your spouse that you understand why s/he has been unhappy with your love life and that you are going to do something about it. If s/he replies, "I've heard this before," don't take it personally. This sort of response is based on hurt. Just reassure your spouse that this time things are going to be different and say nothing more.

2. Get a medical checkup. To eliminate physiological causes for your lack of desire, a trip to your family physician or gynecologist may be in order. Ask if hormone replacement therapy such as testosterone would be appropriate. Evaluate whether side effects from medications or medical conditions are a factor in your situation. Discuss whether herbal remedies or dietary changes may be helpful.

3. Schedule an appointment for you and your partner with a therapist who is trained and experienced in the area of sexuality. If you are a man whose sexual desire has plummeted due to your having sexual problems such as impotence or performance anxiety, a certified sex therapist can teach you many different techniques to overcome these difficulties. You might also consider taking a drug such as Viagra, which will help you have and maintain an erection.

I know it is really difficult for a man to admit he is worried about low sexual desire and even more difficult to ask for help in this area. But I urge you to do precisely that. You need to put your pride aside and get your sex life/marriage back on track. Your wife may be understanding at the moment, but if you put things off much longer, she might not be around. Read what one desperate woman wrote about trying to rekindle the spark in her marriage:

> While it's hard on men to admit when they can't perform they need to get over it and realize that there are more important things in life than their ego. The following incident is by far the most damaging thing I have ever faced in my personal intimate life with my husband and I doubt I'll ever forget it.

On our twenty-fifth wedding anniversary I planned a very romantic evening with him. He was at work and I went out and bought new lingerie, some light snacks, the same wine we had the first night we went out, rented a top floor hotel room of a five-star hotel near where he worked (since it was midweek and he would have to work the next day). I brought a clean set of work clothes for him for the next day and then left the hotel key, panties sprayed with my perfume, and a note hanging from the visor of his pickup and went back to the hotel to wait. I lit candles all around the room, had music with me and around 6 P.M. the phone rang. Picture me, giddy with anticipation at how surprised and turned on he will be and I race to the phone and he says, "What the hell are you doing? I have to work tomorrow!! If you want to get f**ked can't you wait until the weekend??? I'll see you at home." Never in all my forty-nine years have I felt a blow like I felt that night. I hung up, got drunk, and stayed in the room by myself. He showed up around 4 A.M. and wanted to know why I wasn't home.

If you are a woman with low sexual desire, a certified sex therapist can offer you a great deal of knowledge about sexuality and the skills to help you tap into your sexual side. Regardless of your gender, if your partner won't join you, go alone.

4. Care about your spouse's feelings. Although you have had very valid reasons for not being in the mood, I hope it's clear by now that your spouse has probably felt hurt and rejected because of it. I know this has not been your intention. Far from it. But part of the healing that must take place between the two of you involves your active participation in things that will help your partner feel better. (The same goes for your spouse, as I'll discuss in the next section, where I offer tips for the more highly sexed spouse.) Here are a couple of suggestions that might help boost your spouse's morale.

Flirt—If you think back to earlier times in your relationship, I bet the two of you were more flirtatious. I bet there were pats on the butt, a wink of your eye, a kiss blown across a crowded room, lightly touching each other in passing, a suggestive smile, a well-timed compliment about your spouse's appearance, and so on. This kind of playfulness is an important part of keeping passion alive. Put more energy into letting your spouse know that s/he is attractive by flirting.

Don't just say "no"—If you aren't in the mood, and sometimes you won't be, it's okay to say "no." You shouldn't feel bad about it. However, if you do say, "no," it's important that you make an alternative suggestion. Perhaps later in the day might be better for you. Or, just because you aren't in the mood yourself doesn't mean you can't do something to pleasure your spouse. Although your spouse might initially insist that the only way s/he is interested in being sexual is if your heart is totally into it, convince him/her otherwise. Since your sexual desire might always be lower than your spouse's, there is nothing wrong and everything right with the idea of your pleasing your spouse from time to time when s/he is in the mood. It does not have to be reciprocal. Convince your spouse that you really feel good about giving to him/her in this way.

5. Look for the small flutters. Dr. Pat Love, coauthor of *Hot Monogamy*, suggests that it is frequently the case that people with low sexual desire never experience earth-shattering sexual urges as do their more sexually-oriented partners. For them, it's more like barely noticeable, mild tremors. Rather than assume that the Tidal Wave will be the cue that it's "sex time," look for more subtle signs.

For example, have you ever had even a fleeting thought that your partner looks good tonight or that you like his/her cologne/perfume, or that you find yourself attracted to someone on television and it puts you in a slightly sexy mood? If so, great. This is a wonderful starting point. Take an action. "When you feel even the slightest pulse of desire, follow through with it," says Dr. Love.

6. Put on your running shoes. Joggers always say that the hardest part about running is putting on your running shoes. So too with sex. I wish I had a dollar for every time I've heard a person say, "I really wasn't in the mood at all at first, but once we got into it, I enjoyed myself." When people nudge themselves, even halfheartedly, to "get their feet moving," their pleasurable physical sensations often override any reason to resist.

Unlike the last suggestion where you are advised to look for the small flutters, I am now suggesting that you don't necessarily need to feel turned on at all in order to initiate sex or respond to your partner's advances. If you push yourself a bit, you will see whether the caressing and touching *puts* you in the mood. Give it some time. You'll probably surprise yourself. So, get out those running shoes . . . just do it.

7. Focus on the exceptions. In your quest to figure out what turns you on, you should do what I've suggested you do throughout this book, focus on the exceptions. Identify what has worked to turn you on in the past. Recall times you were feeling sexier and ask yourself what you were doing differently then. Were you taking more time for foreplay? Were you having sex in different positions, locations, times of day, week, or month? Were you in better shape back then? Was your partner? Were you using sexual devices such as a vibrator? Were you more active in your life?

As you begin to ask yourself these questions, you will notice that some of the conditions for feeling more sexual are either no longer part of your life or even a remote possibility. For example, some people tell me that sex was better before they had children. As far as I know, having children is an irreversible decision. If some of the conditions are not doable, ask yourself, "What was different back then? How did not having children make things different?"

People often say, "Things were just more spontaneous." Although it's impossible to be very spontaneous when you've added children to your lives, you certainly can plan for some spontaneity. Call the in-laws or close friends, have them take your children overnight. Plan a weekend getaway. In other words, although it may not be perfect, you can rearrange your lives so that you can replicate at least part of what was working for you back then.

8. Experiment with novelty. Sexual relationships often become boring when you do the same old thing over and over. Decide to become adventurous and try things you haven't tried before to see if you find them enjoyable. Explore and experiment until you know exactly what turns you on. Do you like back rubs, hot baths, sexy lingerie, certain kinds of touching, some positions more than others, moving slowly or speeding up? The possibilities are endless.

9. Talk openly about your preferences. As you begin to figure out what you like and don't like, you have to commit to discussing it openly and specifically with your spouse. Don't be embarrassed. Unless you address this directly, you aren't going to get very far. Review the goal-setting chapter to remind yourself about using action-oriented terms. For example, it isn't enough to tell your partner, "I would prefer we 'make love' rather than 'have sex.'" You need to be able to put into action-oriented terms what you mean by "making love." For instance, you might say, "To me, it feels like we are making love when we spend more time kissing and we keep our eyes open," or "When you touch my hair or touch me lightly on my face, it feels more tender and that makes me feel as if we're making love." It might feel strange at first to be *this* specific about your sexual encounters, but your partner won't understand your needs unless you are.

Sometimes it's hard to put into words the things that turn you on. If so, offer a "hands-on" demonstration. *Show* your spouse what to do. If this is uncomfortable for you, consider reading an "improve your sex life" self-help book together at night. It will stimulate some great discussions and who knows what else. Although there are many books from which to choose, the one I most strongly recommend is *Hot Monogamy,* by Dr. Patricia Love and Jo Robinson. If the process of talking things out seems daunting, see a certified sex therapist.

10. Improve your self-esteem and outlook on life. If personal issues are preventing you from feeling good about yourself and your life, it's time to give yourself a boost. You can't rely on your marriage to be the sole source of your happiness. Everyone must take responsibility for his/her own mental health. If you are feeling crummy, it's time to do something about it. Pamper yourself. Spend time with friends. Take a challenging class. Develop a new hobby. Exercise regularly. Cut back or eliminate alcohol and tobacco. Read a good book. Be kind to yourself. Take time to nurture your spiritual side. Find a good therapist.

Along these same lines, many times people stop being interested in sex when they stop feeling good about their bodies. A poor body image often makes people feel self-conscious and they will either avoid sexual encounters or be so tense that they don't enjoy themselves. If you are one of these people, you need to do something to change the way you feel about your body. If you have gotten out of shape and aren't fit, it's time to start eating better and exercising. The benefits of being in shape extend far beyond your improved sex life. You'll feel better, look better, and increase the chances you'll stay healthy.

11. Work on your relationship. If the dip in your sexual desire is due to negative feelings about your marriage or your spouse, it's time to do something constructive about it. *Stop blaming your spouse.* You need to take responsibility for making things better so that you will feel more loving toward your spouse. Sign up for a marriage education class —learn new communication skills and methods for handling conflict. Find a skilled marital therapist to help you uncover real solutions to the difficulties you've been having. Again, if your partner won't join you, go yourself. You must get off dead center!

But don't wait until the issues in your marriage get resolved before you start putting energy into restoring your passion. Your marriage won't last that long. And here's a little secret. When you do, you may notice that the relationship problems and issues about which you were so concerned have totally disappeared.

Although you may not agree, it is entirely possible that your spouse has been acting unkindly and selfishly because s/he is unhappy with the marriage. And the reason s/he is unhappy with the marriage is the topic of this chapter—sex. Since s/he feels unfulfilled, s/he is not being kind, loving, and sensitive in return. Once you begin being more attentive and your spouse becomes more satisfied, I wouldn't be surprised if your spouse starts being nicer to you in return. Let me give you an example.

A while back, I was a facilitator for a group of women who wanted to have better relationships with their husbands. Somewhere during the third meeting, the women started to put their husbands down; the conversation almost bordered on male-bashing. When I concluded that the conversation was no longer productive, I asked the women, "Tell me, how is your sex life?" There were eight women. Their responses ranged from "nonexistent" to "mediocre." No one said "good."

So I asked if they would be willing to try an experiment. They said "yes." I told them that for the next two weeks I wanted them to pay more attention to their husband's sexual desires, to be more affectionate, to spend more time making love. Although they thought it a strange request, they agreed and off they went!

Two weeks later, they returned, giggling like little girls. Curious as to what the hubbub was all about, I asked them what was going on. After the laughter died down, one of them said, "I initiated sex much more often than I usually do and I absolutely could not believe the change in my husband! He rarely does his fair share around the house or with the kids and in the last two weeks he's put up wallpaper, grouted in between the tiles, read the children bedtime stories, and taken them to school so that I could sleep in a little later on a few mornings. I don't believe it!"

Another woman said, "I wasn't sure how I was going to approach him differently when you gave the assignment. Since he was due to come home late that evening I thought I would just take a bath, get myself in the mood. I lit candles and burned incense. Lo and behold, he came home much earlier than expected, found me in my mood-enhancing bath, took off his clothes, climbed in the bath with me, and we had a most sensual experience. Besides having a great time, I swear, this experience did something to him. The rest of the week, he was much more attentive and caring. He made dinner for me several times, something he doesn't often do. I liked it so much that I kept up my end of the bargain and was much sexier with him. Although we had been arguing almost every day when I started this group, we haven't argued at all in the last two weeks. This is good stuff!"

The list of "miraculous" changes was never-ending. Couch potato husbands turned into men these women only dreamed of. Whoever said that the way to a man's heart is through his stomach was dead wrong. (By the way, if you are a man with lower sexual desire than your partner, know that this same dynamic works with highly sexed women as well. Once you start paying more attention to your wife's sexual needs, she will respond more lovingly to you. You will like her more. Trust me on this one.)

By now, the story I just told should not be a surprise to you at all. One of the basic ideas in this program is that when one person changes, the relationship changes. That's Divorce Busting 101. So, all you really have to do is to tip over the first domino. Show your spouse more affection and attention, then watch the miraculous results.

Tips for the spouse with a higher sexual drive

1. Don't take it personally. Differences in sexual desire among couples are very, very common. Although it is hard to have your advances rejected repeatedly without taking it personally, you need to remind yourself that your spouse's lack of interest in sex just may not be about you, your attractiveness, or your qualities as a human being. It may simply be a matter of a hormone deficiency, other physiological problems, or feelings s/he has about himself/herself. Although you undoubtedly still want things to change, try to develop a little empathy for your spouse. Chances are, given the choice, s/he would prefer to feel turned on easily. It's not exactly a picnic to feel disinterested in something your spouse thrives on! S/he probably feels inadequate and questions his/her own sexuality. I know this situation hurts you, but don't underestimate how painful this is for your spouse either. Even if s/he acts defensively, s/he probably spends lots of time wondering why things aren't easier between you. Try to be more understanding.

2. Break free from the Catch-22. If you are a man whose wife is less interested in sex than you, and my description of the gender differences (she wants you to be more communicative and attentive before she is interested in sex) rang true for you, it's time to start paying attention to your friendship with your wife. Many women are wired this way. They can't get turned on unless they feel close to you.

This means that you need to start doing the things that are important to her, like talking about personal issues, spending time together, doing things as a couple, pitching in more at home, being more available to her, and asking her about her day. These are the kinds of things that soften women's hearts. And women adore it when men do small things for them. Bring her a cup of coffee in the morning. Leave her a note telling her you love her. Call her from work just to tell her that you are thinking of her. Bring home a single rose. Make her feel special. Be romantic. Women love it when men show their affection through random acts of kindness. They are much more likely to want to be close to you sexually when you do.

If you're upset with your wife because she's been cold and rejecting, the last thing you feel like doing is being kind and thoughtful. All I can say is that if you really want to improve your sex life and your wife needs to feel close to you emotionally as a prerequisite, doing the things that bring you closer to her is the only way you are going to get there. You can hold out because you're angry, or you can break free from the Catch-22 and be loving. Experiment by being a friend and watch what happens. Friendship is a great aphrodisiac for most women!

If you are a woman and the more highly sexed partner, the same theory applies. So many men have told me that their wives are "bitchy" and naggy and it really turns them off. Men become passive-aggressive, agreeing to your demands but turning off to you emotionally and sexually. Why not approach things differently? Even though you might feel hurt or rejected or unsexy because your spouse has been so apathetic, don't be critical. Be kind. Be complimentary. Catch your husband in the act of doing something right and tell him about it.

Look at your own behavior. Figure out what you might be doing that could make your spouse respond defensively. Ask yourself, "What has my husband been complaining about recently in regards to my behavior?" and start changing. Become more of the person he wants you to be and he might become more of the person you want him to be.

3. Do something different. Without knowing you, I can say with some certainty that your "more of the same" behavior has been to pursue your spouse for sex. And since this has become such a heated, ongoing issue between the two of you, you've gotten into roles with each other. You pursue him or her for sex, and s/he declines your offer. The more you pursue, the more your spouse feels pressured and angry and pulls away. So, it's time for you to try a new approach.

Back off for a while—No matter how attracted you might be to your spouse or how ready you might be to make love, for a certain period of time you should commit to not approaching him or her. Do not initiate sex for a while and see what happens. Don't talk about your plan. Don't threaten. Just back off and wait. Sometimes the lower-sexed person simply needs more time to allow his/her batteries to recharge. When the tug of war has ended, s/he might feel more amorous. It's really worth a shot.

I know that backing off isn't easy, especially if you are feeling turned on.

But if you haven't tried backing off yet, at least for several weeks at a time, you need to put this on your short list of things to try.

Stop talking about sex and focus on yourself for a change—You have been so focused on your relationship (at least the sexual part of it) that you have probably put your other needs aside. Rather than spend time arguing about what is or isn't happening in your marriage, use the time to focus on yourself and find things to do that fulfill you. Go out with friends. Start a new hobby. Join a health club. Go to church. Once s/he sees you focusing on yourself rather than your sex life, s/he might want to be more involved in your life . . . in every way. Here is a letter from someone who piqued her husband's interest when she stopped talking and took action:

Hi, everyone, can I join the no-sex club? This has been an on-again-off-again problem in my marriage too. Things were fine until we got married two years ago. The other night I tried to talk to my husband about my need for conversation, affection, and sex. He rolled his eyes and the only thing he said was, "Here we go again." I stopped there and said, "I know you don't want to hear this but I need to tell you that I didn't get married to live like brother and sister. I want and need sex and I am not happy with the way things are." Then I dropped it. He was quiet and distant.

The next evening I went out to dinner with a friend of mine. (She and I do this every week, girls' night out.) That night when I got home he was very attentive. We talked for a while (not about the hot topic) and he was very affectionate and we made love. I think that going about my business and not trying to discuss this with him anymore made him wonder what I was thinking and made him more interested.

Do a 180—Wouldn't it just blow your spouse's mind if you were to tell him/her that you have been doing some reading and that you now have a better understanding about his/her feelings about sex and that you're sorry about all the fighting? Think about it. Your spouse has been making you feel like a sex maniac and you've been making him/her feel like a celibate.

You're convinced that you're right and s/he's convinced that s/he's right. And where has all of that gotten you? Right here, right? So, while I can't guarantee that telling your spouse that you understand his/her feelings better will make him/her want to jump your bones, I can tell you that making your spouse "wrong" won't. Showing compassion and under-standing might be the turn on s/he been waiting for! Who knows?

4. Focus on what works. Have there been times in your marriage when your sex life was more passionate? Yes, I know, in the very beginning. But read what I wrote earlier in the chapter about the reasons this happens. Newness makes hormones run amuck. That is not the case any longer. So examine your marriage beyond the very beginning. Ask yourself, "What was different about the times when my spouse was more interested in sex?" See if any of the conditions are reproducible. Then do that.

When Brenda asked herself what was different about the times when her husband was more interested in sex, she thought of two things. Earlier in their marriage, they used to give each other long back rubs and this al-ways turned her husband, Jesse, on. They had taken a massage class to-gether and enjoyed the time they spent pleasuring each other in this way. Brenda realized that they had not given each other massages in a very long time. With this in mind, Brenda surprised Jesse with soft music and set up their massage table. Her plan worked like a charm.

5. Touch affectionately without thinking sex is imminent. Women often complain that their husbands never touch them unless they want sex. This turns them off. If, as the man, you are the more highly sexed part-ner, it will serve you well to remember this about your wife. She might want you to hug her, cuddle, hold hands, sit next to each other on the couch, or have you kiss her in ways that are affectionate but not sexual. Lots of women say that men are incapable of hugging without their hands sliding slowly down their butts. Since many women have a strong need for affection without sexual overtones, they get annoyed when each and every touch becomes a means of foreplay.

If this sounds familiar to you, then you might try being affectionate and stop there. Your wife will appreciate it and you. She might even wonder what in the world is going on. And that's exactly what you want to do; break out of old unproductive patterns. When you start doing the things that touch her soul, she will be more inclined to do the things that touch your body.

6. Masturbate. Since your sex drives are so disparate, it's unreasonable for you to expect your spouse to take care of each and every desire. You need to take responsibility for satisfying your own needs from time to time. In all likelihood, you are already doing this and you don't need me to tell you to do it. However, you've probably been resentful about it. That's not good and it's also not fair. Although your spouse needs to do a better job in meeting you halfway, there will still be times when you are hot to trot and s/he isn't. That's normal and you need to accept it. As long as your spouse is making more of an effort to understand and care for your needs, you need to accept your differences and take care of yourself occasionally without feeling resentment.

7. Accept a gift of love. Sometimes, as things improve and your spouse is trying to be more caring about your needs, s/he might decide to become intimate with you even though sex might not be a burning desire. Rather than feel insulted or put off, you should accept this as a gift of love. In good relationships, people do things for their spouses all the time that may not be exactly what they feel like doing at the moment. That's okay. In fact, that's more than okay. That's great. Remember what I told you earlier in this book about real giving? Real giving is when you give to your partner what your partner wants and needs whether or not you understand it, like it, or agree with it. Allow your spouse to show his/her love by being sexual even if it wasn't his/her favorite thing to do at the moment. Accept the gift and appreciate it. Good marriages are built on this kind of caring.

8. Respect your spouse's sexual prerequisites. Here's another really good suggestion from Dr. Pat Love. When a spouse with low sexual desire tells his/her spouse about the conditions that need to be in place in order for him/her to engage in or enjoy sex, the higher-sexed spouse often does not understand or accept the requests at face value. For example, if a wife tells her husband that she prefers making love at night rather than in the morning, the husband might think she is just making up excuses. (For most men, testosterone peaks between 7 to 8 A.M.; women's testosterone levels peak in the evening.) If a husband tells his wife that he feels more turned-on after they take a shower or when the kids are asleep, she may think he is just putting things off so that sex never happens. But the truth is, these may not just be excuses. Although you may have a hard time believing or understanding this because you are ready to go at the drop of a hat, your spouse may really need things to be a certain way in order to feel relaxed, comfortable, and turned-on. As much as possible, you should try to honor these requests and not discredit your spouse when s/he is confiding in you about these preconditions. Take what your spouse is saying at face value. Create the kind of atmosphere that is most likely to be conducive to your spouse's desiring sex.

9. If all else fails, be brutally honest. I've worked with countless couples where one spouse was so dissatisfied with their sexual relationship that eventually s/he decided to have an affair or leave the marriage. You might be thinking of these alternatives too. Affairs and divorce are lousy solutions. Even if an affair satisfies you temporarily, it will only make things more difficult at home. Although an affair or a separation sometimes serves as a wake-up call to the other spouse, you can't always count on this. Affairs and separations are bad for marriages.

However, as the more highly sexed person, you might be at the end of your rope. You might be fantasizing about someone else or about packing your bags and leaving. Before you decide to have an affair or leave, I implore you to make sure your spouse knows in no uncertain terms the seriousness of the situation. Make certain s/he understands what will happen if nothing changes. Don't threaten in the heat of an argument. Don't say nasty things. Don't blame. Don't criticize. Just tell your spouse calmly (or write a letter) that because of the differences in your sexual appetites, you are so unhappy that you are considering doing something you really don't want to do. Spell out what you've been thinking about. Tell your spouse that this is not a threat, but that rather, you are so desperate, you don't know what else to do. Ask your partner one more time to seek help. Then wait and see what happens.

Here is some advice to the more highly sexed spouse from a man with a low libido whose wife was so unhappy sexually, she decided to leave the marriage:

Please do something to tell your husband how serious this is before you complicate matters with an affair. Do everything in your power to explain to him where you are headed if something does not change. I know you feel like you have already, but you have to get his attention. Having been there, I don't think you have his attention yet.

He needs to know how important sex is to you and that your marriage is in serious jeopardy. Give it to him straight . . . "You are considering finding someone else who will give you the love you deserve" if the two of you cannot get it together. Please, for your sake as well as his, give him every opportunity to change. If he can't or is unwilling to change, then you will know in your heart that you tried everything you could to make the marriage work, then separate.

I'd give anything to be able to spend the rest of my life explaining the depth of my feelings to my wife. It would take me that long to beg her forgiveness and to apologize for the idiot that I was. She tried, but I did not understand. I do now! Ironically, just before we split up, we found our sex life. With better understanding on both sides, we were compatible and it was great! It appears, however, that it was too late.

THE PROBLEM ISN'T SEX, IT IS THE THREAT OF DIVORCE!

You may be reading this chapter and thinking to yourself, I now understand the problem more clearly but my spouse isn't interested in working on our marriage, let alone our sexual relationship. Now what?

This is a very tough question to answer. However, here are a couple of tips. If you are the more highly sexed partner and your spouse has half a foot out the door, you can't do too much right now to convince your spouse to see things your way. You don't have too much leverage at the moment. Since s/he is not certain that s/he wants to stay in the marriage, you simply can't expect him/her to meet your needs right now. You have to be more strategic and put your sexual needs on hold at the moment. However, if you follow the advice in this book and are able to turn things around so that you have your spouse's attention, following the advice in this chapter at a later juncture will be a good idea.

If you are someone who has a lower sex drive and your spouse is seriously thinking about leaving the marriage because of this, you can show your new understanding for his/her feelings by dropping hints that you are interested in being intimate. Then wait and see if your spouse is responsive. This is tricky because, as you know, it is important that you not be viewed as being desperate or pushy. If you do, you will push your spouse out the door. So you have to be subtle and see if your subtle advances are well received. Flirt, leave notes, touch him/her lightly in passing, send a "hot" e-mail, leave a breathless message on the answering machine, but do these things only if it piques your spouse's interest. If you keep pursuing your spouse when s/he isn't being responsive, it is very risky. So, you have to keep your eyes wide open and watch the results.

If your spouse is estranged or even separated and s/he seems interested in being physical or making love, by all means, go for it! Even if your spouse has said, "I don't love you anymore," don't necessarily believe it. Don't reject the idea of making love simply because your spouse has been standoffish or aloof. It's entirely possible that your spouse is confused and trying to figure out whether s/he should stay in the marriage or not. S/he may be wondering if s/he can ever have feelings of love for you again. Sometimes being sexual reminds people of the love they have for their partners. It is the glue that pulls them together.

Take advantage of this opportunity to connect physically if your spouse is willing. Don't push it, but if the occasion arises, don't turn your back on it either. Making love may be just what it takes to remind your spouse that your marriage is worth keeping. It's hard to feel distant when you're touching and caressing your life partner. Put your pride aside. Suspend your doubt and insecurity. Let passion connect you and bring back those loving feelings.

CHAPTER FOURTEEN

Expect the Impossible

Well, my dear friend, we have come a very long way together, haven't we? I sincerely hope that you have found my marriage-saving program to be helpful. More than anything else, I hope that you have found your way back into your spouse's heart. I respect you tremendously for valuing your marriage, for honoring the commitment you made as a couple, and for devoting yourself so completely to bringing back your love. You are a very special person. The world should be full of people like you.

Not long ago, I heard of someone who learned that she had a very serious, life-threatening illness. At first, she spent an inordinate amount of time researching how the disease develops, progresses, and the various treatment methods available. Although she found this to be informative, she still felt great despair over the possibility that she might lose her life since this was often the outcome for those who contracted the disease. She felt fairly hopeless.

She began searching Web sites for stories about people with the same diagnosis who managed to survive the odds. Having found several of these triumphant, awe-inspiring stories, she grew determined. "If someone else can do it, so can I," she told herself. And so far, her unwavering belief in herself has paid off. Her disease is in remission.

There are lessons to be learned from this woman. You now are armed with enough information to fight for your marriage. But no matter how well informed you might be, when you face a love-threatening condition, you need all the help you can get. You need to know that many people in your shoes have beaten the odds. Even when reconciliation seemed out of the question, these determined people expected the impossible. And wonderful things happened. I want you to read their stories and imagine yourself stepping into their shoes.

These letters are from people who have become part of the "Divorce Busting" community on my Web site (www.divorcebusting.com). It is there that people put into practice the techniques I write about in my books. It is there people receive love and support from complete strangers who are equally committed to keeping their families together. People tell me that my Web site has been a blessing to them in their darkest hours. They say it's been their lifeline. But the truth is, the person receiving the greatest gift from all of this is me. My life has been incredibly enriched by the knowledge that I am touching people's lives. Knowing that I have helped people make their marriages work and enabled them to raise their children as a team is almost overwhelming to me at times. Hearing from so many people who have successfully avoided divorce is the greatest reward I can possibly imagine.

If this book has touched your life in some way, I'd love to hear from you. I'd love to add you to my wonderful collection of success stories. You can e-mail me at divbuster@aol.com or write to:

The Divorce Busting Center
Michele Weiner Davis
P.O. Box 197
Woodstock, Illinois 60098

I'll be looking for your letter, expecting the impossible!

Dear Michele,

It wasn't very long ago that I was concerned about the lack of passion from my wife. She expressed a desire to go to counseling but her eyes were glazed over when I touched her. There was no response. I think I know where passion starts. It's in the eyes. I began looking into my wife's eyes a lot. When she talked to me or whenever I had a chance I would look into her eyes and think, "I love you." Then one day she reached out and touched my face gently with her hand and said, "I know, me too." It seemed like forever before she actually told me for the first time, verbally, that she loved me. But the first time she REALLY told me was that day she touched my face. I never would have thought that only a little over a month ago my wife said that she thought of me like a brother. That she actually had plans to date other men after her breakup with the current boyfriend.

One thing that has been a determining factor in bringing my wife and me back, at least to this point—a steady dating relationship—is that I have learned what she desires. Things I would have heretofore thought corny or silly are now becoming general fare for our growing "new" romance.

I have learned to tell her how beautiful she is first thing in the morning. I don't just think it now (like before), I actually SAY it. Little things, like asking her what she wants for dinner and then ordering it for her, taking her arm when we cross the street, LISTENING to her and jotting down the things she likes and wishes for and combing her hair fifty times at night just to feel it in my hands and tell her how beautiful it looks. I tell her and show her every day that I love her. I don't let that loving thought just fly through my mind without making it stop for a moment so I can make a statement to her about it before I let it go on.

If I could have only known the incredible responses received from such small tokens of my appreciation, I would never have lost my wife in the first place. Now that I know, I'll never have to face that loss again.

Several months later . . .

I asked my wife to marry me again on the same day as I did seven years ago. She said "yes." It's only words because we never got to the divorce. But we both needed to hear it and recommit. WOW! The last month . . . if I didn't know better I would say I was in the most wonderful dream I could ever imagine. It's not an illusion nor is it a dream.

I thought that there would be some really tough times working on getting back into our marriage and making it work. It's wonderful how easy things become when you have each other's best interest at heart and not your own selfish agenda. There have been a few times when the old selfish me would make its ugly way to the surface (I'm getting really good at drowning that clown). Instead of going with the old behavior, I go with something new. I try another way or point of view. And guess what, most of the time it's great and the rest of the time it's different at least. People should try breaking out of their own self-made barriers and beliefs more. It's rejuvenating.

Miracles happen. You CAN have your relationship back. Your partner may not buy the fact that you changed but you keep changing. You make your belief a reality. You make your belief your partner's reality. You and your partner will get what you want in your relationship. Give the relationship on which you are working everything you've got. Keep a consistent image of the person that you have become and are becoming constantly in your mind's eye. Improve it a little every day, in small steps. Every improvement that is made is proof to the mind that, in fact, there can be further improvement.

To everyone in these (www.divorcebusting.com) forums who has fought and is still fighting to save the most important thing in his/her lives, his/her relationship, I express the most sincere admiration. I just want everyone who is fighting to know that there are incredible success stories. I am one of them. Michele's program can and does work. Keep at it. You have nothing to lose and everything to gain by trying.

Steve

Dear Michele,

In August 1998, my husband and I had been together for seventeen years, married nine, had a two-year-nine-month-old son and a relatively problem-free marriage. Sure we had the usual stresses. You know, with each working full time, often opposite shifts, spending our individual and collective "free time" with our extremely active son, not knowing how to communicate, financial considerations, etc. Nevertheless, our marriage was impenetrable, right! I was so wrong. I had built up resentment for the entire nine years of our marriage and had become the queen of nag! I was GOOD!

On August 19, 1998, we had an argument that led to my husband leaving home (surprisingly, my suggestion that he leave). My gut was telling me that something was not right with him. Well, I was right. He was involved with a girl from work; their emotional attachment started around June. Of course, I did all of the usual don'ts . . . crying, pleading, begging, pursuing, etc. I thank my lucky stars I found Michele in the nick of time. I read her book over and over again, joined this Web site, and regained my positive attitude. I put the 180 and act as if into overdrive. I backslid a few times but mostly held my own. I got stronger and stronger every day all the while my husband maintained that he was not in love with me, hated me, never wanted to see me again, blah, blah, blah. So, after three months, I decided I had given him enough of my time and chances to hurt me so I filed for divorce in the December time frame—this was my last resort. He was served in January and our first court date was set for early February 1999. During this time, we were seeing (still are seeing) a marriage counselor (under the guise of parting as friends, which would be best for our son) so I was fortunate to have a dialogue going with him on some level.

Although a part of me wanted to stay married to him and I loved him, I knew that I could no longer live the same way with the same man. I needed change. I had to change. I started to live life for me and my son. As far as I was concerned, my husband had to live with the natural consequences of his actions. It was during this time that I noticed a difference in his attitude toward me (like Michele says, don't overlook the small stuff). He was not in such a hurry to leave my house after visiting with our son; when he called he started asking how I was doing; he noticed my changes (I lost weight, changed my hairstyle, got contacts, and started wearing different styles of clothes—different for me).

His attitude continued to change, as did mine. The stronger and more independent I got, the more attractive I became to him. WE decided to postpone the court date and work on the marriage in early February 1999. He moved back in April 1999 and things have been good, often great, ever since!

I still have to work hard at staying solution-oriented and not losing sight of the "cheese." I have had my moments, where I thought I made a huge mistake! But somehow WE continue to overcome these obstacles. I've changed, he's changed, and our marriage has changed! We've been through a lot together and still continue to grow and learn.

Thank you, Michele, for all of your wonderful work, commitment to your beliefs, and having the foresight to know that people like me can benefit from both. I do not want to relive any of those days but I have to say I'm not terribly sad they happened. My life is so much more rewarding now and I'm a much happier person for those experiences. I kept the faith! I believe I have the power to change and be happy!

Dear Michele,

Lillian and I are doing extremely well. I never knew I could be so much in love. Everything I give comes back to me at least tenfold. I've never seen so much love in the eyes of another human being as when I look into my wife's eyes. Sometimes, at night, when she thinks I'm sleeping, Lillian will whisper in my ear that she loves me with all her heart. I have to say, even as sleepy as I am sometimes, it moves me to a tear or two to be given so much love by someone who left me, just last year, in November. I hope you know how happy I am that I read your book, found your Web site, and practiced your techniques. Solution-focused living is the best. There is no alternative.

Can you guess what Lillian and I are very thankful for this year? Here's a hint: It has to do with something called divorce busting, and it involves two extremely happy people and how their lives were changed because this incredible woman decided to look at the practice of psychology with a different perspective.

Okay, end of hint.

Thank you for helping us change our marriage, our love, and our lives.

Affectionately,
Patrick

Dear Michele,

My wife asked me to leave about three months ago. She said that it was over and that she wasn't in love with me and that we were never getting back together. We have been married for seven years and together for ten—we have two girls ages three and six. About a month into this I found Michele's book and stuck to it like glue. I had some backslides but I had to learn patience and I realized that time was on our side. My wife was cold and angry, could hardly look at me, and when she did, I didn't see my wife anymore, it was another person. She stopped wearing her wedding ring, which meant so much to her when we got married. She refused to go to counseling or even talk about us.

I was a mess. I cried, I couldn't concentrate at work, I lost thirty-five pounds, I couldn't sleep, I begged, reasoned with her, and nothing worked. At the beginning, she said that she needed time and I didn't give it to her. I think if I had done this I would have been back sooner. This is the hardest thing to do. I remember the doom and gloom feeling not talking to her, how I wanted to pick up the phone and just hear her voice. I thought about losing her and the situation almost twenty-four hours a day. It is like a living hell. But I soon realized with Michele's book that I had to give her time and be her friend. I laid off the calls and she started to call me. I started to sound happy and in turn she started to sound happier. When she felt that I wasn't going to pressure her about the relationship she felt more at ease with me. Slowly things started to change. We spent a little time each week together with the kids with no pressure, no trying to hold her hand, no trying to kiss or hug her. In time she would give me a little hug, squeeze my hand when I left, and call me dear or honey on the phone. We still have work to do on our relationship but I now know that things will work out.

Hang in there, everyone, even though I know that it is hell. Stick to Michele's book, go out and have some fun, be around people even though you feel like going home and crying and doing nothing.

Your spouse is also having a very hard time with this whether s/he shows it or not. My wife acted as if this was nothing for her at the beginning and that really hurt me; she finally admitted the other day that it was killing her and she couldn't work either.

They will also say some very hurtful things to you—I don't love you anymore, I don't know if I could ever be intimate with you again, etc. etc. Don't react to them, it is not them talking, it is the demon of defense inside of them.

Keep the faith.

> Patience and strength,
> Stu

Dear Michele,

I have implemented your techniques over the last three weeks. It worked like a charm! My husband, who was before Christmas ready to divorce because he was "not in love" anymore, was away at school doing something for and "finding himself," asked me last Friday if I would consider taking a leave of absence from my job next year to live with him in Memphis.

He says he is recommitted to our marriage relationship, and I am the person he belongs with. He has returned to counseling and believes that his feelings stemmed from his depression (I knew this, but he was not convinced) and the loneliness of living apart—he found himself attracted to another woman in November.

He has over the last few weeks (after my 180) realized what he wants. I had told him that I knew what I wanted and was going to live my life and when he figured out what he was willing to do to make our marriage work—we would talk. A few days after this he called to ask if this meant I was going to see other people. I think this was the turning point for him to take action.

Since then, he has been trying to meet my needs and has been very attentive. We have seen each other on weekends this month and spent some time together having fun. He is talking about our future together and is remorseful about what happened, answering all my questions and HE is discussing what he needs to do to make our relationship better. I have tried to discuss with him my part in our marriage getting to this point, yet he claims that the only complaint that he ever had is my not taking care of myself first—I let my weight get out of control, and put his needs and worries before my own. NOT ANYMORE!! I have made positive changes in myself and the techniques I have been reading about have really worked. This progress would not have been possible without the things I have learned on this board. I have seen myself in so many postings and learned to focus on solutions instead of "whys." I have followed the suggestions that are given so lovingly and freely, and see a bright future ahead.

I am thankful to all who post here, sharing their painful stories and helpful advice. Michele, you never know how many people you touch. I have been greatly moved by the concern shown here, and will continue to visit to gain insight and wisdom from those who bravely "fight the good fight." My sincere gratitude to all of you!!

Jo Ann

The following letter is from a woman who was absolutely convinced she was going to divorce her husband, that is, until she read my book!

Dear Michele,

I have been working my way through your book a second time and have been trying to apply some of the principles to our marriage. I'm trying hard to figure out what works, and keep track of that. So this post is part of this exercise. At least it has a happy outcome, so bear with me.

One of our many problems was my husband's complete lack of

involvement with the children. Not only did he never attend any kid-related event, buy them presents on his own, etc., he never seemed to take any joy in watching them have fun. It got to the point where I went on vacation with them alone, because it was obvious to everyone, even my nine- and four-year-old that he wouldn't enjoy being with us anyway. It was real sad.

Anyway, with the divorce looming, he made a lot of promises and has been working hard to keep them. This Halloween, for the first time ever, he took my nine-year-old out for the town celebration. I never miss these events, but my four-year-old had a meltdown that evening and was in no shape to go. I squelched the urge to leave Chris with the four-year-old and trusted him to try it with Sam. I kept my mouth shut when Chris mumbled something about dropping Sam off with friends, and said use your judgment, see if Sam would like to have you along and check if the other mom would like help, etc. I truly expected to see Chris boomerang back in ten minutes after conveniently disposing of his responsibilities. Two hours later, a beaming father and son returned . . . bursting with tales of all of the houses they hit, people they met, etc. Sam was ecstatic to get this kind of attention from his dad, and I could tell Chris really enjoyed it too. I told Chris what he did was really important, and that there was no way Sam would have had as much fun without him and I meant it.

In addition to this happy tale, there were other breakthroughs in the family event participation theme this week. Clearly, there was something triggering these events besides my ultimatum or even my agreeing to be friendly/neutral at home rather than constantly fighting. It took me all day to figure out what it was that I did, but it finally came to me.

I work at home, but this fall I had an especially tough travel schedule. In spite of our huge problems, I was forced to rely on Chris to watch the boys this month for a stretch of five to six days. Shortly after this, I had to leave again for the day. I tried to think about something nice about Chris although that was hard to do. I finally conceded that the boys loved him and despite the awful domestic conditions at home, he was hanging in there, taking care of them. I remembered that they could be trying (as cute as they are) and that it must be hard for him to try to handle them at the same time. So, against my better judgment, I called the florist and ordered a dozen roses to be delivered while I was gone. I intended to tell the florist not to put "love" on the card, but "forgot" to. Actually, I was embarrassed to admit that I could be that petty as she knows both of us. When I came home that night, Chris was thrilled. I was still confused as to why I did it and not sure that I had done the right thing at all, but I mumbled that they represented a thank you for the good job he did with the boys.

Well, the 1½ weeks following the flowers have been filled with huge improvements with family participation on his part, so this small gesture clearly was the catalyst. I can't believe it took me so long to make the connection.

Ellen

Dear Michele,

I want to thank you personally for having a big part in saving my marriage. In April, my wife let me know that she wanted a divorce. She said we had grown apart and that she didn't really love me as a lover anymore. We have three kids, ages seven, five, and three. We have been married eleven years.

We started going to counseling together but soon she quit going. I kept going by myself. I knew I could be, and needed to be, a better husband and father. We have had problems, but nothing like fighting or abuse. One of the major issues was her credit card debt. The more she spent, the more I would withdraw into my cave. When I wouldn't communicate, she would spend more. It became a vicious cycle. I knew I still loved my wife, but she said she wanted to go through with this. I kept trying to visualize life after divorce and I hated it. We are both from divorced parents.

I was lost. The counseling helped some but I had no map or plan.

During one session, my counselor mentioned your book. After briefly looking through it, I couldn't wait to get started on it. At last

I had found what I had been looking for. The part that encouraged me the most was that it mentioned that things could still work even if only one partner was willing to work on it.

So I read it and couldn't put it down. Soon after finishing it, I went to work on changing. I started doing the little things. Many days I would get absolutely no response from her. It was so hard, but I kept picking myself up and trying again. But some days it was like trying to love the wall.

Soon after, I got jolted again when I found my wife was having an affair with an old high school friend. I knew I still loved her but I really hurt. I kept going back to your book and rereading parts. I told her two things. One, I still loved her and wasn't going to quit until she walked out the door. And the second thing was, I asked her to promise she would read your book. If she still wanted out, okay. Basically, my marriage was resting on your book. I took the kids away for the weekend, and left her alone.

After reading your book she said she wanted to stay and work on the marriage. Our marriage has never been better. At times my wife will look at me and smile and say, "Who is this man?" We celebrated our anniversary in May, one of the most memorable weekends of my life. I am the happiest guy in the world right now.

So I just wanted to say thank you, Michele. And here is a big hug for you and your book. It saved us.

Sincerely,
Chuck

YOUR SUCCESS STORY POSTED HERE

I am saving this place for you. Envision yourself and your spouse loving each other. This is the place to document your success. Congratulations for solving your marital problems with *The Divorce Remedy!*

Selected Bibliography

Amato, P., and A. Booth. *A Generation at Risk: Growing Up in an Era of Family Upheaval.* Boston: Harvard University Press, 1997.

Berman, C. *Adult Children of Divorce Speak Out.* New York: Simon & Schuster, 1991.

Burns, D. *Feeling Good: The New Mood Therapy.* New York: William Morrow, 1980.

Gitlin, J. *On Divorce.* Charlottesville, Va.: Lexis Publishing, 1997.

Love, P., and J. Robinson. *Hot Monogamy.* New York: Plume, 1994.

Page, R.M., and G.E. Cole. "Demographic Predictors of Self-Reported Loneliness in Adults." *Psychological Reports* 68 (1991):939–45.

Procheska, J.O., J. C. Norcross, and C. C. DiClemente. *Changing for Good: A Revolutionary Six-Stage Program for Overcoming Bad Habits and Moving Your Life Positively Forward.* New York: Avon Books, 1994.

Reichman, J. *I'm Not in the Mood: What Every Woman Should Know About Improving Her Libido.* New York: William Morrow, 1998.

Sheehy, G. *Passages: Predictable Crises of Adult Life.* New York: E. P. Dutton, 1974.

Waite, L., and M. Gallagher. *The Case for Marriage: Why Married People Are Happier, Healthier, and Better Off Financially.* New York: Doubleday, 2000.

Wallerstein, J., J. Lewis, and S. Blakeslee. *The Unexpected Legacy of Divorce.* New York: Hyperion, 2000.

Weiner-Davis, M. *Divorce Busting: A Revolutionary and Rapid Program for Staying Together.* New York: Simon & Schuster, 1992.

Yapko, M. *Breaking the Patterns of Depression.* New York: Doubleday, 1997.

Index